F*cking Magic

F*cking Magic

Clementine Morrigan

Copyright © 2025 Clementine Morrigan

All rights reserved. No part of this book may be reprinted or reproduced or utilised in any form or by any electronic, mechanical, or other means, now known or hereafter invented, including photocopying and recording, or in any information storage or retrieval system, without permission in writing from the publisher.

Paperback 978-1-7640782-0-7
eBook 978-1-7640782-1-4

Editor
Wallea Eaglehawk

Cover designer & artist
Charlotte Penabel

First edition published in 2021 by Clementine Morrigan
Second edition published in 2025 by Revolutionaries

Revolutionaries
Wonnarua and Gubbi Gubbi Country, Australia

Contents

Preface for the Second Edition xv
Introduction 1

Fucking Magic
#1

Swing Set 7
What It's Like to Have a Body 10
Fucking Magic 13
Medicine 22
Sucking Dick is Part of the Process 24
Making It 27
Daddy Issues 29
Opening 32
Raining in Montreal 35

Fucking Magic
#2

Raining in Toronto 38
Principled 39
Fuck Me Up 42
Resolve 45
The Tower 48

Kiss the Ground 52
The Beast at the Bottom of the Lake 57
Cuimhne, Misneach 61
Desire 66
I Remember You Then 69
Je suis prête 71

Fucking Magic
#3

Lifeless Worlds 77
So So Safe 80
To Be Loved 82
Surrender 85
The Chromatic Scale 87
I Push Him Off Me 93
Eye Contact 97
We Are So Brave 99
Perfect Again 102
Tell the Truth 103
Young Girls 106
This is Where I Want to Be 109
You Are Good 111
Trauma Magic 113

Fucking Magic
#4

Neurons That Fire Together Wire Together 121
Sickening 124
My Body Tells Me That It's True 127

Hungry for Love 130
Fucking with Integrity 132
Cock Sucking Bisexual 135
Je t'avais dit non 138
Real Love 142
Sex Maniac 145
This World 148
Indigo and Violet 150
Alchemy 154
Home 157
An Archive of Hollows 160
Transformation 162

Fucking Magic
#5

Taste the Silence 167
Return to the Water 169
Devotion 174
Carnelian4RoseQuartz 176
Like the Moon 178
My Voice Disappears 181
The Magic Comes Back 183
Queer Futures 185
Exhale 187
Melting 189
I Want to Hold Your Hand 191
See Through Blue 193
Freedom 196
Six Years Sober 199

Fucking Magic *#6*

Safe 205
Kill the Misogynist Bro in Your Head... 207
Becoming a Forest.. 211
Remember 214
Write... 217
Listen for Desire... 221
The River 224
What I Need 226
Sluts Can Say No.. 228
Baby's First Play Party 231
Finding My Way Back 235
Sober House.. 238

Fucking Magic *#7*

AnarchaMagic 245
First Love... 248
We Carried This Message 250
The Wholesome Collective.. 253
Careful and Daring.. 255
Last Year... 257
The Distance Between Us.. 259
Letting the World Love Me 262
Time Travel to the Present 265
Hurt 267
The New World Now 269
How I Learned to Relax and Love Eating Pussy 272
You Are Enough 275
Coven 277

Fucking Magic #8

Living Universe 283
Capable 284
I Want Him Dead 286
Calling 289
Joy 292
Two Rivers 295
Remember 297
The Only Way to Love 299
The Same Lesson 301
Gay Slut Life 2019 303
So Fucking Pretty 305
The Fire and the Swan 307
Still Alive 310
The Forest 312
Femme4Femme D/s 314
Still Crazy 316
Something I Can Trust 318

Fucking Magic #9

Love in the Apocalypse 323
For Mary 325
Swamp Milkweed 327
The Beginning of Spring 329
My Beautiful Fucking Life 330
Split Personality 333
Love Water Always 337
Incest Survivor Magic 340
Fingers 342

Power and Desire 345
Listening to Black Metal in My Therapist's Office............................... 346
Straight Girl Trauma 349
I Choose to Live 352
Nervous System Love 355

Fucking Magic
#10

Be Gay Do Crime.. 361
You Are Sucking My Cock and I Can Feel It... 365
River Slut 367
Queer Sober Dance Party 369
Do You Want to Kiss Me?... 371
Violet 374
Punk in My 30s.. 376
Feel It All 378
Waking from a Dream 380
Cutting Fences... 382
Grief... 384
La fin de leur monde 386
I Still Think of You 389
Naked 391
Hitchhiking 393
If I'm Going to Be a Musician I Need to Practice Freedom................... 395
Family 397

Fucking Magic
#11

Lipstick	403
Fucking by the Train Tracks	405
I Need to Write	407
Turn Back Into Stars	410
This is the Change	413
Cancel Me	415
The Fucking Pleasure of Being an Adult	419
Yours	422
We Went to the Ocean	424
Coming Back to My Body	426
My Wild Precious Life	428
We Don't Crawl Before Anyone	432

Fucking Magic
#12

Transformation Again	439
Wild Living Mourning	442
Safe Enough to be Curious	445
Ferris Wheel	448
We Did What We Were Capable Of	450
It Starts with the Water	452
Animal	455
This Love	457
Tell Me About Your First Time	460
The Abandoned One	463
The Tracks	465
Desire is Holy	467
Pandemic	469
Careful and Unafraid	471

Acknowledgments 475
About the Writer 477

Also by

Clementine Morrigan

Rupture (2012)

The Size of a Bird (2017)

You Can't Own the Fucking Stars (2018)

Trauma Magic (2021)

Sexting (2021)

Preface

for the Second Edition

WRITING IS SOMETHING sacred. It is also, for many of us, something transgressive. We write what we know we are not allowed to say. We write the stories we can't find on the shelves of our local indie bookstores. We write the book we need and we do it without permission. In a rush of power from some unknown source, we write the impossible things and then we publish them.

Book deal be damned. Literary legitimacy be damned. Waiting until the writing is *good enough* be fucking damned.

For many of us writing is a question of survival. We shine our words into the darkness like a lighthouse because we know how many are navigating those waters in the dark, trying not to crash against rocks and go under. We shine that light for ourselves too. We write to prove to ourselves that this hard won survival is more than just survival. We don't just survive – we get to *live* too. The writing is how we live, despite everything.

Outsider writers haunt the edges of the literary world with our storm of undomesticated words. With our typos and the edges of the writing cut off by the photocopier. With our staple jams and our scrawled handwriting. With our stubborn, persistent, audacious hope. We are kept out of the literary canon by gatekeepers protecting social capital and defending insider etiquette. Yet our words are passed from hand to hand, found in piles in the bathrooms of squats and punk houses, hung up on little zine clotheslines in bedrooms, gifted from one person to another

Fucking Magic

crumpled and stained – *here, this did something for me, I hope it does something for you too.*

Fucking Magic is outsider writing. It is underground writing. Queer writing. Incest survivor writing. Forbidden writing. It is writing that has travelled the world in envelopes and pockets and backpacks. It is writing that found its way into the hands and hearts of thousands of people around the world without institutional backing – until now. This second edition of the collected issues of the zine *Fucking Magic* has found a home with the indie press *Revolutionaries*. It feels powerful and important for this work to finally break its ways inside mainstream literary spaces.

If writing calls to you, if you hear a whisper or feel a tug, if your heart aches for writing – then write. Don't wait for permission.

Clementine Morrigan.

2025.

For everyone I've been.

Introduction

*I*STARTED WRITING ZINES when I was twelve years old. They were a place for all my secrets, a place where I could put all my fear and pain and desire. I would go down to the end of my driveway and put the little red piece of metal on the mailbox in the upright position, indicating to the mail carrier that there was something there to be sent into the world. I've been writing zines ever since, and I have written many of them. I wrote them during active alcoholism. I photocopied them at the drop-in centre for street involved youth. I painstakingly wrote them by hand when I didn't have a computer. I printed them at the public library. I traded them with strangers I found online or in the pages of *Broken Pencil*. I left them on buses and in public bathrooms. Zines are how I saved my life and how I became a writer. Zines are the place where I can say what's true, what hurts, what I'm grappling with and moving through. Zines are the place where I can pour my anguish and grief and rage and persistent hope and stubborn desire. Zines welcome me exactly as I am, however I am. Zines don't wait for me to be better, smarter, wiser, more healed, less problematic, less broke, or a 'real' writer. Zines welcome me now, as I am. And they always have. To this day I still make my zines like I'm in the '90s: with scissors and glue. I still have a folder with all the hardcopies that I use to make my photocopies. I still fold my zines and staple them and put them in envelopes and send them to strangers.

The book you are holding in your hands is a collection of 12 issues of the zine *Fucking Magic*. This writing is born out of the ethics and aesthetics of zine making. It is outsider writing that did not wait for permission or the backing of a press in order to exist in the world. I started

Fucking Magic

writing *Fucking Magic* when I was 30 years old. I was five years sober and had just left a three-year long partnership. I was breaking open. I felt like I was dying and I was coming alive in ways I hadn't been for years. *Fucking Magic* follows me as I heal from trauma at deeper and deeper levels, as I fall in love, as I claim polyamory and discover my sexuality, as I move cities, and go after my dreams. *Fucking Magic* bears witness to transformation after transformation as I step into my power and become the adult I always needed. I often joke that *Fucking Magic* is a mix of hot x-rated queer sex and super intense heavy trauma shit. It's all that and so much more. It's a prayer and a process and a struggle and a dream. It's me falling on my knees in ecstasy, and grief, and exaltation, and surrender. It is the work of learning to really love, and feel, and live. Hard work for trauma survivors.

And *Fucking Magic* ends at a precipice, at the end of one chapter and the beginning of the next. It drops off into the abyss of the next adventure.

Here is *Fucking Magic* as a book, and a prayer, and a spell.

Clementine Morrigan.

2021.

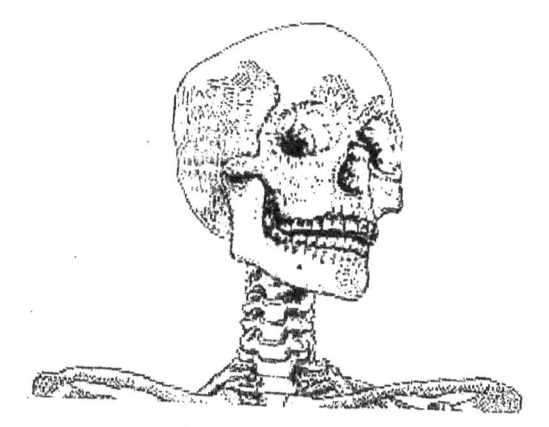

Fucking Magic

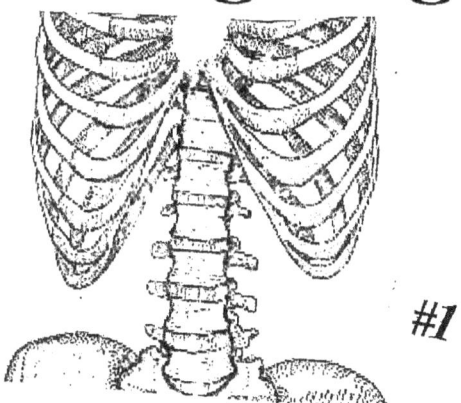

#1

Swing Set

C*AN I WRITE my way back into my body? Can these words work like a softening, an opening? Can I trace them like a string, like a cord, connecting me back to the beginning?*

Years ago we sat on my back porch, my best friend and I. I was new to having friends, new to being sober, new to trusting anyone at all. I was preparing for my criminal injuries compensation hearing and the lawyer had given me a huge file to review. *Read it*, she had said. *Get familiar with it*. As if I wasn't already familiar with everything he did to me. But I had to be prepared. So, I asked my best friend to come and sit with me. I read it out loud so that I didn't have to be alone with it.

You know what he did to me. You know all the gritty details. You know about my childhood. You know. And you were supposed to be trust worthy. You were supposed to be my friend.

I read the words and my best friend listened. They listened while I read about the rapes and the physical violence and the names he called me. They listened while the details were laid bare: the ejaculation and the crying, the *you look so sexy when you're all sad and submissive*. The mattress off the balcony. The hole in the wall the size of my body.

So I fell in love with my best friend. The feelings were reciprocated. It was supposed to be the first healthy relationship of my life. It was the right choice. The safe choice. I chose someone who already loved me. I went to their house and I laid in their bed and they held me.

It feels like all I do is swallow down pain and listen to you tell me it isn't what I think it is. I'm caught in a cycle of loss but I don't know that I am losing. I'm hoping you will remember that you love me.

Fucking Magic

I started to hate femmes. I started to hate myself. I was paranoid all the time. I tried to play it cool. I read about compersion and asked myself why I was so jealous. This wasn't my first time being polyamorous and yet I felt like my insides were being shredded. I blamed myself. I sought a spiritual solution. I surrendered at the altar of my pain. I needed someone to blame so I blamed myself. I took the weight onto my shoulders and I worked hard at being better.

I did all the work. Read all the books. Initiated all the conversations. I dove deep. I started to hate my body. I started to hate my clothes and my hair. I started to doubt my sanity. My sexuality started to shut down but I continued to offer myself up. My sparkle was starting to dull. The lights were going out in my eyes.

Queer power couple. Date night. Selfies on instagram. Make it look good. Make is so believable that even I believe it. Find a place inside to hold the pain. Find a way to bury the truth. Dig a well for all the water. Keep down what can't be true. It can't be real.

Promising things will change but nothing ever changes. You never touch me anymore and when you do it is like I am not there. You say you love me. You say you want to be with me. You say you'll work on it, we'll work on it. But I'm left alone doing all the work. I'm tired of feeling so alone.

Nothing changes if nothing changes. My best friend taught me that. My best friend taught me so many things. My best friend cracked the world open and made things possible. My best friend showed me how to be sober. My best friend loved me. My best friend showed me how to love. But nothing changes if nothing changes. I finally tell the truth to another human being. The words break like a dam and come flooding out of me. My friend listens to me tell what is happening in my relationship, what has been happening for so long.

Years ago I sent my best friend a text. I said I hate how it's awkward when we hug. I said I wish it wasn't. I said *you're my best friend and I'm crazy about you*. The text was not meant to confess my crush. It was just meant to be an attempt at vulnerability within this very important friendship. I knew my best friend was biking home so it would be awhile before they got the text. Anxiety ridden, I went into a park and went on the swings. I surrendered the outcome. I trusted the universe and I let my heart go.

When I got off the swings I checked my phone. My best friend said they felt the same way about me, that they had felt this way for a while and didn't know what to do about it. They had taken the *I'm crazy about you* to mean, well, I'm crazy about you. And they were saying they felt the same.

Years later our relationship is crashing and burning. I have refused to go back into denial and everything is painful all the time. My partner promises to get therapy but doesn't. Months pass. My partner promises to go to meetings but doesn't. Months pass. My partner acts like nothing has changed. Everything has changed. I can no longer hide the pain. We make small talk and I occasionally push this issue. *I can't do this anymore.* More promises. More excuses. I can't do this anymore.

I am riding my bike and I see the park in which I waited for their text message all those years ago. I stop and I enter the park. I am gutted. I know what is happening and I am sobbing. I make my way to the swings and I swing and I pump my legs. I sob these gut wrenching sobs and I know it has come full circle. I pray. I surrender. I give up all my love and all my hope and all my pain. Shaking, I take my phone from my pocket. Sobbing, sitting on the swing, I write a text message. I tell my partner that I am moving out. I am looking for a new place to live. I can't do this anymore.

What It's Like to Have a Body

*L*AVENDER AND NETTLE tea at home. Green tea in my reusable mug while I'm out. An attic bedroom overlooking Kensington Avenue. People walking on the street, checking out the shops, laughing. House plants and framed photographs of people I love. Candles on my altar. Incense burning by the window. Tarot cards. Back on social media. My world is slowly starting to get bigger. I am stretching my wings.

WhatsApp conversations with my best friend: *LMAO OMG nail painting emoji. / You deserve better. / Fuck this date is awful trying to figure out how to leave. / HANGED MAN. / Stay in the town!! / Thank you for witnessing. / Of course, anytime.* Conversations over breakfast with my roommate. Talking about the ghost cat and the fairies, about art projects and essay writing, about trauma and spirituality, about sex and dating, on the floor laughing because there is no cat in the bathroom but we definitely heard a cat.

I can feel my heart opening to the world. I can feel the cool spring air moving through my ribcage. Venus is in retrograde. I have lived here for four months.

Music in my earphones, buying vegetables and walking through the market. Sparrows gather on the pavement. Snow comes and goes. I feel the tension start to melt. I feel the familiar throb of pain. What I tried so hard to stop from happening has happened. Again. I surrender but I don't submit. I let life in again.

What It's Like to Have a Body

Procrastinating on paper writing. Meditating on the Virgin Mary. Reaching deep. Letting go of rigidity. Letting go of what other people think of me. Letting go of trying so hard to be in control. Letting go of trying to redeem myself. Letting go of shame.

Flirting, feeling, working out at the gym, going to my weekly boxing class, feeling the impact of my fist against the bag. Learning to trust, first, myself. Listening and learning the lessons of a responsive living universe. Practicing magic as embodiment. Remembering what it's like to have a body. Following the diet my naturopath prescribed. Cooking my food. Making dinner at 2am sometimes and my roommate comes home laughing, asking me what I'm doing.

Letting my hair grow out. My natural colour for the first time since I was thirteen. I am thirty and I'm going gray. *Your hair is different at your temples. / Yeah I'm going gray. / It looks intentional. / Nope, natural.*

Remembering what it's like to feel desirable, to feel seen. Remembering what it's like to feel desire. Remembering desire like a fire at the centre of my being. Remembering what it's like to love my body, to feel and move and breathe, unrestricted, not anticipating critical comments. Remembering what it's like to feel like I'm enough. Remembering what it's like not to try constantly to be something other than what I am. Remembering what it's like to be a human being. Remembering what it's like to feel safe. Remembering what it's like to feel loved.

Breaking rules, not following suggestions. Going to therapy and telling my therapist that I'm not just a slut, I'm a feelings slut. Making the choice to date. Making the choice to start connecting with my sexuality again. Going on dates. Starting things. Ending things. Trusting my gut. Telling people when I don't want to see them anymore, with kindness, and without excuses. Asking for what I want. Saying with clarity what turns me on and embracing the fact that it's pretty vanilla tbh. Practicing ethical nonmonogamy, with the emphasis on the ethical. Catching feelings. Doing the 'no strings attached' thing. But either way, staying grounded in my humanity and the humanity of those I am engaging with. Remembering that sexuality can be healthy and good.

Fucking Magic

Coming back into my body. These muscles. These curves. These arms. These hips. These breasts. This skin. Starting to feel like myself again. Catching my reflection in the mirror and liking what I see. No longer feeling like my body has betrayed me by not being able to be several different attractive models at the same time.

One of my best friends tells me they never knew me before, that I seem like an entirely new person now that I am free. My other best friend tells me that my light has come back on, that she saw me lose myself in that relationship, that I became a shell of myself, unrecognizable. Who is this new person? This old person? This sociable, confident, kinda even extroverted person? This brave person? This loved person?

Reading fiction for fun, wondering how far I can push my procrastination before it's seriously a problem. Cutting myself a lot of slack. Letting joy be a priority. Letting pleasure be a priority. Spending a lot of time laughing. Using my library card again. Trying not to get late fees but not totally succeeding. Looking out the streetcar window, feeling the wind in my hair, against my skin. Smiling at strangers, feeling a stir of something.

I am starting to recognize myself. Structural dissociation integration work. I am not either exactly, I am both. Processing my feelings. Letting myself make mistakes. Letting myself breathe. Letting myself cry. Holding space for the pain which is breathtaking. Trusting that I'm where I need to be. I am exactly where I need to be.

I open my heart and I find that the world opens to me.

Fucking Magic

WHEN I WAS a little girl I watched my grandfather want me. I watched his eyes on my body. I felt the strength of his arms when he grabbed me. The greasy stubble on his face. I lived in a constant state of normalized terror. Always waiting, watching, wondering. Always heart in chest and head spinning. The oldest girl, I felt responsible not only for myself, but for my sister and my cousins. I grew up in an environment of sexual violence, incest. His constant sexual comments and stares. The game they all called 'slippery slobberies'. Him standing over our beds while we pretended to be asleep. He was after us, and the other adults did not care.

Do I have to start here? Does it always come back to this? How much therapy do I have to do until this is no longer my origin story? But it will always be my origin story. I can't change what happened. I can keep digging and I can keep finding new layers of fucked up. Some things I can't even write despite how open I am. I can keep coming back to it and I can find new ways to relate to it. I can grow. I can change. I can heal.

At the same time, my body was changing. I remember the pleasure, wonder, and terror of it. I remember the tufts of hair under my arms and my tiny new breasts. I remember the bursts of pleasure, sickening and addictive. I remember promising myself not to touch myself and then doing it anyway. Feeling sick and awful afterwards. I remember shame. Deep, permeating, all-encompassing shame. And that shame stays with me today. Gut level. Bone level. Sex is terror and violence. Sex is wrong, dangerous, invasive. Sex is all around and never named. Sex is the root of my trauma and yet I am still a sexual being.

Fucking Magic

I'm in her bed and we have both come, wrapped in each other's arms, bodies pressed into each other. It feels good and I love the little breath she lets out as she runs her fingers over my shivering body. She changes positions, moves between my legs. Suddenly, she shoves fingers inside of me. Too big, too much, too fast. I want her to stop but I don't have the language for stop. I say my secret prayer that she will read my body language, my sudden silence. But she goes on fucking me and I leave my body. I can feel it happening but I also don't feel anything at all. I have moved backwards, out through the back of my head, into the mattress and down into the bed. I can feel the words but they are more like sounds and they are unspeakable.

I was a queer kid sexually attracted to girls instead of boys. I discovered porn on the internet and was horrified by how gay I was. I was deeply in love with my best friend and she was a girl. Sex was bad and dangerous already. Incest was the context in which I first became aware of sexuality. Homophobia put the nail in the coffin. I was disgusting. Sexual. Wrong. A boy in my class said *let me see your hand* and he smelled it. *Is this the hand you write with?* I gave him my left hand. *See! It smells like fish. You touch yourself. You masturbate.* I was mortified. I started putting ziploc bags over my hands when I touched myself, rubbing my skin raw with soap afterwards. The shame was so big and so wide it swallowed up my whole being. I wanted to die. I didn't want to have a body anymore. I didn't want to feel those sick sweet feelings that I liked so much.

I was drugged and date raped by a woman when I was seventeen. Another woman told me the reason I needed to use my hand to come was because I was fucking dudes, that what I needed was to be fucked by a woman. She fucked me on the ground there in the park and it was awful. I couldn't come and she treated me like shit from then on. I can't even count how many times men have raped me. How much sex I just laid there for and stared at the wall. How many things have been shoved up inside of me as my eyes glazed over and I chose to be somewhere else. How much sex I was too drunk to consent to. How much sex I don't remember at all. How much violence and coercion, name calling and terror, love and broken hearts,

Fucking Magic

violation, humiliation, hands around my throat, condoms taken off without permission. I time travel. I rise above my body. I exist and I don't exist at all.

    I learned to love fucking as a drunk, a slut, and a sex worker. I don't want to glamorize those years because they were depressing as all hell. I romanticized my pain. I acted like I didn't care at all. I let men use my body and disrespect my humanity, mostly for fun, less so for work. I had a hard line with work because I knew that people kill whores. So I worked sober and I was more choosey. But for pleasure I surrendered myself to the violence of men. I sought love from men who thought of me as trash. I didn't know what else to do. I didn't know how to find actual love, I didn't know what it looked like, what it felt like. I didn't even know that love was what I wanted. I was assaulted often. I was told *I don't kiss sluts* by dudes who loved fucking me. I spent days in front of the toilet vomiting, dry heaving, and shaking.

    But during those trauma years I learned to love fucking. I learned to come like crazy pressed against a perfect stranger. I made money sometimes and sometimes I just got off. But I learned to love fucking. I didn't get rid of the shame but I put it out of sight somewhere. I became someone who could be sexual. Someone who could feel desire and act on it. I learned what I refer to as my *slut skills*. I navigated danger with ease. I was brave and brazen. I carried condoms in my purse or tucked into my knee high socks. I played music in the other room to make the dude think someone else was home or left some other shoes by the door. I got the money first and put it out of sight. I found my way back from the strange places I ended up in. I discovered this sparkle, this vast expanse of pleasure. I found a way to feel my body, to pull myself close to the person I was fucking and crack open the pain.

    I'm at the doctor's office getting treated for an STI. The nurse is really cool. We are talking about fucking and risk and how I should go about disclosing to my partners that I caught something. She says No one ever talks about the risks associated with not having sex. *And I love her for saying that. Getting an STI has flared up my shame, reminding me that sex is dirty and dangerous, inherently bad. That I am fucked up and dangerous for having caught something. But yeah, what about the risk associated with not having sex? For some people not having sex is healthy and good, not risky at all. For me sometimes what I need is to not have sex. But abstaining from sex is always painted as risk free (even as it is also framed as abnormal) and having sex, especially certain kinds of sex, is loaded with risk. Sexless years spent shut down and cut off from my body, years spent choking on shame, unable to touch myself, riddled with self-hatred and disgust, like yeah, there's risk there. There's risk for me in re-inscribing the narrative that sex is bad and dangerous. As an incest survivor, as a rape survivor, I cannot afford to buy into the narrative that sex is bad, dirty, disgusting, dangerous. I tell the nurse* I've been reading safer sex literature since I was a teenager and honestly no one says anything about scissoring. Like really how risky is it? *She laughs,* That mythic lesbian sex act, either it's all queer women do or it doesn't happen at all. *I laugh, give her a look,* It's definitely a thing though. *She smiles,* But really, there aren't studies on this. No one invests money into researching the sexual health of queer women. So the answer is, we really don't know.

My first love was bisexual and slutty too. He was a survivor of child sexual abuse too. He had done sex work too. I held him in my arms and I didn't judge him when his trauma stuff came up. We had queer sex and we held space for each other. I told him about my sexual history. Laughing and playfully I told him about all the sex I'd had. It seemed safe to do so because he was open about his. It seemed safe to do so because it was obvious I was a slut and he was into me anyway. He taught me how to ride a bike. We spent the summer riding around the island. I had never been loved before and neither had he. We had sex sober. We held hands and smoked weed in the park. I loved him fiercely, deeply, truly. And then, slowly, suddenly, it started. His rage, his violence, his hatred. Flipping the furniture. Grabbing the bong out of my hands and throwing it off the balcony. It came on suddenly like a flashflood, apparently unprovoked, but always for the same reason. *You're a fucking slut. It's fucking disgusting. Running your pussy all over town. Do you think any man could love you after what you did?* My first chance at true love, my soul mate, the love of my life. This beautiful, broken human being. This person who knew deep down like I know the terror of violence, the unspeakable horror of violation. This person who I loved so much and he was slipping away. He couldn't love me because I was a slut, he hated that he loved me because I was a slut. That's what he told me. I adamantly disavowed my past. I swore up and down that I would take it all back, trade it all in for his love, if I could, and I meant it. I meant it deep in my bones. Our love was the only thing in the world that mattered, it was the only thing that was true. *Fucking slut, do you know who you're fucking with?* On the ground with him on top of me, knee to my chest, cutting off my breath. I loved him so much.

She kisses me on the beach in the freezing cold. We walk along the shore talking about how much dudes suck and looking at the winter sculptures. On our third date I invite her over to my place and we drink tea. I am terrible at expressing desire for other femmes. She is beautiful and smart and cool. Sober dating and lack of gender roles makes this difficult. But more than that, and deeper than that, my all pervasive sexual shame is more pronounced with women. Men seem to absolve me of responsibility for my desire by being so obvious about their own. And homophobia, queerphobia, biphobia, heterosexism, misogyny, and trauma have left their mark. We talk about the awkwardness and the difficulty of hitting on other women. She kisses me goodbye at the door. I text her to say maybe next time we'll make out. She says she'd like that. It takes us seven dates before clothes start coming off and I enjoy every minute of it. I enjoy the slow process of feeling each other out, of feeling safe enough to go for it. I find a kind of desire I haven't known before. It is slow, unrushed, multidimensional. I look into her eyes.

I got sober when I was 25. 12 step meetings every day for more than seven months. No more alcohol and no more drugs. Lots of therapy. Lots of work. My sponsor told me to change my number, to get rid of the numbers of all the guys I was fucking. It was a painful and difficult choice but I wanted to stay sober more than anything. I wanted to change my life. So I did what she asked. I stopped having sex for the first time in my adult life. At five months sober I went through my rape trial. A five day jury trial in which I had to say all the awful details while he was in the room. I didn't look at him. I looked at the defense lawyer or my little cup of water. I didn't exist. In some ways I had never existed. He was found not guilty and he raised up his arm in celebration. I went home and I laid in my bed, the same bed he raped me in. I didn't drink. At seven months sober, against the advice of a lot of people, I started dating. I loved it. I had some fucked up experiences. I let a random dude pick me up at a library and went to a cheap motel and fucked him. The sex wasn't good. The sponsor I had at the time said *If you want to be promiscuous in sobriety, you can do that. My advice is to find people with good sobriety who are promiscuous and ask them about it.* I love her for that response. I didn't know if I wanted to be promiscuous. I didn't know what I wanted. Sexual shame was still crushing me and now I didn't have the booze to dissipate it.

I can't write my proposal for my final research project for my masters degree until I have figured out what to feel about sex. Maybe it doesn't seem related but it's related. Sex is sequestered off, partitioned from the rest of my life. I have survived by keeping sex separate. All this integration work, plus leaving an unhealthy relationship, plus close to five years of sobriety, has unleashed sex from its trappings. I am undone. I am fucking people again. I am feeling things. And it's driving me crazy. It's making me feel crazy. Can I be a sexual person and still write this research project? Can I be a sexual person and still read fiction for fun? Can I be a sexual person and still be a good person? I talk to my therapist about it and I tell her I might be a slut after all. I am surprised to find that I am down for hookups. But it feels different from my drunk days. It feels different because I am present, because I am being honest with myself and the other person, because I am not pretending to be okay with being treated with disrespect. It feels different because it is coming from a place of love and care, for myself and the other person. Even though I don't know the person well, we are sharing intimacy, we are communicating in a language I remember deep in my bones. I don't ghost. I am careful. I do my best to be careful. To handle both of our bodies and hearts with respect and care. My therapist is mostly supportive but she worries about my safety. I almost want to roll my eyes at this. I tell her about my slut skills. *I tell her about the knowledges I've developed from sex work and sluttiness. I tell her* I know how to do this.

I started dating my best friend. They were six years sober and I was not yet two. I put them on a pedestal. I didn't yet know who I was, who I could be in sobriety. I still thought of myself as the girl in a blackout, glazed over eyes, screaming incoherently. I still considered myself to be trash. I believed I was lucky to have them. I was used to being the disposable drunk slut. I was used to being screamed at, hurt. I was used to 3am texts, *You up?* I was not used to being cared about. My best friend cared about me. They told me they loved me long before we were a couple and I didn't know what to say. What was love without sex? What was care? But once we started dating things started to change. They were emotionally unavailable, avoidant, cold. Preoccupied with other people, dismissive of me. I started to float away from my body. I started to desperately try to figure out how to be lovable again. I put up with so much shit but I thought I had so much more than I deserved. Years passed and my body shut down. I disappeared again. I developed a hatred for my body and sexuality that I didn't even have during my drunk days.

We matched on bumble and have been messaging on and off for a few hours. Now I'm at the gym on the stationary bike and I'm still messaging and laughing to myself and smiling at my phone. After getting to know each other a bit and flirting we get to the whole What are you looking for? *thing and I tell him* I'm nonmonogamous and open to a number of different things. I can do casual but only if it's respectful. *He says* We should get together some time. When are you free? *I say* I'm at the gym right now, in your area actually. I could come by tonight. *He is into this idea. So I shower and throw on my clothes and start walking to his place. I stop at a convenience store to buy condoms just in case. I remember this. I feel like a slut and it feels good. At his place we talk awkwardly, both of us shy. I laugh a lot. I ask him how he's feeling and if he's feeling good about this. He says he is. So we start making out. He pulls me on top of him and we kiss and it feels amazing. We have absurdly hot sex, stopping periodically because it's too intense and sometimes I dissociate when it's too intense, so I need breaks. He is cool with this. After a bunch of orgasms he gives me some pajamas and I sleep in his bed.*

What if sex is a practice like magic? What if there is no shame in desire? What if sex no longer needs to be separate from the rest of my life like a dirty secret? What if it's possible to be sober, spiritual, ethical, happy, healing, and slutty, all at the same time? Sometimes I like to hook up with people I have only just met. Sometimes I like to go slow and won't even kiss on the first date. I just like to tune into my body (my body which still exists). I just like to feel the vibe between me and the other person, the energy flowing between us, and to do what feels good for both of us. Practicing sluttiness in sobriety has been a practice of learning, of navigating, of unlearning. It has been a practice of being careful, of making hard choices, of handling rejection from both sides with as much grace and respect as possible. It has been a practice of presence, of courage, of embodiment. It has been a practice of facing my deeply embedded shame. It has been a surrender to deep pleasure healing me at a cellular level and finding the courage to believe I deserve this. Finding the courage to believe that it's okay to want this.

My trauma history leaves you speechless and that's okay because I don't need you to say anything. I don't need you to be shocked or to assume anything. Sexual trauma is a language I know well and I'm not worried about it. I try to explain this to my therapist and I can tell she doesn't get it but I don't need her to get it. I don't need anyone's validation to know what I know deep in my bones. I am a survivor. I don't mean that in any kind of cliché way. I mean I have already survived. I mean another rape won't kill me. I mean I understand the ins and outs of assaults. I know what it's like. I know how to protect myself to the best of my ability and I know how not to blame myself when I fail. I know that I am fucking magic, that it's magic I am here at all, that it's magic when I can pull pleasure from the depths of my traumatized bodymind. When I can pull myself into the moment, feel the pleasure cracking the shame wide open, feel the space created when I surrender the shame, feel myself becoming new again.

Fucking Magic

It's magic that I'm healing and changing and growing. It's magic that I have reinvented sluttiness. That I have shaped it to the curves of my sobriety, that I have mixed and mixed and created a kind of alchemy. I have found new applications for my slut skills, *new possibilities for pleasure grounded in a practice of love for myself. It's magic that I still have this huge heart, that I still feel all these feelings, that everyone I touch I touch with care. It's magic that I'm writing these words, that I'm using these words to trace the lineage of my traumas, to find the electric sparkle of my pleasures, and the power of my survivals. I am remembering sex as magical practice, trauma magic, all the things I've learned from everything I've lived through, combined and recombined, used with intention to create transformation. A liminal space of embodiment. A practice of collaboration. Presence. I am returning to myself, to my body, to the goodness of feeling good. I am kneading the shame in my hands, squeezing it, wringing it out. I am casting a spell, setting an intention, using the power and energy of my body, my being, to create something powerful and new. It's fucking magic.*

Medicine

The hottub at the Y and the steam room. Working out. Boxing class. Reading fiction. Reading poetry. Reading theory. Writing in my diary. Writing poetry. Writing essays. The cats. Their purrs. Riding my bike. Sexting. Leaking my own nudes. Conversations with the roomie. WhatsApp for hours with my friends. Tea. Coffee (lattes actually). Walking in my neighborhood. Making Spotify playlists. Emo. Tarot. Practicing magic. Approaching everything like a practice of magic. Self-reflection. Honest conversations. Taking risks. Taking time to be with the plants. Keeping my room clean. Bullet journaling. Trusting myself. Going to therapy. Going to 12 step meetings. Not going to 12 step meetings. Bold lipstick. Laughter. Oversharing on facebook. Being myself. Asking for what I want. Trusting that I'm okay if I don't get it. My vibrator. Drinking lots of water. Magnesium bi-glycinate. B2. B6. B12. Ginger. Turmeric. 5-HTP. Vegan omega3. Surrendering perfectionism. Being okay with not being able to do everything. Study dates. Friendship dates. Expressing affection. Telling the truth. Supporting other addicts and survivors. Practicing patience and kindness. Condoms. Getting tested. Talking about sexual health. Ranting about biphobia to my nurse practitioner. Self-advocating. Asking for help. Texting crushes. Being playful. Being flirtatious. Feeling cute. Getting enough sleep. Standing up for myself. Saying the hard thing. Setting boundaries. Prayer. Solitude. Hope. Joy. Sorrow. Grief. Anger. Pleasure. Contentment. Feeling my feelings. Smiling to myself. Being flexible. Making plans. Travelling. Faith. Holding space for complexity. Integration work. Letting myself be a contradiction. Finding the middle ground. Admitting that I don't have

Medicine

all the answers. Admitting that it hurts. Doing healing work for myself and others. Ancestor work. Mourning. Lifting up. Trying. Trying again. Practicing forgiveness. Knowing that it's not my job to forgive everything. Sunlight. Noticing. Paying attention. Watering the houseplants. Getting a massage even though I can't really afford it. Stretching. Meditation, maybe. Walking for the sake of it. Letting go of what I no longer need. Practicing gratitude. Giving myself permission to make mistakes, to grow and change, to leave, to say no, to say yes, to desire, to want, to ask, to process, to change my mind. Healing. Learning. Resting. Going for it. Letting go.

Sucking Dick is Part of the Process

*L*AUGHING WITH MY roommate in the kitchen. *It's all part of the process! Like procrastination is part of being an artist. It's like a seed germinating underground. And honestly, I had to figure the sex stuff out. Like tinder and having sex and all that, it was all part of the process. I can't write honestly about trauma with my sexual shame completely unprocessed. It's like, Professor: I was sucking dick and that was part of the PROCESS.* And we're laughing and we're both procrastinating and we're both late on assignments but we are feeling our feelings and we are living our lives and we are honestly brilliant.

I walk up the staircase to my bedroom and I am struck by the beauty of my life. This new life. It manifested out of nowhere. I manifested it. I faced the deepest pain. I am often surprised by the depth, dimension, and diversity of pain. Just when I think I've felt it all there is some new pain, some whole new type of pain. I broke the dysfunctional promise. I walked away from what at one time I thought I did not deserve. I learned that I deserve so much more. I deserve this new life. I deserve people who love me and support me. People who listen to me and hold space for me and share their own vulnerabilities. I am meeting myself for the first time. I am meeting myself by saying no to that which is bad for me. I am no longer abandoning myself. This is the magic. This is the secret. This is the work.

Integration can feel like swinging. My therapist explained it like a pendulum. As I come closer to myself the pendulum will swing more rapidly. It will feel strange. Sudden. Abrupt. But I am learning to ride these waves. I am learning to love all of who I am. I have saved my own life so many times. In so many different ways. So much of my behaviour over the years seems completely insane, but these were the ways that I survived what was impossible to survive. I am learning to forgive myself for the ways I fell short of my values. I am putting an end to intergenerational trauma by healing it here in my own body, here and now, lifetimes of pain.

My joy is like this shining light, it's like this tidal wave, it's like this bend in spacetime. My joy is a rebellion, it's a powerful elixir, it is healing, healing, healing. I spend so much time laughing, literally laughing my ass off, just laughing for no reason or because something is really funny or just because I just love to laugh. When I type LMAO I really am laughing my ass off. I am healing, healing, healing. Friendship lights up my life, enlivens me, gives me new roots and new earth to plant them in. Friendship is that good soul medicine, that kindness, that witnessing, through the good times and the bad. By showing up for myself and showing up for my friends and letting them show up for me I am learning what love is. Something I never knew. I am learning the language of care, of presence. I am healing those childhood wounds and surprise surprise, the answer is not dysfunctional romantic love.

My joy isn't something you can take from me because it isn't something that you gave to me. My joy is hard earned and hard learned. My joy is the bravest thing I've ever done. To lose it all again. To tear my fake life to the ground. To smash the pedestal I put you on and the public lie of our relationship. To dare to imagine that I deserve better. To show up and do the work and tell the truth even when it felt like my heart was literally being ripped the fuck out. I felt new depths of pain. I didn't know that was possible. But now I have felt joy. I have felt the pureness of joy that isn't anyone's but mine. You aren't the best thing that ever happened to me, even though there was a time when that's what I believed. But the pain I went through turned out to be a passageway through which I found my way back to myself.

Fucking Magic

I wrote a paragraph of my proposal today, the proposal I've been procrastinating on for months, at the coffee shop with my best friend between intense convos about dating and sexuality and misogyny and #slutlife and loving ourselves and each other in a world that's always trying to tear us down. Refusing to believe the bullshit lies. Uprooting the toxic shame. And the words started to loosen and they started to come and I remembered, or maybe learned for the first time, that being a sexual being is not in opposition to being successful in other areas of my life. There is no separation. I can be both. I can have both. And deep down in the core of my trauma I can feel the beginnings of my split starting to heal.

So I love the process. So I love the pain. I tell my roommate *Yeah so we're brilliant. Disorganization and procrastination are just signs of being brilliant. So don't even feel bad about it!* And she tells me *Feeling bad about it is part of the process too.* And it all comes together and crystallizes and we are laughing and we are happy and we are feeling our feelings and we are living our lives and we are in it. We are in it. And this is the process and this is the work and it feels bad sometimes and we dive into the depths of our traumas and our greatest pains and we carve out the space that we need to hold that and we create joy and beauty and power and change. We make something new.

We are laughing and our laughter is magic, it is stirring everything up, it is changing it. We are laughing and our laughter is healing, it is the secret we were looking for, it is the answer to the question we didn't know how to ask.

Making It

*F*UCK CAPITALISM AND the crushing pressure of it. Fuck the tick-tock clock that says *You're 30 you should have achieved more than this*. Fuck pretending like the living world isn't suffering, crying out, just like we are, because the times we are living in are unlivable. Fuck the whole business as usual thing. It is okay to struggle. It makes sense to struggle. Fuck Canada for celebrating 150 years of genocidal violence and hiding behind words like reconciliation while Indigenous women and two-spirit people and men and children continue to experience unbelievable amounts of violence. Fuck pretending like this isn't happening, fuck the lack of acknowledgement of violence as the starting place, as where we are. We are here and this is what is happening, what has been happening. Making space for the pain of it, for the complexity of it, for the responsibility of it, that's the work. "Making it" within this system doesn't change anything and we need to stop leaving each other behind. Fuck success if it means forgetting, if it means pretending, if it means denying. I want success that feels heartfelt, that feels like the work I was put on this earth to do, that feels like part of the struggle, like we are in this together.

    I am trying to heal. I am working so hard to heal, and not just myself, not just this deep sever within myself, not just the dissociation and the alienation from my own body and the intrusive thoughts that say *rape* and *get off me* and *don't fucking touch me*. I am trying to heal this world, this beautiful, dying world. I think on some level we all are. Either we are trying to heal or we are trying to forget. Because we know the hour is now. Because we know this is real and it's come this far. And the work is healing, remembering, restoring, transforming. Listening. Taking responsibility. Lifting up. Trying. Going back, going forward, holding still. The work is to try and to fail and to try again. The work is to love in the face of despair. *The work is to love in the face of despair.* It is ancestor work. Remembering who we are and where we come from. Healing intergenerational trauma. Stepping into our power as human beings, as creatures of this earth, and renouncing systemic violence. Healing the earth by remembering the true names. This is Tkaronto. Where the trees stand in water.

The only way for me to heal is for me to love this world. The only way for me to love this world is to name and resist the violence of capitalism and colonialism. I can only love this land which has loved me all my life if I resist the violence through which I came into relationship with this land. It is time. And I can't do this work if I am distracting myself with narratives of success and failure, if I am anesthetizing myself by believing there is a way to "make it" in a dying world without making saving that world be the work.

Daddy Issues

Hands grasp at hollowness. There is a devotion. There, I said it, *devotion*. I am undone by the possibility of care. It's the withholding. There I said it, *withholding*.

Holding. My heart is in my throat, is in my hand, is buried somewhere deep in the flesh of my body. If I love enough, if I am good enough. I'm thirty years old. Not a little girl anymore but still. Maybe there's hope for me yet.

How many times have I been told I have *daddy issues*? They say I have a god-shaped hole. Maybe I have a dad-shaped hole. *I am a traitor for writing these words.*

Bad daughter. Black sheep. Runaway.

I try to figure out the calculations. What can I afford to lose? What can I stand to give up? Turns out it's a lot. I walked into the jaws of a shark, I walked off the dock, into the lake. I walked into certain danger thinking *Maybe this will make me good.*

But nothing did. There are secrets still, there are things we don't talk about. Unspeakable things. My body is stiffened and sickened, still. I can tell the truth but it feels like a lie because the truth is *I don't know*.

Touch me. *Don't touch me.* Touch me. *Don't touch me.*

Don'tfuckingtouchmedon'tfuckingtouchmedon'tfuckingtouchmedon'tfuckingtouchmedon'tfuckingtouchmedon't.

My body is an empty space. My body is an unanswered question. My body is a bargaining chip. My body is a tree marked to be chopped down. My body is your desire. My body is the site of terror. My body is the site of pleasure: mine or yours?

Fucking Magic

But I never said *I love you dad* because I knew love was slippery and dangerous, love was the doors we weren't allowed to lock, and the curtains we had instead of doors. Love was nothing but respect. Love was nothing but standing together, as a family, never telling the secrets, never believing what the other people said about us. Love was the secrets and the ways we kept them. Love was submission, cornered like a dog.

Old junk cars all out in our second cousin's yard and all the dogs tied up on ropes all day. It makes me sad to see them tied but it's not allowed to ask about it. My grandfather in nothing but his tiny underwear all the time. My professor father glaring at me *It's a class thing*. He's a Marxist and he uses his political ideology to make excuses for incest.

My father was fierce in his devotion. There, I said it, *devotion*. All the things he rebelled against by running to the university are the very things his books brought him back to. Turns out his father was a working class hero. Lumberjack. So my father, the professor, found his roots.

I found the roots of trees on my hands and knees when I went out to the forest because it was safer than the house. I am the daughter of professors. I know the fancy words they taught me but not a single word for what is happening to me.

They make me cry at the dinner table. Sometimes they forget I'm just a kid. My father screams and calls me *disrespectful, ungrateful, selfish*. My body buds breasts and I feel the pressure of my grandfather's eyes, hands, face. I am disappearing. I am going into the night.

So now when I talk to men I think *Dad is that you?* Because I don't talk to my real dad. Because the pain is too much and the secrets weigh down on my spine making me look at my feet making my neck ache. Because his eyes are sad and he smiles and *he has done nothing wrong*.

Just because your grandfather did that to you doesn't mean you have the right to drag your father and your brother into this.

So now I don't have male doctors or teachers because I keep looking at them like *Dad is that you?* And even when I'm dating men there's this little part of me that's like *Dad is that you?* I know it's a terrible thing to admit and a little cliché, maybe a little pathetic, but it's the truth.

There is a devotion. There I said it, *devotion*. There's a way in which I lay my whole goddamn body in the middle of the highway. Just for a glimpse of that kindness. Just for a glimpse of that care. Just for a tiny little comfort so that I can feel some relief from the terror.

Because I don't understand. I still don't understand. Years and years of therapy. Books upon books. Self help. 12 step. Addiction. Spirituality. Feminism. Intergenerational trauma. A culture of sexual violence. Colonialism. The nuclear family. Class. Race. Gender. Child abuse. Incest. Sometimes I think I get it. I think the pieces are coming together and power and violence and trauma are starting to crystallize and make sense. But I still don't fucking understand. I don't understand.

I don't understand child sexual abuse. I don't understand incest. I don't understand and I want so badly to understand. I want a way to know why. I want a way to ask *how could you?*

The floorboards are creaking. The doorknob is turning. The adrenaline has stopped time. But it isn't my dad, it's his dad and I'm on the floor pushed between the bed and the wall because there aren't words for the things that I fear.

Maybe there was a gun under the bed. A rifle that he used to shoot at his own brother, oh that caused quite a stir. And maybe the woodstove is hot and it burns me when I touch it and maybe there is a bucket of hot coals. Maybe the spring runs clear and cold and maybe there are animal heads all over the walls: deer, bear, fox, their glass eyes glistening, their bodies gone. Like mine.

So when I'm feeling good, when I'm feeling cared for, when the world cracks its hard exterior of stress and fear and terror, when I feel soft, when I can laugh, when the touch is welcome, when the words are kind, when I can believe that I'm not just a body, when I feel even, maybe, for a moment, safe, oh my god I feel this fucking devotion. There, I said it, *devotion*. For one fucking second I feel like maybe I am loved.

And yes. Yes. That can be taken advantage of.

Opening

MAGIC IS A way of being in the world, of being open to relationship. Magic is the practice of recognition: seeing the liveliness of the living universe, seeing the liminal. It is a practice of wonder, curiosity, remembering.

I am tired and delirious, haven't had enough sleep. Maybe it's my Mars in Pisces but I am driven by faith in possibility. We talk about death and this is pressing. What happens when we die? What's beyond the horizon of that great unknown?

I try to explain my thought process. Being twelve and having a brain condition which the doctors initially perceived to be brain cancer. Facing death. Staring at the tree branches and wondering what will become of me when I die.

I don't believe the world is just material. I have faith in the immaterial aspects of existence. Yet this does not in any way degrade or deny the sacredness of the material. It is both.

I am exhausted by binaries. I am exhausted by scholars assuming that affirming the liveliness of materiality means we no longer have to 'rely' on belief in the immaterial. This way of thinking makes no sense to me. The material and immaterial are bound up with each other. Both are sacred. Both are here.

Dogs can hear frequencies that I can't hear and bees can see colours that I can't see. The world is far more complex than my capacity to perceive it. So science cannot prove the existence of the immaterial. But science cannot prove its nonexistence either.

Opening

I see the sparrows flitting about. I listen to their voices, watch their movements. I am enchanted. Capitalism requires disenchantment. To remember enchantment, to reconnect with a pulsing, living world, is to resist capitalism and environmental destruction. We are caught up, entangled, connected. We can allow ourselves to be awed and enlivened by the strange wonder of the world.

When I remember I can feel how strange everything is and how familiar. I ask myself, *how long have I been here? How many times?* I hear the seagulls crying out and circling. I run my fingers against the brick of buildings. I watch city people and city creatures and city plants. I pay attention.

Despite everything I am a fierce optimist. Despite everything, love is still the driving force in my life. I want to hold space for healing. I want to do work which reminds us of our own and each other's inherent worth. I want to resist capitalism through magic. I want to resist capitalism's attempts to commodify magic. I want to remember this practice, this language that saved my life.

It was the fox who broke across the field, the loon who broke water in front of the boat. It was the birch with the shining white bark and the shelves of fungus. It was the night sky with its changing moon. It was the sound of crickets, the sound of bullfrogs.

It was the raccoons on my balcony with their fast hands and cautious eyes. It was the squirrels chasing each other in circles around tree trunks. It was the synchronicity of hearing someone say out loud something I was thinking. It's that moment when I'm sure I've been here before, sitting in the darkened bar across from her.

Violence severs me, turns me into an object, turns the world into a series of objects. I lie on the ground and I feel its aliveness. I remember my aliveness. I remember there aren't words in English for so many of the things that I know.

My friend tells me he sees the fairies with me, their light glinting just beside my shoulder, in his peripheral vision. He wants me to know that they are with me, the fairies, my ancestors, these beings who cross fields.

Fucking Magic

I know that they are with me but it is comforting to hear him say it. He smiles at me and tells me I have fairy blood. I am one of them. They are my ancestors.

I keep my eyes on the lookout for mushroom patches. I try to treat every being I encounter with care. I am full of hope and wonder and yes, also fear. But we are in this together, for better or worse, this is what we have and we are here. My heart fills with gratitude, with profound, boundless love.

I insist on the legitimacy of enchantment. Magic is an opening. It is the antidote to despair.

Raining in Montreal

WE SIT ON your bed sipping our tea. Your lip quivers when you say you want to make out with me. Sobriety stretches around us like perfect clarity. The air is electric and I remember to breathe. I fall into the swamp of desire. I feel the hard edge of you. We talk about consent and we make out. I watch the expressions on your face and I give into the feelings of my body.

Your fingers are in my mouth while you fuck me. I press my heart against the bones of my ribcage, feeling things only poets feel. Feeling things only addicts feel. Feeling things only incest survivors feel. A certain magic of having a body. A certain magic of expansive impossible pleasure. You go down on me and I try not to cry.

In the morning you give me my coffee in a cup that says *Slut* on it. I smile for the power of desire, for the simple joy of not being shamed. I watch you dress and I know I've caught feelings. I sip my coffee and I keep my feelings to myself.

Catching feelings is dangerous territory. We send dirty texts and I play it cool. I tell you that the bruise on my collarbone makes me think of you. I tell you that it turns me on to think of the impact which produced it. I don't mention the pull of pleasure, the power in surrender. I don't say a word about my heart.

You respond with a confession of a crush. A little spark of feeling that neither of us know what to do with. But I smile. I tell you the feeling is mutual.

I have a long bus ride home. It is raining in Montreal.

Fucking Magic

#2

Raining in Toronto

My eyes are brave enough to ask the question, my words hesitate. Your eyes respond to mine and I spit out sentences trying to say what I mean. You ask me *If you could have what you want what would that be?* I'm embarrassed by my vulnerability. I am in dangerous territory. You ask me if I want to be your Toronto date. You don't do long distance but we are definitely doing something. *Yes, I really want that.* Cities apart but we are here together in my bed.

We walk Toronto streets, heading east. You start and stop your sentences when the conversation turns to what we're doing. Your eyes tell me more than you're saying. You kiss my forehead at the corner of College and Spadina. I say *Fuck me up, universe, just fuck me up.* We laugh.

You ask me about my first love. I tell you about the girl I loved from the age of five to the age of fifteen. I tell you about the boyfriend who put me through a wall. You tell me about yours, the one who moved away, the one you moved to be with.

As we walk block after block we unfold story after story. Listening to the details of each other's childhoods, each other's traumas, the winding roads that brought us here. The sky threatens rain but we are brave and we keep walking. At Sherbourne we turn south and the sky cracks open. We duck under an awning, sit on cement and watch as the world is washed clean around us.

We talk about gratitude. We talk about trauma. We talk about the miracle of even being here at all, after everything that's happened. *What are the chances of this moment, of any moment, even happening at all?*

Principled

PRINCIPLES BEFORE PERSONALITIES, we say to each other knowingly, with a little flicker in the eye. I want to be principled. I want to be my best self, live my best life. I want to live a principled life, grounded in love, not motivated by fear. I think about shame and what it's done to me. I think about fear. I think about how I was unable to forgive myself for the years of active alcoholism, for the years my behavior caused harm. I know that shame and fear are rooted in trauma. I know that shame and fear are not good motivators for a principled life.

We walk to the meeting and we talk about causing harm, and the shit we've done, and the shit we've been accused of, and the shit most people don't know. I tell you how scared I was. I tell you about how, when I first got sober, I wanted to kill myself so bad. I didn't know how to live with myself after the years spent causing harm and straying so far from my values. I tell you I'm afraid if people knew about the person I used to be they'd drop me. We talk about disposability and exile and how hard it is to admit to fucking up when the consequences loom so large. I tell you I want friends who wouldn't drop me. I tell you I want to be brave. We go to the meeting and of course it's step nine. We listen to people grapple with the harm they've caused and struggle with how to set things right.

I want to feel my body again. I want to feel safe enough to sink down into my skin, not just with a stranger, but with someone I care for. I want to know what it's like to be free from shame. I want the courage to be seen, not just here in my writing, but in person, sprawled out and crying, my body tensing and releasing. I want to fucking relax. I want to feel safe enough to ask for what I want. I want to believe I deserve it. I want to believe that I am deserving of care, that I am not a bad person.

A sponsor I had for awhile told me I have toxic shame. She told me that the level of shame I felt over the harm I caused during my drinking days was not proportionate to what I had done. She told me that my strong desire to kill myself and the fact that a fifth step brought no relief indicated that the shame I felt was not about the harm I'd caused. She told me that when a child is abused they have to make sense of it, so they make sense of it by believing they are inherently bad. I took the violence into me. I turned myself into the cause, the source, so that I could feel some control. Because if it's my fault then maybe I can stop it. Of course I couldn't stop it. I couldn't redeem myself from the shame of being unloved. So when I grew up and acted fucked up that was just proof of what I'd always believed: that I am bad.

We sit in the grass and I listen to these beautiful people who have been broken like I have been broken and who are being reborn like I am being reborn tell each other that they are good. You are a good person. You are a good person. *You look at me and tell me* You are a good person too. *I can feel the collective pain in this circle. I can feel the pain of loving addicts, of being addicts, of living with what we've done, doing the best we can with what we have and never feeling like it's enough. I fucking love us. I love us so much. I know that we are miracles. I know that we should be dead but we're not. We're here sitting in the grass being kind to each other and helping each other heal.*

I want to be a principled person grounded in the certainty that I deserve care, that we all do. I want to love myself enough to ask for what I want. I want the openness in my heart to be grounded, not to dissolve into oblivion. I want my mouth to form words and to say out loud my desires. I want to know what my desires are and I want the guiding principles to be kindness, patience, curiosity, care. I want to breathe deep and not feel like I'm going to die. I want friends who have my back, who wouldn't drop me. I want communities where we don't live in fear of exile, where we stay and work through the hard shit, where we help each other heal.

Principled

I know it's fucking hard and I know it isn't easy but I also believe it's the work. None of us are infallible and none of us are disposable.

On the way back from the meeting, as we walk the streets of Montréal, I tell you I'm scared that I'm a bad person. That somehow the things I've done set me apart, make me irredeemable. Somehow there is a line that divides inside from outside and I am on the outside. I can't make my way back. I have made direct amends wherever possible. I live my amends every day. I have done everything I can to set things right. I have changed. I continue to change. But I worry sometimes that I am defined by my past. I worry sometimes that there is no way back. You look at me. You tell me I am a good person. I know you are a good person. I believe you.

I keep learning and relearning these lessons. I keep going deeper and now I've reached the place where mind meets body, the place heart meets mind meets body, the place where I furrow my brow and squint my eyes and try. The place where my poems and the curve of my belly and my hands and my sexuality and my principles and my huge fucking heart are colliding and creating sparks. I say *I hear you universe, shame is clearly up for review.* I can't heal and grow and secretly hate myself at the same time. I can't heal and grow and believe that I am bad. I am not bad. I am a good person, worthy of love and care. I have to heal the shame in my body. I have to forgive myself for my past. I have to extend the compassion I so freely give to others to myself.

I want to stay with the complexity. I want kindness, forgiveness, goodness. I want communities of care and justice, not shame and fear. I know in my body when my actions are grounded in love and justice. I know in my body the difference between accountability and shame. I know in my body what it feels like to be grounded in my principles. I want to live a principled life.

Fuck Me Up

*I*LIE ON THE tattoo table as the artist tattoos *Fuck Me Up* inside a heart on the side of my butt. He asks me about the pain and I tell him it barely feels like anything. He laughs *You've been fucked up so much that now you don't feel anything.* I laugh. If only he knew how true that is.

Later, in a bright room on a bed with white sheets, I watch a beautiful person fuck me. White sheets, bright lights, beautiful human being. My eyes drink in the sight. Their hands on my hips, their eyes meeting mine. That fucking curve of their lip. I am enraptured. I am captured by the sight of them. I am unraveled, undone, but I can't come. I can't enter the depths of my body. I can't slide off the edge of that cliff.

Frustrated, I rub my clit raw. I swear I can come in under a minute. I swear I can come thirty times in a row. *You know how I told you I get a concussion if someone looks at me the wrong way? It's the same with orgasms.* But if I catch feelings I am severed from my centre. If I catch feelings the door to my pussy is locked.

Trauma is tricky and this seems backwards as fuck. Meet a stranger on tinder and I am a wriggling mess of pleasure. Fuck someone I have feelings for and I can't come. It's like my heart sends off a warning signal, a flashing light that immediately shuts down my connection to pleasure.

I remember when it stopped being fun to fuck the love of my life. I remember when pleasure dissolved into terror. I remember learning how to conjure pleasure from the terror. I remember sex as an offering, a way to keep the peace. I remember choosing the violence I would endure, and rape was not the worst.

Fuck Me Up

I remember other things, things I don't remember. There is a silence I keep in my stomach. It is an endless well. I drink the water to keep it full. I don't go to the bottom. I look at my reflection rippling on the surface of black water and I don't dare go down there.

I told the universe to fuck me up. I said bring it the fuck on, universe. I laughed hysterically and felt the fullness of my heart. I tattooed that shit on my body. *Fuck Me Up* in a heart on the side of my butt. I surrendered to the wild mystery of my life. I took the risk because I knew I would survive it. I knew I would survive it because I have already survived. I gave in to pleasure, to possibility, to hope. I let myself follow my desire, I learned the lessons, and I hit a brick wall.

I want to be soft. I want to relax. I want to feel safe. I want to open like a flower. I want to turn toward the sun. I want to breathe and feel my breath in my fucking toes. But I can't let go. I can't surrender. Despite all my talk of surrender I am holding the fuck on.

My naturopath thinks my digestion issues are rooted in trauma. She explains to me that our bodies shut down nonessential functions like digestion when we are in a flight or fight response. She suggests that my body has simply forgotten how to digest due to a lifetime of complex trauma.

She wants me to sit for a few minutes before eating, to breathe deeply into my belly, to look at my food. When she tells me this I feel how much I don't breathe into my belly and so I try.

I want to cry. I feel sick and terrified and deeply sad. There's this well down there, this deep, deep well full of water. It feels like if I breathe down there I will open up a flood. I will open up and flood and I won't stop flooding. I feel like a little child curled up in a ball, trying to make myself disappear. I feel a terror and a sadness so big I'm afraid I'll disappear into it.

Lying in bed with this person I'm crushing on. They have been asking me hard questions lately like what my favourite foods are and what I'm into sexually. They want to know what I *want*. What my desires are. I tense up with terror at the possibility of this vulnerability. I tell them how

Fucking Magic

I'm locked outside my body. How fucking hard it is to try to get back in. I tell them I hate that I have to do this work.

They say *You* get *to do this work. Most of us can be kinda in our bodies, kinda not, and go through life that way. But you have the opportunity to really be in your body. You* get *to do this work.*

So I surrender. I give in. I do the work. I try again. Fuck me up, universe. Fuck me up.

Resolve

When I was seventeen I lived alone in a bachelor apartment in Toronto. I left my keys in the door and I woke up to find a man standing over my bed. He bolted when I opened my eyes. I didn't know if it had really happened. I called my mom, which is something I almost never did. She agreed it was probably a dream and I went back to sleep. When I awoke again I found that I had been robbed. My keys and purse and all my cash were gone.

When I was seventeen I used to fuck myself up with a razor. In my tiny apartment all alone I would cut my arms and legs to oblivion. It was the only thing that gave me any peace. It was the only way to translate the urgency I felt within me. It was a fight for life in the face of death because suicide loomed large.

I wanted to die. I wanted to fucking die. I looked at the bridge. My mother's father jumped from a bridge and he died. I thought about the lake. I thought about the traffic, the subway tracks. And of course there were the pills. Bottles of them. One by one I would swallow them down. Then I'd feel the panic rising up in me because I didn't want to die.

I don't want to die. *You might not want to kill yourself but you're going to.* Intrusive thoughts. Suicidal ideation. A desperate desire for respite from this obliterating nameless pain, this shapeless void that drags me down, this unbearable feeling, this desire to destroy myself. But I don't want to fucking die.

I'd take the pills. Then I'd drink the charcoal. Get hooked up to the wires. And pray for my fucking life.

Fucking Magic

Sitting in the park eating ice cream, she asks me where my resolve comes from, my courage. She asks me how I learned to be brave. I think for a second and tell her *My resolve was born in my confrontation with death.* I came so close to the edge and there, in that surrender, I found a desire for life. I found something inside myself that insisted: *Live. Live fucking live.* I fought for my life because I knew I could die. If I didn't fight I knew I would die.

I found a way to live despite the pain. Simple things. Small things. The hardest things. I wrote the truth down. Even just in my diary. Even just in secret notes to myself that only I could decode. I tried to make sense of what happened to me. I tried to find a way to speak the unspeakable. I gave myself explicit permission to break all the rules. I would do anything, everything, I would do whatever it took to stay alive.

And that meant being fucking crazy. It meant cracking open and screaming and being completely insane. It meant pouring the pain from inside me into the world. I did it for years because it was all I could do until finally I could do something else. But I refused the lie, the lie that would kill me. And to this day I stand by the truth even when everyone else pretends it isn't real. I remember and I write down the truth and break all the rules and that's how I stay alive. I tell the truth. I stay alive.

I tell her about the way I loved him in the courtroom. I took the stand and I couldn't look at him. I loved him. I will always love him. She asks me how. How can I love him and never go back? Where does my resolve come from, my willingness to surrender who I love? I tell her *I realized he would kill me unless I stopped him. I realized he wasn't going to stop himself.*

When he put me through the wall and then used my body to clear the furniture out of the way to throw me on the floor, when he put his knee on my chest and cut off my breath and screamed in my face *Do you know who you're fucking with?* I knew I could die. I knew I would die unless I stopped him.

So I loved him and I let him go. I loved him and I did whatever I had to do to make sure he didn't kill me. I never spoke to him again. I gave

Resolve

up everything, everything, and I decided I wanted to stay alive. I will do whatever I have to do, surrender everything I love, break every single rule, I will turn it all over, throw it all away, to live.
    Live. Fucking live.

The Tower

J UNE IS THE month of the Tower. My Saturn Return isn't over yet. Despite all the growth and all the work, or maybe because of it, more is being revealed. It's time to burn some things to the ground.

June is the month I break up with my best friend. It's the month I grow into boundaries and let go of people pleasing and avoiding conflict. I stand up for myself, communicate my boundaries, and when they aren't respected, I walk away. I love her but I walk away.

June is the month I realize I forgot my body again. It slipped out of my hands, a ghost again. But I find my body, face down on the vinyl couch at a sex club. I find the pleasure deep down at the root of me and for a second I remember. This man is massaging every inch of me. I am blissed out and my skin is alive with desire. Everyone keeps telling me *breathe, breath. Breathe, Clementine, breathe.*

June is the month I realize I left my heart in Montréal. I long for those streets, that city. I struggle against what it would mean to leave Toronto, the place I've called home for fifteen years. It's June. I am hot and I love the heat. I walk everywhere. I walk for hours, all over Toronto, as if I am lying with a lover I am leaving, memorizing every detail one last time. I listen to my headphones, the same songs over and over, I am trying to feel something, there is something I am trying not to feel.

June is the month of the Tower. Face those fears, the ones that really scare you. Get activated by romantic feelings and slowly lose your mind. But I find it again. I find my mind running circles way up in the sky outside of my body. I have only two priorities: be good, be loved. And I know that it's crazy. I dig deep into the earth to remember who I am. June

The Tower

is the month I forget. The story seems to have culminated, concluded. I seem to have lost my place. I seem to have been redirected. Two priorities: be good, be loved.

June is the month I tell my therapist about the well inside of me. *It's so hard to surrender, so hard to let go, once I feel happy, no not happy, loved. Once I catch a glimpse of love. It's all I want. To be loved. What am I supposed to do? I can't go back in time and make my parents love me.*

She asks me *Do you think your parents didn't love you?* My response is impassioned, verging on anger, covering up the terror, the ultimate betrayal. *No they didn't love me. Maybe they thought they did but that isn't love. When you love someone, you protect them. Especially a child. If you love a child, you protect them. You fight for what you love. My parents did the opposite. My father punished me. He called me disrespectful, ungrateful, selfish. My mother did nothing.*

They knew how terrified I was. They knew what my grandfather was doing. After he did that to me I told my mom and she didn't do anything. She didn't protect me. She didn't love me. My parents couldn't love me because their parents didn't love them.

June is the month of the Tower. *Breathe, breathe.* Feel that air deep in my belly. It makes me want to puke, sob, cut myself to ribbons. It makes me want to build a monument to my terror, but I can't talk about my terror. I can talk around it but I can't even begin to explain.

Breathe, breathe. So I do. My neck aches and I get a massage. I lie on the table and I try to breathe. I go to the Y and use the hot tub, the steam room. This is the passageway. This is the next lesson. It's time for me to do this work and it's work I'm terrified to do.

Breathe, breathe. I drop my shoulders because they are at my ears again. I breathe into my belly. I put my hand on my belly. Maybe I am gaining weight again. Maybe my body is a tool to achieve my priorities: be good, be loved. Maybe my body is an animal, a living creature. Maybe the child I was is still here in the flesh and she's scared.

Breathe, breathe. Make the tea, holy basil, lemon balm, lavender, steep it in a glass jar and write on the lid: *I love you, you are safe, I will protect you no matter what.* I tell my therapist I'm a ride or die and I realize for the first time that I want to be that for myself. I want to have my back no matter what.

June is the month of the Tower. I realize there's a child in me. She's scared. She has two priorities: be good, be loved. These are the only things that matter. She takes me over. Emotional flashbacks. Terror, desperation. I forget the rest of me, the rest of who I am.

Breathe, breathe. I realize there's an adult in me. There's this adult I've grown into. This person I've become. When the trauma is activated I can forget who I am. I forget that I have more than two priorities. I forget I don't care about being good, I care about living a principled life. I care about loving myself. I am so fucking strong and brave. I have already survived and I will protect myself no matter what.

When I remember the adult in me, this person I've become, I am proud of myself, I am happy. What I need is to love the child in me, not run in fear but love the fear until it's soft enough to breathe into, soft enough to heal. I am strong enough and I'm fucking ready. I can no longer pretend I have only two priorities, I can no longer pretend I don't have a body, I can no longer treat my body like a means to an end.

June is the month of the Tower. It is the month when things burn. I light a match and drop it. I lose my place in the smoke. I forget where I'm going, what I'm saying. But the heat wakes me up. I'm afraid to lose, I've already lost so much. I grip and hold on. *Love me, don't leave me.* I let people treat me badly so that they won't leave. Lightning strikes and I let go.

June is the month of the Tower. I neglect my divinity, treat my body as a means to an end, a shell, a nuisance. I get angry at myself for my trauma. Why can't I come? Why can't I ask for what I want? Why am I so scared? Why do I have to be like this? I forget to be gentle. I forget to go slow. Lightning strikes and I let go.

Breathe, Clementine, breathe. My body is tense with fear, desperately holding on, trying to keep the terror at bay. I am clench up, all shallow

breath and raised shoulders, unwilling to find out what would happen if I let go
    The lighting strikes and I let go.

Kiss the Ground

I WALK HOME FROM the show after dancing and singing and hearing all my favourite songs. I walk home through the hot June Toronto streetlight, passing big blossoming bushes heavy with sleep. I walk along the dirty sidewalks of this grimy city (I keep telling people Toronto is grimy and they tell me it's not, but it's the grime of this city that I love). I want to kiss the fucking ground. I want to get down on the dirty sidewalk and press my face into it. I want to feel the weight of my body pressed into the cement and I want to kiss it. I want to somehow merge my very being with this city, because I know deep down in my heart that I am leaving.

I did kiss the dirty Toronto pavement when I was released from the psych ward all those years ago. That was for my freedom, for the pleasure and privilege of being in the world. But this time I want to kiss the ground because the truth is I'm really sad. My heart is breaking. I'm really sad because I know that I'm leaving. I look at the CN tower, cheesy but it's always there, especially now that I live downtown. I look at the city skyline. I walk these streets, these alleyways. This is my home. This is the city that raised me, feral runaway, high school drop out. Drunk, fuck up, panhandling and screaming at strangers, pissing rivers all over the dirty ground. This is the city that saved me.

This is the city where I have been my worst most fucked up self. Yeah I was assaulted and yeah people treated me like dirt. Yeah the cops were called and yeah I got thrown off the streetcar face first. But I existed here, crazy like that, drunk like that, broken like that. The city itself held me. The concrete held me. The alleyways and the sidewalks were the only places I could really come to, the only places that could really love me back. I slept under cardboard reeking of old piss or hiding in the bushes because I was less likely to be assaulted there and this city loved me back.

I love this fucking city and this city loves me. We've been through it all together. Cockroaches and bedbugs, the don valley which holds all my secrets, the funeral for my broken heart, the fox who came to witness, the lake that stretches to the horizon, all the secret places to get warm when it's freezing. This is the city where I destroyed myself and it's the city where I saved myself. It's the city that I ran away to, scared incest survivor queer kid runaway, from a dirt road, a place where you don't lock your doors. I came to Toronto alone, sixteen years old, and I learned.

I never meant to stay. Not this long. When I was eighteen I had a dream of making it to the west coast. I wanted to get the fuck away from my family, not just away to the nearest city, but away, gone. But then my little sister said I couldn't leave her in my parents' house, said it wasn't safe to leave her there, so I took her. Me, nineteen years old and her, sixteen. I couldn't take her to the west coast so I just took her to Toronto. I tried my best to be her quasi-parent/drinking buddy. I did my best, which wasn't very good at all. We got a shitty apartment at Sherbourne and Dundas and I worked forty hours a week at a sex store and she went to high school and we survived.

We lived together for six years in a number of shitty apartments and when I got sober I severed the codependence and moved into a sober house. I slowly built a life in sobriety, a life here in Toronto. The Toronto twelve step communities got me sober and saved my life. The people in those rooms showed me how to start living again. Now I'm five years sober. I've lived in ten places in the close to fifteen years I've lived in this city, four in the past five years. I've literally seen it fucking all and what they say about Toronto housing is true. We have no housing security. Everywhere is being gentrified. We have no rights. Cockroaches and bedbugs are a constant looming threat. And the rent is absurdly expensive. But it's all I've known and I've always made it work somehow. We make it work somehow.

Fucking Magic

And now I live in the best apartment I've ever lived in. It's a fucking dream. A beautiful, giant attic room overlooking Kensington Avenue. A roommate who became a best friend. Two precious cats. I found this place like a fucking miracle after leaving a dysfunctional unhappy relationship and having to move. I saw 25 places in my hunt because that's what Toronto housing is like. When I saw this place I wanted it so bad I was terrified of my desire. I had to surrender it. I had to want it and let it go. When I got the place I couldn't believe it and I built a home here. I built a life here. I have only lived here for seven months and already it has changed me. I love it here. I want to stay. And I know that I am leaving.

I want to roll around on my bedroom floor, press myself into the walls. I want to run out into the streets and press my face into the pavement, lick the fucking cement. I want to somehow merge my body with this city, with the home and life and love and history I have here. So that somehow I can stay. So that somehow I can always be here. My ghost will haunt the city. In the alleyways, in the valley, at the corner of College and Spadina, there will always be a piece of me. I pretend like I'm indifferent but I'm not indifferent. I pretend like I'm spontaneous and daring but really I'm deeply sentimental and it is so hard for me to let go. I love this fucking city and I love my home so much. I love my life here. I want to stay. And I know that I am leaving.

I am almost done with my Saturn Return but not quite. I left a three year long relationship and out of the ashes I built this incredible, beautiful new life. I fell in love with myself and the world and my life. I made a home in this beautiful apartment, in Kensington Market, and in my body for the first time in years. I started to laugh and to have sex again and to feel things. I thought I'd found everything I was looking for and it's true, I did. But I'm not quite done with my Saturn Return and there are more big lessons on the horizon. I thought after all these huge changes that I could settle at least for a while. The universe had other plans for me. I got my poems in a journal and in April I went to Montréal to read them at the launch. It was just a trip to read my poems at the journal launch, and maybe read some tarot and make some money while I was there. It was just a little trip to Montréal, that city just a six hour bus ride away.

Montréal which I came to with my abusive ex partner after he got out of jail, all those years ago. It was the trip to start things over, the trip to solidify our love once his bail conditions were no longer an issue. We smoked weed and walked around the city putting up stickers and taking pictures. He taught me how to skateboard in the streets of Montréal. There are videos of me. 23 years old, trying to skate. Laughing, happy, desperately in love. I always wanted to travel but as a drunk I never got very far. So this trip with the love of my life to this city six hours away meant everything to me. It was the adventure of a lifetime in a life like mine. Of course, he got angry. Of course my devotion couldn't stop his rage but I tried.

I didn't come back to Montréal for years. When I was just over a year sober I was awarded money through criminal injuries compensation. The first thing I did was take the bus to Montréal alone. I didn't know anyone in the city then. Being new to sobriety my life was a lot smaller than it is today. I had never travelled alone and I was terrified. I stayed at a cheap hotel. I was so scared that someone was going to break into my room. I pushed the dresser in front of my door and slept with my keys in my hand. I spent the days wandering for hours and getting lost. I certainly didn't have a smartphone. So I just walked and walked and I loved the city.

Eventually I started dating the person I would be with for three years and we started taking semi-regular trips to Montréal. We would come for the Anarchist Bookfair or Queer Between the Covers. We stayed with people in different parts of the city. I started to get to know Montréal and I loved it even more. I would say to my then-partner *I wish we could live here.* And they would tell me their work is in Toronto. And I chose love, of course I did.

But then maybe that isn't true. I chose a particular love. I chose the love for my partner, for the relationship, and I continued to choose it even as it crashed and burned in dysfunction. I also loved Montréal. I loved that city and I kept being called back there and I kept fantasizing about living there one day but I couldn't choose it.

So now, this year, the year I've finally built the life I've always dreamed of in Toronto, this is the year I choose Montréal. I went to Montréal just to read my poems at an event. I read tarot for tons of people to make some money while I was there. I laughed with cute queers and listened to their secrets. I wandered into the many churches and spent time with Our Lady of Sorrows. I found the church of my dreams. I hung out with friends and saw people I never get to see. I reconnected with my sobriety at a radsob meeting and I felt excited about sobriety for the first time in a long time. I hooked up with a cute person and developed a crush, which gave me an excuse to come back sooner rather than later. I left the city knowing that I left my heart behind. I didn't mean to fall so hard for Montréal but I did.

Toronto I will always love you. You will always be the city that saved me, the city I was my most fucked up self in, the city I got sober in, the city that held me through all that. Toronto I will never believe the haters. People who don't see your grime just don't know you like I know you. People who haven't loved you through cockroaches and piss drenched cardboard and fucking in Nathan Phillips Square. Goddamn Toronto I fucking love you so much. I love our history and I love this beautiful life that I've just built. I love Kensington Market. I don't care what anyone says. I fucking love Kensington Market and I feel so fucking blessed to have this beautiful home here. I am so fucking happy here. I don't want to leave. I wish I could have two lives. I can never tell you how hard it is to walk away from what I love.

But I also know that I am leaving. Even though the timing seems all wrong, I know that it is time. Even though it seems sudden, I realize this is the last major lesson of my Saturn Return. I have to fucking leave. I have to leave what I love to be with what I love. I have to leave what I know to be with what I don't. I have to choose. I have to finally choose something else. I have to follow this flirtation with this city a six hour bus ride away. I have to let myself love Montréal.

The Beast at the Bottom of the Lake

*I*DREAM THAT I am sleeping in the bed I really am sleeping in, in the room I really am sleeping in. In the dream I don't know that I'm asleep. I think I am just lying there in the bed, maybe dozing off a little. Then, adrenaline. I see someone in the room, someone standing there in the dark, standing over my bed. Terror. I don't think, I just act. I just move. I bolt out of bed, try to get away. I wake up standing, shaking, my heart racing. I have turned on the bedroom light in this state. I have done this alone and with my ex partner in the bed. I wake up disoriented and unsure if it really happened. My whole fucking body is shaking with terror.

I have these dreams and I had one during the three week trip to Ireland I took with my mom and my sister. I am mostly estranged from my family but I do have a relationship with my sister and my mom even though it is hard. I never spend extended amounts of time with them though, especially my mom. But I agreed to this trip because I wanted to see Ireland, the land of my ancestors. I said yes before I really thought about how hard it would be.

The three of us are sleeping on single beds in one hotel room. My sister awakens to me throwing myself off the bed, stumbling around in the dark, confused. Once I realize what has happened I say *Sorry I fell off the bed*. It doesn't make sense because obviously I was moving around, not just falling on the floor but that's the only explanation I offer. In the morning I tell them about my dreams and we laugh about how weird it was what I did. My sister asks me if I've ever talked to anyone about it. No one says anything about why I might have these night terrors,

Fucking Magic

with their particular theme of someone standing over my bed. No one acknowledges what kind of trauma would make a body react like that, come alive like that in sleep.

When we are in Sligo we talk to an old man who works as a woodcarver. He knows the old Irish stories and he tells them to us. He tells us a story about a beast at the bottom of the lake. *We all must face the beast,* he says. *That one thing we are afraid of facing, we have to face it. But we can't face it alone. We need someone who understands, a friend, a community, even the land itself.* I listen to him intently, hearing his soul medicine in the stories of my ancestors, feeling it hit me deep in my being where I most need healing. I know I need to face the beast.

Later while my mom, sister and I wait for a bus we start talking about what the man said. My mom says *Isn't it cool what he said about the beast, how we have to face it but we can't face it alone, we need someone who cares about us, someone who understands. When he was talking about the beast, I thought about your dreams. I thought about the nightmares you have.* She looks at me when she says this and I want to scream *What the fuck are you talking about? What do you think those dreams are about?* I am angry and triggered and exhausted and in pain. In my family we never mention the abuse. I can never speak of what happened to me. If I do, my mom becomes hysterical. Yet here she is, acknowledging my night terrors, saying I need to face the beast, while being completely unwilling to hear me speak of it. I can't understand how she can listen to that soul medicine, how she can hear about the beast and be reminded of my night terrors, and not put together what the beast is. I don't understand how she can be here with me in Ireland, seeing what I see, hearing what I hear, and still remain so deeply in denial.

The beast at the bottom at the lake is incest. It's my grandfather's strong arms pinning me down and his tongue in my mouth. The beast at the bottom of the lake is my twelve year old body hiding under a blanket in the middle of the lawn in the middle of the day because I was so fucking afraid. The beast at the bottom of the lake is the fucking betrayal. My mother, the feminist, the women's studies professor, who teaches feminist mothering, who is a renowned scholar of feminist mothering, didn't protect me. *You knew and you didn't protect me. You knew and you didn't protect me.*

My father saw the cuts covering my fifteen year old arms and the question he asked was *How could you do this to your mother?* I got beaten up at a show when I was nineteen and my mother asked *Why do you always do this?* When I was seventeen and wouldn't shut up about the sexual abuse my mother yelled at me *I was a good mother. This one thing can't erase that. You can't take that from me.* Any conversation about the sexual abuse turns into a conversation about her and her pain. These days we don't even talk about it but if it's even implied I see the pain in her eyes. The pain isn't about me, it's about her. It's about what she lost. Her fantasy of being a good mother, better than her own mother. Her fantasy of being the feminist mother who has it all. It is too painful for her to admit what she sacrificed in those pursuits. What she sacrificed was her daughters, our safety, our bodies, our hearts. She can't face it. She can't name it. She won't face the beast.

No one has ever said to me *I'm sorry*. She has never said to me *I'm sorry I didn't protect you. I'm sorry I didn't take you away from the danger. I'm sorry I kept making you see him. I'm sorry I got angry at you when you told me.* She pressured and coerced me, telling me that people will die because her father died, jumped off a bridge when she was eighteen and made her face the finality of leaving on bad terms. I sit with my mother's trauma, my mother's pain. I have come to understand why she didn't protect me and I do understand it. She is traumatized. She was never loved. She does not know how to love. But I still want the love she never gave me. I still don't know how to deal with the pain of this betrayal. I can't stand to have her look me in the eye and talk about the beast at the bottom of the lake without realizing her betrayal is the beast. She can't help me face the beast because she won't face the beast herself. No amount of soul medicine will do any good without the truth. The soul medicine is the truth. The truth is the soul medicine.

Fucking Magic

I can only forgive when I am no longer trying to get what I need from someone who can't give it to me. I want my mother to love me. I dive deep. I let myself see her trauma. I carve out a huge space in my heart and I find the capacity to forgive her. But the past is not the past when it's ongoing, when I keep getting hurt because I want her to give me something she can't give me. My friend asks me why I even see my mother. *I love her and she's traumatized and she did the best she could.* I always think of my mother, 25 when she had me, 30 when I was five. I always think of my mother, eighteen when her father jumped off the bridge. I know she is traumatized. But I also see the life she has, tenured professor, world traveler, and I know that none of this would have been possible if she had insisted on my safety and taken me away.

I changed my name so that you won't know who my mother is. I changed my name so that she can have her life and I can have mine. I changed my name so that I can tell the truth without naming her. But I still feel like a traitor for writing these words. I still feel guilty, ungrateful. I still feel her pain, her panic, her sad eyes. I still hear her telling me she is a good mother and I don't know what to do with the truth. The fundamental responsibility of a parent is to protect their child. I was not protected. My body and my safety were traded in for other people's comfort and convenience. No one wanted to do the work of naming incest so they forced me to take it on instead. My body is heavy with the weight of intergenerational trauma, with the silence and the shaming and the guilt. I sometimes wonder if I will ever be free of it. I changed my name so that I could write these words, so that I could face the beast on my own terms.

Cuimhne, Misneach

*I*LIT A CANDLE in the cathedral and left my petition to Our Lady of Perpetual Help. I wrote on the little piece of paper *Please help me heal from the pain of child sexual abuse, please help me know love.* I lit a candle inside Saint Bridget's Well. I got on my knees and drank from the holy water of the well, I took it in my hands and placed it on my heart. I asked Bridget to help me, to heal me. I let all my pain rise to the surface and I prayed *Please help me heal, please show me how to heal my heart so that I may know love.* I came upon the grotto, the place of prayer, on an Irish country road. I saw Our Lady lit by candle light and I got on my knees, tears in my eyes, all the pain I could never speak heavy in my heart. She held it for me, arms open, She welcomed me. I surrendered my confusion, my pain, my desperate desire for love. I surrendered my hope, my terror, my belief that somehow I could make everything alright. I gave it over, I asked for Her help.

Here on this land, talún, I found the stories of my ancestors. Here in this place I found the language of my ancestors living on people's tongues, spraypainted on walls, *misneach, courage*. My sister and I tattooed these words on our ankles: *misneach, courage, cuimhne, memory*. I chose the words because they were offered up to me by my ancestors. Remember and be brave. Here on this land, with my ancestors, with the hunger of starving mouths that split them from this land and put them an ocean away, with English that I think in, plastered all over everything, but Gaeilge on street signs, graffitied and remembered. I am trying to remember.

Fucking Magic

Remember: remember. What they want me to forget. My mom smiles and laughs and her eyes panic when we get anywhere near the truth. I learned to forget, like my ancestors before me. The pain is better out of sight. Generations of sexual abuse, alcoholism, violence. Generations of people who never learned how to love. And we lost our stories, we lost our connection to the land, we became colonizers and split others from their land, covered even more land with English. We forgot who we are. We had nothing to heal us or teach us, nothing to remind us of the old ways. *Cuimhne.* And so I remember.

It has always been against the rules to say what happened to me. When I was a child I was screamed at, called disrespectful, ungrateful, selfish. I was a bad daughter because I did not submit, so I learned to submit. When I got older it was the psych ward for me. I was marked as crazy. I was never allowed to say my pain, my terror. I have never been allowed to give voice to the betrayal. So, like my ancestors before me, I filled that hole up with booze, I drank away my pain, I became abusive and fucked up, I became a giant walking wound. I drank away the memory, *cuimhne*, and I drank for courage, *misneach*. Alcohol did for me what I could not do for myself. Alcohol gave me the power to say fuck off, to say *no*. I was never allowed to say no.

I sit at the edge of the ocean which reaches out to the sky, The Cailleach is present in Her form of mountain, Her face visible in the rock. The Cailleach, the old woman who made the world by dropping rocks from her apron. The Cailleach is older than time, She is the creatrix. She is the land itself, talún. She stares at the sea, Her gaze unwavering. She has seen it all. She has been here all along. I give Her my heart. I ask Her for courage, *misneach*. *Cailleach show me how to be brave. Cailleach help me remember who I am. Cailleach grant me cuimhne, Cailleach grant me misneach.* The land, talún, the ocean, farraige, are big enough to hold all the pain in my heart. Even though it is crushing. Even though it feels impossible, unresolvable. Even though it has driven me to drink, to suicide, to death. Even though it almost killed me and I carry it with me still. The Cailleach has seen it all before. She is wise enough and strong enough. She will teach me to remember and be brave.

Prayers are answered and magic works. I am walking the streets of Galway and slowly, suddenly, I remember. I remember who I am. I see the candle in the cathedral. I see the water in the well. I see the rock face overlooking the sea. I see myself as a child hiding on the front lawn. I see my mother and my father and I know my love can't free them. They have to choose that for themselves. I see my mother and my father and I know my love can't heal them. They have to choose that for themselves. I see my mother and my father and I know nothing I do can make them give me the love I need. I have to get it somewhere else. I remember Mary's open arms. I remember the flowing waters of Bridget's well. I remember the Cailleach's unflinching gaze. I remember what the woodcarver said about the land itself. I remember that the land has always loved me, not just Ireland, the land of my ancestors, but also the stolen land we call Canada which has yet to be decolonized. The land I have lived on my whole life has always loved me. I am learning how to love.

I was afraid I would never know love because my ancestors forgot love many generations ago. But I am reminded of *cuimhne*, I am reminded of *misneach*. Love is in my very dna, it's in my bones. Love is the way the world opens to me, holds me. Love is the loon landing on the lake, the mist above the water, the raccoon rooting through the trash, the blossoms that scent the summer air, the water that keeps me alive, the trees that keep me breathing. Love is the way I find my courage and face down a man twice my size who's trying to hit his girlfriend. Love is the way we keep trying, not perfectly but genuinely. Love is the alcoholics who show up for me and show me that I am worthy, no matter what I've done. Love is memory and courage, willingness to fight for what we love. I was afraid the pain was endless like the ocean but the ocean is bigger than the pain. The pain will never go away. It will always be there like the memory. The pain will always be an opening, a well, a prayer. The pain will always connect me to my ancestors, connect me to the love. The pain helps me remember and it helps me be brave.

Fucking Magic

The answer comes on slowly, it dawns on me suddenly, like it's been there all along. It isn't this easy, simple, groundbreaking thing. It's hard and it's complicated but I know my heart is big enough to hold it. My prayers are answered as I remember what I know. I can't trade in my safety in an attempt to secure love. I can't do it anymore. I can't do it ever again. I can't hide the truth, buy into the lie, because it's fucking killing the child in me. I can't abandon her anymore. I can't laugh and smile and die inside. I can't go along with the lie like it's not hurting anyone. Because it's hurting me. I won't play along anymore. I can't do it to protect my mother. I can't do it to protect her from her pain. I can't walk around like a terrified child saying *lovemelovemeloveme* surrendering up my safety because the truth is it doesn't work anyway. It never has. They say that safety is the fundamental human need but I know that the need for love is greater. I have chosen love over safety every single time. But the trick is that if it demands a sacrifice of safety it isn't love.

My ancestors speak through me with the scraps of language I have managed to remember. My ancestors speak through me from the mouths of caves, from the Otherworld, where they live now. My ancestors speak through my hands as I type these words. I know that I am here to end a cycle. I am here to start something new. I am here to remember and be brave. The only way to do that, they tell me, is to insist on protecting myself. I can never again trade in safety for love. I feel them when I remember this. I feel my prayers answered, the magic working, the relief. It isn't easy. It isn't fixed. It's hard and it's painful and it isn't the answer I want. I want to believe that by some powerful act of forgiveness and self-sacrifice I can secure the love I'm desperate for. But I can't. I can't.

So I surrender. So I grieve. So I feel the fucking pain that I've been running from my whole life. The pain of an unloved child, a child hurt the way no child should ever be hurt. I feel my twelve year old body on the front lawn under the blanket terrified and hiding and helpless. I feel what it feels like to go to my mom and tell her and have nothing change. I bear witness to this pain and it fucking hurts and nothing is ever going to fix it. And knowing this, remembering this, clears the space and grants

Cuimhne, Misneach

me the courage to start doing something new. Now that I don't have to fix it, now that I know I can't, I can start something new. I can begin to know love that is rooted in safety and a refusal to ever abandon myself again. I can remember my ancestors, their stories, their magic, I can begin to find my way back to who I am. I can feel the relief. I can feel the strength that flows with this surrender. I watch the sun setting over Galway and I walk the streets with my head held high. I love myself. I am deeply, profoundly loved, here and now and always.

Go raibh maith agat.

Desire

I'M AT THE sex club and it's foot fetish night apparently. Well, okay, I'll roll with it. My friend has gone back to the pool and I don't feel like it. I get myself a glass of water and walk up to the third floor. I sit alone, sipping my water like a champ. A guy approaches me and asks me if he can give me a foot rub. I say sure. And so he does. I sit there sipping my water enjoying the sensations of his hands on my feet. After awhile he asks if he can massage my whole body and since it's been good so far I say yes. We move over to the bed area and I lay face down on the vinyl. He works me over and I relax. Various men are watching, a bit of a crowd is forming. Some ask if they can watch and I say *Sure, why not.*

His hands on my body feel so fucking good. Tension melts away and I am breathing. Slowly, I can feel the pressure building. Here on my stomach I find a way back into myself. I'm not putting on a show, even though clearly I kind of am. What I mean is, I'm not trying to impress anyone. I am completely relaxed and from this place I feel a depth of pleasure. I am breathing deep and my whole body is being worked over. Another man who is watching asks if I need another set of hands. I tell him *Yes, but I might put the brakes on at any moment.* He says *of course.* So now these two guys are working me over, touching me all over. By the time one of them makes his way to my cunt I am drooling on the vinyl, a mess of pleasure. He whispers in my ears *You are so fucking wet.* And I just say *I know.*

I'm in downtown Galway swiping left and swiping right. I match with a cute femme and we start chatting. I tell her I'm visiting from Toronto. She asks what I'm doing and I say not much, just wandering Galway. She

Desire

asks me to come join her and her friends at the local gay bar. I google map it and it's a seven minute walk so I say *I'm on my way*. I arrive and introduce myself and we all play bingo. I tell her and her friends about my paper on queer, feminist Marian devotion that I'm presenting at a conference in Galway. We talk Irish politics and religion and the repeal the 8th campaign. I go to the bar and get myself some water.

Later she walks me all over Galway. She shows me the university I'll soon be presenting at. Eventually we end up at the beach. The moon is huge and so is the ocean. Everything is dark blue. We take off our tights and shoes and wander down to the water. It's cold but not too cold. We are starstruck by the brilliance of the beauty that surrounds us. We keep wading deeper until our floral dresses almost touch the water. We laugh about how convenient femme clothing is. We keep repeating how beautiful everything is. Finally I turn to her and say *So I think you're really cute...* And she says *Should we be like really gay and make out?* And we are both laughing and we start kissing under the moon. We wrap our arms around each other and I run my fingers through her purple hair. My favourite thing is when I pull away a bit and look at her and her whole face is lit up with a smile. She is beautiful.

Somehow we decide it's a good idea to take off all our clothes and leave them on the shore and run naked through the night into the ocean which seems a lot colder when we are naked. We let the darkness of the water submerge us and we press our bodies together for warmth. Seaweed floats by and I am terrified it's a fish. She reassures me and we laugh and her smile lights up the night. I wrap my arms around her, press myself into her, listen to the sounds she makes. When we decide to get out of the water we run across the beach stark naked holding hands and pray to god that our clothes are where we left them.

I'm sitting in a restaurant in Galway when the text comes through. My date who I haven't seen in way too long is asking me to tell them a story. *The setting is your new apartment, with nothing in it, and you are wearing only a dress. I walk into the room.* I read the text and realize what I'm being asked to do. I have such difficulty verbalizing my desires, asking for what I want, saying what turns me on and I am being asked to put that into story form. But, I'm a writer. So in some ways this is perfect. Writing has always been a safe place for me to explore my feelings. I decide to take the plunge. I decide to give it a shot. I start typing.

The words pour out of me and I am propelled by them. My hands are connected to my heart which is connected to my cunt. I describe a scene in detail in which I am being ordered around and told to be quiet, a scene in which I eagerly obey these orders until I accidentally fuck up and then am put to a test. My fingers are crashing over my phone screen as the scene plays out before my eyes. I can feel myself getting turned on. The restaurant has disappeared from view and I am in an empty apartment, with my hands above my head, getting fucked against a wall. By the time I press send I have written a really long, detailed story.

My date reads the story and finishes it off with a really hot, really sweet aftercare scene. I'm like wow this is bdsm in sexting form and I feel super cared for and seen. I'm weirdly turned on but unfortunately in a public place. But whatever. I decide to live my best life and I go to the bathroom and get myself off, listening to really bad radio music, playing the scene I just created over in my head, relishing every detail which I created from my own mind. I come hard. Afterwards I tell my date I just came in a public bathroom. They applaud this behavior and say that we are great. I tell them *I feel all relaxed and chill now*. I tell them *I deeply appreciate the way you bring out my inner perv. You make me feel safe enough to do so.*

I Remember You Then

I'M LYING ON my bed with one of my oldest friends. She's lived on the other side of the country for years and so we haven't seen much of each other. We are friends from back in the day. We are friends from back in my drinking days. She's seen the worst of me and the craziest. I've screamed at her for no reason. We did acid covered shrooms and I talked her down from a bad trip. We were ghb'd and almost raped and we ran for our fucking lives, escaping together. We panhandled up money for the liquor store. We rolled around in the dirt and made out under the moon. And now I am 30 and she is 29 and we are all grown up.

She's lying on my bed and telling me how much she appreciates my friendship. I thank her for forgiving me. I say *I know I was so fucked up to you back when I was drinking.* She tells me *Remember when you called me a couple years ago? When you were doing that thing, I don't know what they call it...* I say *Amends.* She says *Yeah amends. You sounded so nervous and I just wanted to tell you, you didn't need to be. We were so fucked up but we loved each other and we took care of each other as best we could. You got down on your knees while I was trying to fuck that guy on that person's lawn and you gave me a condom. You told me to put a condom on it and that stayed with me. I can count on one hand the number of times I've had unprotected sex and that's because of you. I remember you then.*

She starts talking about what I used to be like. She conjures up my days of active alcoholism, that version of me I'm so ashamed of. She says *You didn't take any shit from anyone. If anyone fucked with you, you fucked with them right back. Like when you were really young and those guys attacked you at that show, you fought back. I remember when you told*

Fucking Magic

me the doctor asked you how much you drank. And you said fourteen litres a week. Like it was no big deal. Like you were proud of it. Because that was how you survived. You weren't ashamed of how you were. You were loud and you screamed at everyone and you survived. And now you're older and you're sober and it's good. And I'm so glad I knew you then and I'm so glad I know you know.

I listen to her words and I don't even know how to take them in. I feel her love and I don't even know how to take it in. I feel the way she sees me, and the way it heals me. This fucking crazy girl, this friend of mine who can't believe I've forgotten how to pick up dudes on the street. She's like *Come on Clementine! You give them the look!* And I know exactly what she means. I'm so fucking grateful for her forgiveness and I'm trying to grasp what she's saying when she says I don't need it. I feel the person I was and the person I am and the person I'm becoming coming together, connected by her witnessing and her love. I feel myself begin to accept myself, deep in my bones. I feel myself surrender self-rejection and shame. I look at this beautiful being laughing her ass off on my bed and I am grateful.

Je suis prête

I AM READY. I am ready for the life I've always wanted, the life I've always dreamed. I am ready to drop the dead weight of shame, stop second guessing my worthiness. I am worthy.

I feel it in my body, this shift in my bones. My shoulders drop, my head lifts up, the tension in my belly releases. I breathe. The air is so good, so sweet and nourishing. The city is warm and the sun is setting and I am saying goodbye.

I am ready. I am writing my final masters project, wrapping up two years of research on trauma, magic, and more than human worlds. I'm reading the things I've written and I'm like fuck yes Clementine, good job. I am ready to commit myself to my work, to my writing. I am ready to call myself a writer. I am done joking that it's not a 'real job.' I am ready to move to a city where the rent isn't atrocious, where it is possible to live that writer life and still survive. I'm ready to follow my dreams and these are my dreams. I want to fucking write. It's what I've always wanted. It's what I love.

I am ready to love myself. There is no shame in being happy. There is no shame in living my best life. I have spent so much fucking time feeling so much fucking pain. The worst things, the things I couldn't believe could ever happen, well, they happened. And I am ready to stop defining myself through the pain. I won't apologize for my joy anymore. I won't tiptoe around or make myself smaller. I will only cultivate relationships with people who encourage me to shine. Because that's what I fucking deserve, that's why.

Fucking Magic

I am ready to stop calling the person who put me through a wall the love of my life. I am ready to surrender that title and let myself be free to love again. I will no longer organize the story of my life around a person who almost killed me. I will no longer romanticize his violence in any fucking way. What he did to me was unacceptable, end of story. And he is not the love of my life.

I am ready to have boundaries, to walk away from people who consistently hurt me. I am done believing that my love is big enough to change anyone. Everyone is responsible for changing themselves. If I can help, I will help, but not at the expense of my safety or health. I'm fucking done with that shit.

I am ready to surrender my search for parental love. I am ready to surrender the belief that if I am good enough I will secure that love. I am ready to surrender the belief that if I forgive enough I will secure that love. I am fucking done. My parents couldn't love me, true story. I forgive them but I won't pretend it wasn't what it was. It's not my job to fix it for them. It's not my job to lie. It's not my job to face their demons for them. And I can't make them do a single thing.

I told my therapist about the unconditional love of Our Lady of Perpetual Help, how She forgives everyone, how She turns no one away. My therapist reminds me that I am not Her. It's not my job to forgive every fucking thing. Kesha reminds me that 'some things only god can forgive' and I collapse on the floor and cry because I'm fucking done. I am done trying to fix everything with my huge fucking heart. I am ready to give myself that love.

I am ready to own what's mine and I am ready to put down what's not. A dude tells my friend to carry his bag and she yells *Carry your own load bitch!*

It takes courage to change and I am ready. It takes courage to dream and I am ready. It takes courage to claim my desires and I am fucking ready. I'm ready.

I'm not afraid anymore or if I am the fear doesn't matter. I feel the old thoughts rise to the surface, the guilt and the shame for having

Je suis prête

boundaries or having desires, and I surrender that shit. I'm so over it. I am so fucking done.

I lie in my bed and I make myself come over and over and over again. I'm saying shit out loud and I am reveling in the miracle that is my pleasure. It's not easy to come back into my body after incest and multiple rapes and all the bad shit that happened. It's not easy to feel like it's okay to want sexual pleasure. But I'm fucking ready.

I'm ready to do the work, to show up for my life. I refuse to abandon myself no matter what. Whatever fucking happens, even if I lose fucking everything, I will still have me and I will never abandon myself again. I am ready.

Lifeless Worlds

There is a part of me I don't recognize yet. A part of me that rises up to meet your fingertips. There is a part of me which I cannot speak, an answer to your question, the shape of silence. I curl into the curve of you. I surrender to you.

I'm five seconds in the door and my back is against the wall and you are kissing me. We are in the backyard and we don't even have a moment to enjoy your romantic set up. You are taking off my dress. You are on the ground between my legs, looking up at me, your hair falling over your shoulders.

You ask me if you can slap me and I say yes. I feel my pupils dilate. I feel my attention sharpen. You pull me into the moment and for a second I forget everything else.

You look so fucking good running your fingers over my fishnets. Later I will try to tell you. Later I will try to tell you about my desire, the way I turn myself toward your femininity, the way I fall apart when you turn toward mine. I don't have words for it yet. I don't know who I am as I rise to the surface, as I come up for air from the depths of this desire.

In the bed in the darkness the shadows play across our skin. My clothes are still in the backyard and you are in my arms. My favourite part is pressing my body into yours. My favourite part is the little breaths you take.

We stand naked on the roof and I wrap my arms around you. I look up at you, hold your gaze. You tell me I am hard to read. I laugh. Everyone says my face gives everything away. But I don't know who I am when I'm with you. I don't know what I'm revealing. It is a surprise even to myself.

Fucking Magic

The CN tower is there like you promised me. But the moon, oh the moon. Just past ripening and starting to wane. We are naked and the August heat is welcome. The city stretches off in all directions.

We talk about astrophysics. You tell me about the planets. You look off into the distance and you call up their environments. What's it like to be a planet without an atmosphere? What's it like to be Jupiter's storm? You are called to these worlds and I am called to you. You tell me

you don't understand this quest for life, this obsession with water, with the possibility of bacteria, something *alive*. I recognize in myself this longing for life and I am enraptured by your ability to love these lifeless worlds.

Unrecognizable, alien, so unlike these fleshy bodies we inhabit here under the moon. Strange worlds that call to you and call to me through you.

We sit on my porch another day, the busy crowds of Kensington market passing us by. We talk about sex. We talk about desire. We talk about how good you look in your crop top and shorts. You tell me how much you like my dress. I think of you on the bed in the darkness. I think of my hands against the fence as you strip off my fishnets in the backyard. I wonder who I am, who I've been, who I'm becoming. I wonder what is happening that I don't have words for yet.

Your eyes, your smile, your warmth. I tell you in a text message *I'm this big public personality, but there's a secret vulnerable part of me I'm scared to show you.* You say *I know, I can feel it.*

I tell you about the expectations and the pressure. The women who demand proof of my queerness in the form of sex. The way my queer card is always on the brink of being revoked. I tell you about the trauma, about the way I feel expected to perform my desire, about how hard it is for me to say what I want. I tell you I don't want to have to prove it, I don't want to have to be anything other than a bisexual femme. I tell you how much I desire femmes, how much I desire to be desired as a femme, by a femme, this pent up, repressed desire.

Lifeless Worlds

You laugh. You smile and your eyes sparkle. You give me that look. You're flirting. Teasing me. *Oh I had no idea you had a thing for femmes.* You have me.

Tonight I am a strange and lifeless world, wild and storming. Tonight I am Jupiter's storm, forever caught up in its own wildness. Tonight I am a world without water, without life. And in my depths, and in my strangeness, this unrecognizable, unarticulated rising, wanting, I am met. You meet me here.

So So Safe

You throw me on the fucking floor. My hands fly out and I break my fall against the floor boards. I am not helpless. I am full of this moment. I am keeping up with you. I want to be good. You let me be good. You let me.

My heart is as big as the sky. I am safe here. Here on your bed. Here on your floor. I trust you. I trust you enough to give you this, to let you throw me across the bed, flip me over, hit me in the face. I trust you enough to follow your orders, to be quiet, to stay still, to show you this part of me that so badly wants to be good. You hold me down and I let you. I let you.

You ask me what, for me, would constitute taking it up a notch. I tell you the next step is more communication. I tell you I'm a baby sub, I'm just learning about this part of myself, and I need to talk about it more. You say that's hot. I write a list of my desires and I am terrified. I am terrified to be so vulnerable, but I trust you to hold them, and I press send.

We talk about desire. You ask me about mine. You tell me about yours. I am brave and I tell you how it makes me feel to submit to you. I tell you about the pain and the way that I like it. I tell you about how badly I want to be good. You tell me I'm good, I'm good, I'm so good.

This desire makes me brave, it fills me up, sends me down into the deepest parts of me. I am finding language for unspeakable things. I am finding silence that sparkles with its fullness. I am recognizing parts of myself I'd forgotten. You pull me up off the floor and my eyes fly up at you. I see you see the way I see you.

So So Safe

We talk about consent, communication, the practical details of exploring this. You tell me you want to explore this with me, but you want me to be so, so safe. You have my heart and I feel safe with you. I trust you. I feel seen, I feel whole, I feel here. I am safe with you. I feel so, so safe.

You order me to tell you what I want. You ask me if I like it and when I eagerly nod my head you order me to answer you out loud. I fucked a dude who took my hand off my clit during sex and I tell you how much that fucked me up. Next time you fuck me you tell me *I want your left hand on your clit and I don't want you to take it off unless you ask me first or I tell you*. You dom me into finding my voice. You dom me into owning my pleasure. You work your magic and I take it like the grateful sub I am.

You tell me I'm such a good sub and at first I assume that means I'm so good at taking what you give. But then you tell me that I'm so good because I use my words when I need to, because I use my body language, because I communicate to you my boundaries and desires. You tell me I make you feel safe topping me, you tell me you trust me. I trust you. And I want you to be so, so safe.

In this surrender I find my power. For the first time, I can choose to give myself over because it really is a choice. You hold my gaze and I hold your gaze and I am really here. Here, held, and so, so safe.

To Be Loved

My greatest secret is my hunger for love. It's more embarrassing than the number of dicks I've choked on. It's more shameful than all the cum I've guzzled down. I play it cool. I breathe through my terror of abandonment. I love the child in me. I love the child in me so that I can be loved. I love the child in me so that I don't project my terror of abandonment onto others, so that I don't make the people I care for responsible for my feelings or my past.

My greatest secret is my hunger for love. So here, I'll write it down for the world to see. I'll tell you how scared I am, how brave I am. I'll tell you that I am transformed by pain, my very being is transformed by it, created by it. I am rooted in pain and I do not try to be rid of it. I love my pain so that I can be loved. I love my pain so that I can know what I know. I crack my ribs to make a space big enough for everything I feel. I won't make you responsible for my pain. I won't make you responsible for my past. I won't make you responsible for my feelings. They are mine.

I wonder who I am when I am loved, when I am safe. I wonder who I could be if I surrounded myself with those who treat me with care. I wonder what would happen if I finally found my people: friends, community, partners, lovers, who love me, who have my fucking back, who challenge me and care for me, who would fucking fight for me. I want the softening of love and care. I want to finally feel safe, not just because I know I've got me, but because I know that I am loved. By other human beings. By my people. I want my people. I want family. I have wanted family my entire fucking life.

To Be Loved

We are walking back to your place and my family comes up. The conversation turns to my childhood, my grandfather, the sexual abuse. So I tell you. I tell you the details, I tell you the truth, what happened to me. I rarely say the specifics to anyone, and whenever I do I feel the terror come over me, my breathless voice, the urgency. I can't talk about the details without feeling it in my body, without feeling like I am back there. I tell you I was so scared and when I say that you reach out and take my hand in yours.

I have a heart with an X through it tattooed on the inside of my wrist. In another life when the guys I was fucking asked me what it meant I would tell them that I don't need love. *I'm not looking for it, I don't care.*

I was always a secret. Fucking married men and guys with girlfriends. I was always trash, used for sex and treated with disrespect. I took it because it was all I could get. I took it because I had no idea what care was. I had no idea what love was. I took it because sex was all pervasive in my childhood. I knew what it felt like to be held in my grandfather's gaze. I didn't know what it felt like to feel loved or safe. So these guys would fuck me and I'd promise to never make it complicated for them. But sometimes when I was really really drunk and they'd refuse to kiss me because they *don't kiss sluts* I'd start to cry and sob and scream and all the pain of being unloved would come pouring out of me.

Now I love myself. I love myself so fucking much. I have my fucking back. No matter what. Whatever happens. I will never abandon myself again. I will never settle for less than I deserve. I will never pretend that I am okay with disrespect and violence. I will never deny that I am deserving of love. I am deserving of love. Inherently. Fundamentally. And I'm finally ready to admit that it's what I want.

I want to be loved. I want to find my people. I want to let them love me. I want to surround myself with people who really truly have my back. I want to breathe life into my relationships, my communities, my friendships, my partnerships. I want to be brave, braver than I've ever been. Because I can face down a man twice my size, I can stare violence straight in the face. But love, love is the scariest thing. It's the great unknown. My heart is softening. I am surrendering. I am letting down the walls that have protected me all my life. Love makes me brave and I am braver than I've ever been.

Surrender

I GET ANXIOUS ABOUT my health, about my career, about my relationships. I get anxious about my loneliness, about my mental health, about the things that haven't changed yet. I feel the tightness in my chest, the subdued panic, the need to control. The need to control outcomes. The need to be safe. To be loved. It is easy to forget the way that the neurons in my brain always crisscross their way through trauma networks. It is easy to forget the way that trauma lives in my body, in a visceral experience of feeling *unsafe*.

I don't feel safe.

I attempt to address this feeling of lack of safety, vague and ominous, all consuming, through anxious rumination. Maybe if I think about it a million times it will be resolved. Maybe if I just turn it over in my mind one more time I will feel safe. Yet this process just generates more anxiety. I forget the primary magic, the foundation of my recovery, what makes it possible for me to live today. I forget to surrender. *Surrender. Let go and let god. Take the right actions and let go of the results. Let go of the results.*

I have to remember to be gentle with myself, to have compassion for myself. I have to remember that these fear spirals are rooted in trauma, rooted in a visceral embodied memory of what it means to truly be unsafe. When I feel like this I hold space for it. I say *Clementine you are triggered and that's why you're feeling this way.* I say *Clementine I love you, you are safe, I will never abandon you no matter what.*

And I turn it over, I surrender the results, I trust the universe, I trust that what will come will come and it will be what it needs to be.

Fucking Magic

I surrender my desires, my hopes, my fears. I surrender my worries, my secrets, my pain. I give it all over. I turn it all in.

Living universe I give you my health, my career, my relationships, my mental health, my loneliness, the things that haven't changed yet. Living universe I give you my desires, my hopes, my fears, my worries, my secrets, my pain, my love. I give it all to you.

The Chromatic Scale

I AM HAVING A work date with a new friend. They're a composer and they're working on a composition. They have a tuning fork and they show me how to make the sound of A vibrate in my bones. My hand is like a seashell against my ear, my bones carrying the current of sound.

I tell them I don't understand music. They are so kind and supportive, so generous with music. They tell me I do understand music, I understand more than I think. I tell them about guitar, about my guitars gathering dust in my room. They say *You play guitar? Of course you understand music.* They say *There are so many reasons to play. Because it's therapeutic, because it feels good, because it's fun. Being good isn't the only reason to play.*

I tell them about the joy of playing, the joy of singing, the *joy*. I go home and listen to my old recordings. I post a video on facebook of me playing guitar and screaming when I was 23. I write *I miss playing*. A friend of mine sees the video and sends me a message. They tell me they have always felt like they aren't good enough at music too. They tell me they liked my video. They ask me if I want to start a band.

I am fifteen and I am friends with all the older boys in bands. My friends and I all have crushes on them. We go to the shows. We try to look cute. We watch them play and keep our eyes on the one we are crushing on. We feel the music of eighteen year old boys vibrating in our bones and we don't know what we are feeling. We want them. We want to be wanted by them. We don't know what we want. There is a secret desire. A secret desire to sing. A secret desire for strings. A secret desire for forbidden things.

One of the boys has his dad's car, an 88 Oldsmobile, baby blue. We all pile in, sit on the plush seats with the windows rolled down and the boys play

Fucking Magic

cds from the cd book in the car. The wind is in my hair, the sounds are in my ears, in my heart. I have no control. The boy with the car, he is awkward and shy, he plays electric guitar. He picks me up from school, drives me to the mall instead of class. He likes me. I tell him I want to be in a band. I tell him I don't play anything but I can sing, I can scream, I can write. He says yes and we start talking about making music. I write poems to make into songs. One day on his bed he takes my clothes off. He shoves his fingers inside me and I am shocked. Somehow he becomes my boyfriend. He says he can't be in a band with his girlfriend. My dreams disappear just like that.

My friend and I sit on the picnic table in their backyard. Me on the bench, them up on the table top, smoking a cigarette. They tell me the story of their music trauma, the guitar they wanted and never got, the way it felt like it was too late, the broken guitar they glued wrong, trying to fix not only the guitar but themself. I tell them the story of mine. We talk about the way music has been kept from us, obscured, held secret and separate. We talk about the desire, the longing, the fingers we pressed into strings, never feeling good enough. We pull up pop songs on youtube, listen to Selena Gomez, Tina Turner. We talk about what kind of music we might want to make. We encourage each other. We laugh. For the first time in my life I am talking about making music and I feel fucking safe.

I am sixteen and all I want for Christmas and my birthday is a guitar. I don't get it. I can't play my now-boyfriend's guitars because I am left handed. I listen to him playing. He writes me love songs and I listen. He has sex with me and I lie there. I tell myself I'm in love. I tell myself I am happy. I push down the crushing disappointment of not getting a guitar. I listen to him play. I listen to him play. I listen to him play. I stare at the wall while he fucks me.

My friend finishes their cigarette and we go inside. We sit on their bed in their bedroom and I get out my electric guitar. They have a bass that they are just starting to learn, and an acoustic guitar that they can play. We try to plug into their amp but it's not working. They tell me they've been fiddling with the wires. *Oh well, we'll plug in next time.* We talk about what we might want to play. How maybe we should turn pop songs into punk songs. I show them the songs I've written. The simple little songs. I sing and play. They strum along on their acoustic. They harmonize with my vocals. They tell me they like my songs and write down my strumming patterns. I have never in my life felt so fucking safe and held and seen with music. I have never in my life felt like I could be a musician. They show me the chords to this pop song they've been learning. I pick it up and we start playing together, singing and harmonizing. We change the lyrics, transforming the song from a song about dancing to a song about dumpster diving. We make it punk as fuck. We can't stop laughing.

I'm eighteen and I have a guitar now. I take lessons once a week. My guitar teacher is a kid around my age. He is dismissive and condescending. I don't understand how to play and he tells me I will just 'get it'. I feel awful. I feel like an imposter, a failure, a fake. I feel like I have started learning too late. But I am determined. I keep coming back. I never miss a lesson. I sleep with my guitar next to me in bed, my arms wrapped around it. I work at HMV at the mall. I help the local punks special order their cds. I am an alcoholic already. I use alcohol to feel like I can take part in things, to feel less afraid, to not care what people think. I go to shows and I get in the pit and act crazy, and I wish, I wish, I wish I could get on stage.

My sister and I go to a show. We sneak in beers. We are already drunk. I am acting crazy as I usually am when I'm drinking, throwing my body around, letting the booze obliterate my fear. The singer in the band says *The girl with the red hair really needs to shave her fucking armpits.* Kids are throwing shit at me, laughing at me. I am drunk and defiant. I lift up my arm, show off my armpit hair and walk around the room giving the finger to everyone. I am caught off guard by a punch in the face. I grab my glasses which go flying and attempt to swing back at the guy who hit me. My arm is caught, pinned behind my neck. I go into a panic, a rage. I attempt to escape. I struggle. I am shoved, pushed, hit, dragged. I am screaming. My sister tries to help me but she is held back. The band plays on as I am pushed to the ground. I get away and climb onto the stage, incoherently demanding that people help me. I am pushed off the stage. I'm on the ground. I am *dragged by my pigtails across the floor as I struggle and scream. I am dragged by my pigtails down the stairs, my head slamming against the steps. My head is smashed into a pole as teenage boys drag me to the door and throw me out into the snow. My sister is thrown out right after. We are bruised, traumatized, horrified, shaking. One of the guys in the band is a regular at HMV who special orders cds off me. The crowd of kids who watched me get my ass kicked are all people I know, it's a small town show. My guitar teacher is among them. Only my sister tried to help me. Everyone else just watched.*

I go to work at HMV with a bruised face and a guy is staring at me. He says You really shouldn't have jumped up on the stage at that show. *I go to work and kids pass the HMV and yell* Shave your fucking armpits! *My coworkers just look at me.*

At our second band practice my friend is telling me about how they learned a secret that all the music bros either wouldn't or couldn't divulge. They learned that when playing bass, you find the root note that is being played on guitar, and add a fifth and an octave. We follow the pattern of notes on the neck of the guitar, moving along the length of the neck and moving from the low string to the high string. We realize that the twelfth fret with its double dots is where the pattern starts again at E. Suddenly I say *The chromatic scale!* Because those words are buried in my mind from various times I have tried to understand music theory. But here it is, alive on the neck of the guitar, alive in our fingers, obvious, because no one is shaming us, no one is obscuring the knowledge. We are laughing. My friend says they feel like a music detective. *Yeah we are music detectives! Sleuthing out the hidden knowledge music bros have been hoarding and liberating it!* We are learning, together. We are having fun together. And for the first time in my life I can touch my guitar without shame. For the first time in my life music is bringing me nothing but joy.

I'm 21 and I'm a full time drunk. Trauma has stacked upon trauma. All I do is smoke weed and drink and fuck. I don't have much money but I start taking guitar lessons again. I go every week and I try. For the first time, I learn how to play a couple songs. I sing and I play and it feels good in my bones. I know I'm not very good. I know there is so much I don't understand.

The Chromatic Scale

My life is on fire all around me all the time, but my fingers have learned the shape of chords.

I'm 22 and I carry my guitar on my back to the jam space at the drop in centre for street involved youth. I'm getting some food and a dude approaches me. You play guitar? *he asks me.* Yeah *I mumble, already feeling like an imposter, already feeling terrified.* I'll believe it when I see it *he says.*

I'm 23 and my boyfriend takes my guitar and smashes a coffee table in half with it. After the table breaks he keeps swinging, smashing it into the floor, trying to break its neck. Trying to hurt me in any way he can hurt me. Trying to get in as much damage as he can. I am screaming and crying. My sister hears the commotion and comes into the room, takes one look at what he is doing and runs to him, wrapping her arms around the body of my guitar, stopping him. He takes my amp and throws it down the stairs smashing the glass of the sliding door in the living room. There is glass everywhere. The wires in my guitar are fucked, but he didn't break its neck.

I am 25 and newly sober. I am broke as fuck and living on welfare. But for the first time in my adult life I have time and energy to focus on things other than drinking. I am no longer drunk, high, and/or hung over all the time. I want to play guitar. Deep down in my guts I want to play guitar. So with the tiny amount of money I have I pay for lessons. I eat mac and cheese and peanut butter from the foodbank and sometimes I don't eat. But every week I ride my bike across the city with my guitar strapped to my pack. Every day I practice.

I'm 26 and I decide that no matter how hard I work, no matter how much I want it, I'm not good enough and I'll never be good enough. I decide I'm a writer and that's enough. I decide to bury my dreams of making music in the ground. I stop playing.

I'm 30 and I've had two band practices with my friend. I'm playing guitar again. I'm waking up saying *the circle of fifths!* I'm recording myself and sending the videos to my friend and my girlfriend and my partner. I am being brave. I am having fun. I am laughing a lot. I am not worrying so much about whether or not I'm good. My friend says they love my voice.

Fucking Magic

My girlfriend calls me badass. My partner says I'm punk as fuck. I feel good in my body. My calluses are coming back.

The day after band practice I meet up with my friend and my partner who is also my friend's partner, and my friend and I are talking about music and band practice and how much we love making music together. I am walking in the sun with these two people I love and I am talking about music. We are telling my/their partner about the things we are discovering. About how the chromatic scale revealed itself before our very eyes like magic. How we stumbled upon the reality that the twelfth fret with its double dots is where the chromatic scale starts again. How this very obvious and easy to explain piece of information has never been explained to us. How music has been hidden and obscured and hoarded but together we are discovering it.

It's been there this whole time! They've been hiding it from us, but it's right there! I'm ranting at imaginary music bros saying *It's always been there, right there on the neck of the guitar, you goddamn liars!* And we are all laughing, laughing, laughing. And we are happy. And deep in my very bones I am healing.

Maybe it's never too late to follow my dreams. Maybe it's never too late to heal. Maybe I'm a late bloomer. Maybe I've always been way more punk than I gave myself credit for. Maybe it's okay to not be that good, to be learning, to be having fun. Maybe all I've ever wanted is the life I'm living right now.

My friend and bandmate stick n' pokes the chromatic scale on my body. We sit for hours all needle and ink. And now when I want to figure out a note on the guitar I have a little cheat sheet on my upper thigh. Now when a music bro tells me where a note is, I don't have to take his fucking word for it. Music doesn't belong to him exclusively; finally I know that it belongs to me.

I Push Him Off Me

THE THREE OF us go to the park, me, my partner, and my dear friend/bandmate/partner's partner. We bring snacks and we sit in the grass in the sun. I take my 5htp and drink water and eat carrots and cucumber with hummus. We're laughing and it's early fall, cool but bright and sunny. We are here to practice systema before the actual class later. I've made the decision to try to learn a martial art. I've made the decision to try to learn how to fight. I want another option besides fawn, freeze, or submit, when fleeing is not an option. I want to feel strong and confident and safe in my body. I want to feel like I can defend myself or someone else, like I can show up to violence prepared. Because in the life I've had, the life I have, violence is not a mystery, it's a reality, but it's a reality I am not trained in. I don't know how to fight and I'm scared.

But I want to learn and the sun through the leaves of the trees is soft and green and I am here with these two beautiful human beings who I really love and I really trust. So we practice the Turkish get up and we learn how to roll and how to fall. I pay attention to instructions and I move my body and I try. I'm covered in grass and I'm dirty and I'm rolling around on the ground, collapsing and landing on my butt, paying attention to my body. Laughing, having fun. I feel safe. We start to practice a move called threading the needle. It's a move to get someone off you if you're on the ground on your back.

He's got me on my back again. I'm exhausted. My body hurts from being thrown into things but I don't feel it. All I feel is the electric energy of adrenaline, the rushing urgency of going full speed without breaks. I'm on the ground again, my legs were kicked out from under me and I ended up here, curled into a ball trying to protect my head from his kicks but now he's come down to my level. He's on top of me, the full weight of his body, his knee pressed against my chest. I can't breathe. His face is in my face, close, he is screaming Do you know who you're fucking with? *I can't breathe. I can't breathe. I can't breathe.* Everything else disappears, any attempt at saving a shred of dignity, any hope to make him see that what he's doing is not okay, any love, any hate, just fear, all encompassing, the shape of space, the shape of where my breath should be but I can't breathe.

In the park I feel my thoughts start to skip. They keep crashing into the wall of this memory. I lose focus. I can't pay attention. I don't see the green light through the leaves, I don't feel the peace of laughing with people I love. I can't concentrate. *I can't breathe.* But I remember I promised to communicate, to share my feelings when I start to feel them, so that I don't fall off the edge of a dissociative cliff. So I tell them. I say *I'm feeling upset.* And we sit and we talk about it and I tell them. I tell them that the thought of being stuck on my back, unable to breathe, it's sent my mind into a memory which is repeating, an intrusive thought spinning in on itself, repeating the same outcome again and again and again. *What if his knee is on my chest, what if I can't breathe?* The memory enters the present. I'm not alone with it, alone with him on the floor of my bedroom. I am here in this park, with these people who I love. The moments come together, coincide. They are there with me on the bedroom floor. The three of us, my partner, my friend, and the future me, sit on the floor and watch him as he presses down on me, breaking blood vessels and bruising my chest, stopping me from breathing.

We talk about it. What can I do? How can I get him off of me? And I decide I want to try it. With my friend, first, because they are smaller. I get on my back on the grass and I show them how he was on top of me. *Like this, with your knee here, like this.* And my friend tells me we can stop at any time and they get on top of me like he did, put their knee on my chest like he did. I feel the wave of helplessness. *I can't breathe.* But I can breathe and I am safe and this is someone who I love and trust, someone who is helping me. They tell me that this position doesn't feel

I Push Him Off Me

very strong. They don't have good balance. They ask if I want to switch positions so I get on top of them like he got on top of me and I see it from his perspective. My friend is right. Even though he weighed so much and was so strong, he wasn't in a strong position. We switch again and my partner helps by watching and directing my movements. Together we find a way to move my body. I thread the needle. I push my friend off of me. *I'm on the floor. I push him off of me.*

We do it a few times, a few different ways. Then I ask my partner, who is bigger and has a body more like the person who did this to me, to get on top of me. They do and I feel the weight of them. I feel the terror and the helplessness in my body, but I also feel the power and the strength and the love of the present. My friend watches and directs. Together, the three of us, we create a space for me to find the strength in my body, the movements that will tip my partner and get them off of me. *I'm on the floor. I push him off me.*

Afterwards I ask to hug them both. I sit on the ground with them and I thank them. I tell them that this is trauma magic, trauma time travel. That the three of us just went back in time, to that moment, and we changed it. My friend says I'm so brave. I tell them *I feel so safe with both of you. I felt safe enough to go there, and I feel like it changed me.* I make a heart with my hands. My mind is no longer spinning in circles, coming up against the terror of that memory, because that memory has changed. It is not rushing headlong to an inevitable outcome. Another outcome has opened up, another possibility. *I push him off me.* The three of us talk. My friend and my partner share about their triggers, the things that set them off, the things they are working on learning. I feel held and seen and supported. I feel strong and fierce and full of love.

I want to learn how to fight. I want to learn the language of violence from a place of profound love. I want to be able to fight for myself and for other people. I want to change the outcome, to find another possibility. This experience has changed me. It's just a beginning; just a small piece of a journey that I know is going to be very difficult. But I have found the courage to take the first steps and I have the support that I need to take

Fucking Magic

them. The light shines green through the leaves and I am safe and I am learning to fight and I am happy.

Eye Contact

We take the door off its hinges. I lie on my back and you look at me. You tell me my eyes are like marble, the blue of my eyes matches the grey of my hair. Your hair falls over your shoulders, I push it out of your eyes. I look at you. I hold your gaze and we look at each other. We make out. I wrap my arms around your waist, run my fingers up and down your arm, move myself toward you. You hold my hand in yours, kiss my neck, look at me.

You look at me and I look at you and I'm smiling and then I start laughing and you're laughing too. I say things like *Yeah* and *Definitely* and you ask for no explanation. You just laugh too and look away and then you go back to looking at me. Your eyes are inquisitive but I ask for no explanation. I say *I think you're nice* and you laugh and say *I think you're more than nice.*

We are both a little shy and we are careful with each other. I was brave and asked you if you wanted to kiss me. You said you did. It's nice to move slowly, to talk for hours drinking lavender tea, to feel a little shy, to get a little bolder, to know that tonight all we're going to do is kiss. Kiss, and look at each other.

The other night across the picnic table you wouldn't look at me. We talked for hours in the dark but your eyes were mostly looking somewhere else. It made me wonder if you liked me. It made me wonder how you felt. But tonight in my room, lying on my bed, your eyes are not shy at all. You look straight into my eyes, hold my gaze uninterrupted, you look like you're looking for something, like you're trying to really see me. You tell me you are taking it all in. I say *Yeah take it all in.*

Fucking Magic

    I feel good in my body. I feel good in your arms. I feel safe and comfortable and happy. You tell me *I know I don't know you well yet but I really like you.* I really like you too.

We Are So Brave

I SEE A SQUIRREL make a run for it across a street full of moving cars, so huge and violent compared to their tiny body. Time stops and I watch and it is close, so close, but the squirrel just misses the crush of the tires and makes it to the other side. My hands are on my heart and immediately I start to cry. I want to laugh at myself because I'm ridiculous. I want to throw myself on the ground and cry my eyes out. I want to find language for all the love and all the pain inside me but I don't have words. I'm a writer and I don't have words.

Later I tell my friend about the squirrel and I say *The squirrel was so brave.* My friend laughs at me. *Come on, Clementine, that's going a bit far, the squirrel was just crossing the street.* I'm laughing and I'm crying again and my friend is teasing me saying *You probably just follow people around telling them how brave they are, like I'd get a bagel and you'd tell me that's so brave.* And I know I'm ridiculous but this is actually a very accurate description of me.

My body is a cauldron. It's a place where things go to transform. For so long I couldn't change because I couldn't face anything. The pain was on a loop, like an intrusive thought perpetually repeating itself. But now the pain comes and it changes me. The pain comes and I change it. But I am still overwhelmed by all my feelings. I am slayed by them. Splayed open. I am revealed and transformed and undone by them. I feel so much and that's why I felt nothing for so long. When the pain comes I try to pay attention to its texture. I try to be open to it, curious. I try to welcome the pain and let it change me, let it be changed by me.

Fucking Magic

I'm not who I was yesterday, that's for sure. And no, you can't actually tell what's going on from my facebook status updates, even tho it's true, I def overshare. There is so much more going on, things I'm not saying, things I don't have words for yet. I try to write about it. The way that things which would, at another time in my life, have destroyed me, which would have sent me spiraling into shame and bottles and blades, now these things come and they change me, but they don't destroy me.

I am changed over and over and over again. I put my hand on my heart because I feel so many things. I watch the squirrel run for their life, for the freedom to move from one place to another, despite roads which have been imposed. And yeah I think it's really fucking brave. I think we are really fucking brave. I actually want to cry so much of the time because I think it's fucking beautiful the way we try to stay alive, the way we fight for what we love, the way we have survived so much. I am undone by the courage of living in the face of violence, of risking death in order to live.

I am a practitioner of trauma magic. Over and over again I take pain and I go inside of it and I change it and I let it change me. Over and over again I find a way to be with what was done to me, a way to be with what I've done. I use my feelings and my words and my tarot cards and my body to get up close to the pain, to get inside it. I feel the shattering and the splitting and I change my relationship to it. I build containers with which to hold it. I become a cauldron, a space of transformation.

I watch the plants push through cement, the photosynthesizing leaves which clean the air we breathe, the way the world keeps offering up its love, its dangers and its love, its cycles and its beauty, its reasons to fight. My friend tells me that plants are what they believe in, when they can't believe in people they believe in plants. Plants are so generous. They give us so much. Plants have their dangers and their boundaries and their lessons. They teach us so much.

I don't have the answers but I do have a process. So many people write to me to tell me about their processes, about the journeys they are on, about recovery, abuse, addiction, pain, about wanting to stay alive, fighting to stay alive. And I bless them and I thank them and I tell them *There is only one you in this whole world. You are irreplaceable and we need you so fucking much.* And it's true. We need you. And there is no one else like you in this whole world.

You are so brave. You are so fucking brave.

Perfect Again

*I*WALK THE STREETS of Montréal and she walks the streets of Toronto. We text each other pictures of the sunset, pinks and purples, blushing clouds, *Same sky*. I miss her smile, her hands, and the way when I compliment her she blushes and says *C'mon*.

She sends me a picture of the moon and I look for it above me. *I can't find the moon* I text her, *there are too many clouds*. She tells me *Even if you can't see it, the moon is always there, always changing, but always constant.* We can depend on the moon. But the moon is also free to change, to go away, to have its rhythms and cycles. We can love the moon when we can't see it. We know it's there.

When I am back in Toronto again we walk the streets together, holding hands. It's still warm, late summer, and we talk about the importance of boundaries and having so many feelings and what it's like to have an ocean for a heart. We turn the corner and there is the moon, bold and bright and almost full, filling the sky with light.

She says with surprise *There's the moon! And it's perfect. I mean, it's always perfect but it's perfect again!*

It's perfect again. And we go back to her place and lie in each other's arms and she tells me earnestly that she loves tornados. *Of course you do* I say. She has eyes for storms and skies and she has eyes for me. And even when we are in different cities we are under the same sky.

We love the same moon.

Tell the Truth

THE MOON IS a sliver less than full. My heart has opened into the void of pain. My hungry hands still search for parental love. I am taking the back way from Saint Henri metro to my friend's. It's dark and I am alone. I'm in Montréal, this beautiful fucking city that I now call home. I have this beautiful life that I have built. I have people in my life who love me, truly, who show me in action what it means to be loved. But my mom sent me an email *Happy thanksgiving. Miss you.* And now I feel like I'm going to die. I laid on my bed motionless for hours but then I texted my friend and said I felt sad and lonely and they said *Come over* so now I'm walking under the sliver-less-than-full moon, through the lane way to them.

The moon is in Aries and I am impulsive. I suddenly know what I have to do. The thing I've been afraid to do. I've been afraid to tell the truth. Even though I've already told it. I told the cops and children's aide when I was fifteen. I told my mom when I was twelve. I smashed glass and cut my arms in front of my parents when I was seventeen and drunk out of my mind, screaming about incest. I said it by running away, by refusing to come home for Christmas or any holidays or at all. I said it with booze and pills and razor blades and suicide attempts. I have said it so many times.

But since I got sober, I don't say anything about it. I write about it in my zines. I hide the facebook statuses that mention child abuse from my mom. I don't go home. I never go home. I keep my distance. I talk about surface things when I talk to my mom. I avoid it. I tiptoe around it. In the rest of my life the fact that I am an incest survivor is common knowledge.

Fucking Magic

My work is about trauma. Everyone knows what my trauma is. But in my family it is not spoken of.

Tonight the moon is telling me that I can't live a lie. Not even a little bit, not even at all. Tonight the fear and terror and immense crushing guilt I feel when I consider telling my parents the truth are diminished by the reality of what it does to me to lie. To hide. To pretend. To play along. I can feel the child in me. I can feel her impossible pain. And I know that when I protect my parents I am abandoning her again.

Right there in the dark on the path on the way to my friend's place I type out an email. It is long and detailed and true. It is generous and kind but it is unbending. I tell the truth. What happened. What my grandfather did. What my parents did. How they didn't protect me. How that made me feel, then, now. How I tried to drink away the pain. How I tried to kill myself. How I have saved my life and how hard I have worked to live and to stay sober. I tell them I have been diagnosed with complex post traumatic stress disorder which results from sustained, repeated trauma and an inability to escape. I tell them I can no longer pretend that the truth isn't the truth. I tell them I can't have an honest relationship with people who do no work on themselves and take no responsibility. I tell them I am done carrying the weight of the truth alone. I am done protecting them when it was their responsibility to protect me.

My finger hovers over the send button and I try to talk myself out of it. It feels crazy. It feels wrong. It feels selfish. It feels terrifying. It feels like I might die. But I know why. I know that appeasing my parents is how I survived as a child. Taking care of their feelings. Taking on the weight of what they did and didn't do. Carrying it in my body. Making me sick. I felt all the pain so that they didn't have to, and I had to, because I was a child, I was trapped. But I am not a child anymore.

I am a fully grown fucking adult. I am brave and I profoundly trust myself. Despite all the fucking shit I have been through, I am a good fucking person. Despite all the fucking shit I have been through I am well-adjusted as fuck. I built this beautiful life. I saved myself. I am sober and I am happy and I am grateful. I have people who love me for real. I have power and strength inside of me that are truly fucking unbelievable. And I don't need my parents' love. I have survived without it all this time.

I can't betray myself anymore. I can't trade in my safety for other people's comfort. Not even a little bit. Not at all.

I press send and I feel a breaking, a severing. I feel profound grief and profound freedom. I take the child in me into my arms and I tell her *I love you and I will protect you, always, at all costs, no matter what.* I feel the strength of the adult I am, the person I have become. I walk to my friend's place where I am fed and loved. And I know that I will be okay.

Young Girls

YOU WERE FIFTEEN years old and you were such a badass. Your bedroom was painted pink plastered with posters of rockstars. You were so punk rock with your bleached hair and your red lipstick you could apply without a mirror. I was two and half years older than you, your older sister then and I always will be. But I looked up to you. You were braver than I was and you made me brave. You showed me how to give a shit and how to not give a shit in one breath. You showed me a secret way into the boys club. You knew your bands in and out, you could talk about music. You were my little sister and you were my best friend and you were so cool.

We were kids. Drunk on beer and vodka. Smoking bongs on hay bales. Running through small town streets, smoking weed off pop cans. Pissing rivers as the cops pulled up. Getting wasted on the bus to the city, chugging vanilla extract in bathroom stalls. Then we moved to the city and the stakes went up. Crack and violence and all the guys we loved who were always going to jail. All those years, those fucked up years. There are things we've seen and things we know and things we've done that no one can understand. But we were kids.

I always talk about how fucked up those years were, how scary. I always talk about how I was my worst self, violent and awful, and it's true. We'd get drunk and fist fight. Screaming at each other, hurting each other. But in the morning, in the sick blur of the hangover, forgiveness was never a question. We were family, the only family we had. I always talk about how dysfunctional it was, how awful. And it was. The truth is we were in so much pain, more pain than anyone could bear, and we bore it with alcohol and weed and acting crazy. We did the best we could.

And even though it's true, those years were awful and fucked up and crazy, that's not all they were. The other day 'Young Girls' by the Distillers came on my earphones and I started to cry; I thought of you. Yeah we did a lot of fucked up things but we were also brave. I remember that dude taking pictures of a sex worker trying to work the corner and the way we put our middle fingers in his camera and screamed *Take a fucking picture of this!* The way she joined us and the three of us screamed at him, telling him to fuck off, to get the fuck away from her. He screamed at us *I have a gun!* And without blinking the three of us screamed *Fucking pull it out then!* We didn't fucking care. We were crazy brave.

You were the only one who stood up for me at that show. You punched the singer in the face. You had my back, even though they grabbed you, restrained you. You saw them drag me out by my hair, you were there. And I regret so much of the way I treated you. The drunken rages we would get into, how I was always telling you I was going to sleep right there, on the side of the road, in a snowbank, and you wouldn't let me. You loved me. And I fucking loved you. As best I could which wasn't very well because we were fucking crazy. But crazy isn't all we were. We were brave too.

I don't know if you know what a fucking force you are. I don't know if you know that you are the most punk rock person I know, still, always. I don't know if you know that you are perfect, brilliant, brave. I don't know if you know what you did for me, how you saved me, how you showed me who I could be. To this day you remain my sister, by blood and by choice. To this day I remain crazy brave in the face of anyone who might try to fuck with you. I would fucking kill them. End of story.

We were kids. Young and crazy, drinking beer by the case, wine by the litre. Holding all the secrets, the generations of trauma, in our bodies. Drinking it down and creating drunken spectacles to bear witness to the impossible, to that which we have always known. We were fucking magic and we remain magic and all I want in this world is for you to pick up your fucking guitar. Pick up your guitar, we can still write the songs we always wanted to write. There is no one in this world more punk than you.

This is Where I Want to Be

I AM LISTENING TO Tigers Jaw with my earphones and I hear the line *This is where I want to be.* The sky is perfect blue and the leaves are changing, vibrant yellow against the sky. It's cool enough for my jacket and I got new boots. I am walking the streets of Montréal.

I have lived here for a month and a half and it feels like home. I feel my feet through my boots against the pavement and it feels so good, it feels like home. I am starting to know my way around. I have developed an internal compass aligned with Montréal's tilted map. North West is North and my body knows that.

It was so hard for me to go. So hard for me to leave Toronto, the place I called home for fifteen years. When I go back there every street corner holds a memory. So many chapters of my life. I walk through the park where the cops were called because I was drinking 40s in the men's bathroom. I see my ex where he stood against the wall as the cops searched him. That was the last night of our relationship. The night he hit me under the bridge.

The streets are streets I've biked down, walked down, cried my eyes out on. Neighborhoods where I've lived and loved and had sex and got drunk and got sober and wanted to die and tried so hard to stay alive. Toronto the city that held me, that changed me. And to my surprise I don't miss it at all.

I am home in Montréal. Practicing my French which is still really bad. Taking the metro to St. Henri where two of my best friends live on the same street. Coming home to my apartment. Walking for hours. I am full of love and ease. I am where I want to be.

I am building a new life in a new city. I am making new friends. I am falling in love with myself all over again. Sometimes it's scary and I feel lonely because I don't have strong roots here yet but I am planting them. I am cultivating relationships. I am creating the life I have always secretly wanted and deserved.

I am lost in the rain trying to make it from Saint Henri to Vendome on foot. It's dark and there's so much construction. I take a selfie and write *I'm lost in Saint Henri but I don't even care. I love my life*. My friend is like *Why are you lost in Saint Henri? Come over* and I do and they give me dry socks and drive me to the workshop I was trying to get to. They're trying to smoke a cigarette and they can't find a lighter and they say *My chapstick to lighter ratio is way off*. And I laugh. We laugh. The rain is falling on the windshield. The red of brake lights. My friend is in their pajamas behind the wheel of the car.

I feel a feeling I have never felt. I feel like a different person. I feel safe. I feel generous. I feel loved. This city and these people make me feel at home. I'm home.

This is where I want to be.

You Are Good

*I*AM SOFT AND I am strong. I am honest and I am brave. I am good. You tell me *You are good.* You hold me, you change me. You are soft and you are strong. You are honest and you are brave. You are good. I tell you *You are good.*

I couldn't have predicted this. I couldn't have foreseen it. You told me to meet you and your friend at Saint Henri metro and I turned the corner and there you were. Looking cuter than I was prepared for. You were kinder than I was prepared for. You were better than I was prepared for. You were good.

You sat across from me drinking mint tea. You walked me to your place. Every step of the way you gave me a way out. *I can walk you to the metro or you can come inside. We can hang in the living room or in my room.* I wanted to come inside. I wanted to hang in your room.

I wanted to kiss you. So when you asked I said yes. You made me feel safe and you made me feel good. Right from the beginning you treated me with care. You made me feel seen.

Now here I am in this city and the seasons are changing again. Now here I am in this city that I call home, building the life I have always deserved. You hold me and you change me. You listen to me and you push me. You tell me about your feelings and I tell you about mine.

Love lifts me up, love gives me roots. Love is the bravest thing I've ever done. And to my surprise, I feel powerful in love. I feel strong. I feel full. I feel free. Love is not a cage, love is not a trick, love is not a trap. I used to trade in pieces of myself in order to secure what I thought was love. You show me that love makes me more myself, not less. Love holds me, changes me, makes me brave. Love encourages me, affirms me, pushes me to grow.

Love is the scariest thing. Love is the bravest thing. Any time I've dared to fall in love my heart has been obliterated, my trust has been betrayed. But for the first time I can trust myself, for the first time I have done the work to show up to love already in love with myself. I can trust you because I trust myself. I can love you because I love myself. But it's still scary. It's still brave.

You lie in my bed and you tell me about the ways that you love the people in your life, the way that you fight for them. You tell me that the individual is a myth. And you fucking mean it. You mean it so much that it hurts you and I don't want it to hurt you but this is why I fell in love with you. I love your love. I love the way you put love into action, the way you help me lean further into my love, my courage, my integrity. The way you show me over and over and over again that it is always worth it to be brave.

I am soft and I am strong. I am honest and I am brave. I am good. You tell me *You are good*. You hold me, you change me. You are soft and you are strong. You are honest and you are brave. You are good. I tell you *You are good*.

Trauma Magic

*I*FIND BRUISES ALL over my body from sex and learning to fight. My clothes are covered in grass stains and dirt from rolling around on the ground, crawling, body pressed against the earth. My hands are stained pink from beets and cabbage, yellow from turmeric. I make vinegar tinctures and home ferments. I drink holy basil and lavender, mint and nettle.

I make my bed every morning and brush my teeth every night. These things used to be hard for me to do but I've learned them. I've changed my brain so that now I want to do them, now I do them for me. I put a drop of lavender oil on the end of my nose and breathe. I mix tea tree and lavender into coconut oil and rub it into my skin.

I take 5htp for my sadness. I talk to the people I love about what I am feeling and I write about it. I feel a pain deep down, a panic. I slip into shame spirals. I worry. Deep down somehow I still feel unworthy. I still feel horrified at the prospect of owning my power, of taking responsibility for my desires but I'm getting there.

I am learning how to talk about sex. I ask my partner for advice on how to talk to new dates. It's #slut4slut life, feeling safe enough to ask my partner these things, trusting my partner's knowledge of good consent practices and communication skills. My partner tells me it's okay if I need to text people to talk about sexuality and boundaries and sexual health stuff and consent and desire. They tell me I'm really good with writing these things even if it's hard for me to say them. They tell me *Think of it like an access need.*

Fucking Magic

I drink green tea with ginger. I take l-glutamine to heal my guts. I use an app on my phone where I grow little trees to stop myself from getting sucked into endless scrolling. I practice my French: *Désolé pour mon français. Je suis en train d'apprendre.* I practice setting boundaries: *Last night during sex you took my hand off my clit. This isn't acceptable. My pleasure is important and I have the right to experience it on my own terms.* I am committed to loving myself.

I practice guitar, press fingers into strings. My fingers are regaining their calluses. I practice falling and rolling. I learn how to move my body, I learn how my body moves. I think about movement, motion, becoming unstuck. I drop my shoulders. I drop my shoulders again. I try to find the words that are frozen in my throat. I try to thaw them, say them. I talk about dissociation. I try to take in the reality that I am loved, wanted, welcome. I give myself permission to be here, again and again.

I'm proud of myself for how far I've come. I am sinking into this beautiful life I've built and learning to believe that I deserve it. I am working on being present, remembering to breathe. I am trying to get out of bed earlier. But I also have compassion for my sadness and my pain. I'm not trying to eradicate them. I try to slow down and be gentle. I try to remember that I've been doing so much hard work, that trauma magic is hard work, that I'm doing my best, and it's enough.

The leaves are red and yellow and scattered on the sidewalk. My boots make me feel grounded with every step I take. I listen to punk or emo or straight up pop, whatever I feel like. Or I take off my headphones and try to be present to the world around me.

I buy groceries and cook food for myself. My friends and loved ones cook for me. They show me different ways to make food, different ways to relate to food. I take pictures of the food I make and send them to my partner who replies *Yum*. I'm learning not to feel shame about food. I'm learning how to feel safe nourishing myself. I'm working towards cooking food for the people I love, nourishing them.

I am trying to feel my body, feel pleasure in my body, feel the way it feels to be touched, to come, to be loved, to love, to eat good food, to stretch, to struggle, to move. I am trying to stay with the feelings in my body and it's the hardest work of my whole life. I'm trying to learn how to say *I want this, I like this, I love this, Not like that, More like this, I changed my mind, Slow down, Pause, Stop*. I'm trying to learn how to say *I'm sad, can we cuddle? / You're hot and I want to fuck you / Sometimes I need to slow down or stop / When was the last time you were tested? / Can I hold your hand? / This is what I'd like to eat / This is what I'd like to do*.

 I am well trained in being unloved. I know how to survive unbearable things. I know how to live with violence and rejection and betrayal. My body expects these things. My body is bewildered by and suspicious of the life I currently have. It's scary to be happy. It's scary to be at peace. It's scary to have the life that I've always secretly dreamed of.

 I try to engage in masturbation as a spiritual practice. I try to embody the fact that my hand on my clit is fucking holy. I try to feel my pussy getting wet, I try to stay connected to the heat and the tension and the want. I try to believe that it's good, not shameful. It is good, not shameful. It is magic. I am taking my body back from rapists and pedophiles, from every person who touched me or fucked me like I was an object rather than a human being, from all the messages that say my desire is only acceptable when it takes the shape of another's desire.

 I am engaging in desire as a path toward healing. I will only accept touch that is intentional, connected. I still dissociate but I am working on coming back. I am working on being honest about what's happening and asking for what I need. I may accidentally fuck someone who doesn't deserve me but I am working hard on eradicating that practice from my life.

 I sit in coffee shops drinking soy lattes and writing poetry. I have work dates with cute queers and we get shit done. I post about my feelings on facebook. I read tarot for people and spend hours walking the streets of Montréal. I am happy.

 My sadness doesn't scare me anymore. My joy doesn't scare me anymore. My hope doesn't scare me anymore. My pain doesn't scare me anymore. My love doesn't scare me anymore. My life is a magic spell, a process of transformation, a practice of gratitude, and my heart grows ten times its size, over and over again.

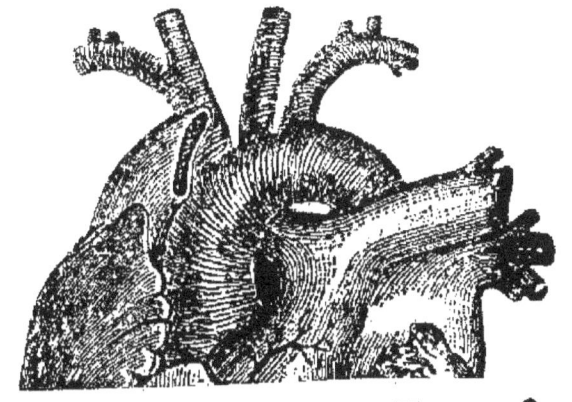

Fucking Magic

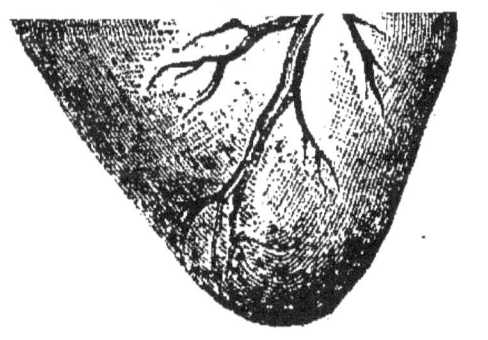

#4

Neurons That Fire Together Wire Together

NEURONS THAT FIRE together wire together. In my brain there is a network of ghosts. In my body I feel the familiar paths of cortisol, well worn grooves, electric rivers. My mouth is the shape of silence, my throat an empty channel. I try to speak, to revive some other truth, to find my way back to something that was before.

But maybe that's the wrong direction: *back*. Maybe it's not so much back as it is: *out*.

My thoughts are prayers, they are spells, they are magic. I create my feelings in the forest of connections firing. I am now on my knees at the altar of this trauma, all I've ever known is the repetition of abandonment, the certainty of betrayal, the presence of panic, slow and steady and lighting myself on fire from the inside. But this pattern is boring, wearing me thin, making me tired. I can't believe what's right before my eyes because it doesn't match the story told by a network of ghosts.

I tell my partner *I compulsively play out in my mind what it would feel like if I lost everything, if everyone I love betrayed me, abandoned me. I feel like I have to do it. I have to prepare myself.* They look horrified by this. They tell me *If you're going to do that at least promise me that you'll also think about what it would be like if everything worked out just fine.*

I start to imagine a future without betrayal, without catastrophe. I try to imagine the steady safety of community and love. It is easier than I expected. Less terrifying than I expected. But there's still a tiny voice that tells me this is dangerous, that I need to know how to survive without this. I tell this voice *I already do.*

I tell my friend that the way I have survived is by telling myself I can lose it all and still be okay. I can watch it all burn to the ground around me and I will survive like I always have. I can be betrayed and violated in the deepest and most fucked up ways by the people I love the most and I will be okay. I tell myself this is what I'm good at, this is what I know. I can lose everything. I tell my friend *I'm only just beginning to admit that I don't want to lose everything, that I don't want to feel that pain anymore, and it's scary.*

I sit in a coffee shop with my partner and my friend/my partner's partner. They both study and work on schoolwork and I write. I feel this ease and peace that I have never known. I feel this goodness, kindness. I keep laughing and calling everything wholesome, because it is. My life is so fucking wholesome right now.

Neurons that fire together wire together. New networks are forming in my brain, old ones are falling away. I am finding a way to tell a new story because I am tired of the old one. I am exhausted by the pain and I am bored by it. I have built this beautiful life where I am held in love and in community. I have built relationships grounded in trust. I trust myself. I trust my body. I trust the people I love. And all of this I trust because it is trustworthy.

So I am building a brain that can know this. I am creating new connections which are capable of holding the truth. I am letting go of ghosts, leaving the past behind me, and stepping into the present. This beautiful life. This safe life. This life where I am happy and I am held and I am loved.

I tell my therapist *It's so crazy. It's so intense.* She tells me to stop saying that. She says *Clementine, I think the phrasing you are looking for is: It's so good.* And she's right. It's so good.

I breathe. I let the breath fill my body. I look around. I see people I love working away on their schoolwork. I see Montréal streets and the grey skies of early December. I feel my feet on the ground. I feel the electric current of cortisol, the neurons firing in their ghost networks and I choose to think something else. I choose to feel something else.

Sickening

*I*CAN'T SAY WHAT I need to say. The words are tangled in the back of my throat. The words are not words, they are sounds. I stand over the sink. I wash the dishes with scalding hot water. Suddenly I feel it, the push from somewhere deeper than my stomach. I grip the counter with wet soapy hands and I let out some kind of sob. My body is heaving, tears are squeezing out of my eyes. I feel it in my guts, some kind of strangled sound trying to make its way up. But then it stops. It never lasts more than thirty seconds.

I lie on my back and press my vibrator through my pants. I don't want to take my pants off. I don't want to feel myself with my fingers, all wet and slippery, voracious. I find it sickening. I tell myself I don't find it sickening. I'm trying to concentrate on a thought but I keep thinking something else. I'm trying to remember not my own pleasure but yours because I know that's what will do it. And my vibrator is buzzing away and I'm trying to push myself over that edge. I'm trying to concentrate.

Did I ever tell you about what it was like under his bed? What kind of daring it would take to choose that as a hiding spot in hide and seek? But kids are crazy. The danger is real. Did I ever tell you he was a hunter? Did I tell you about the severed animal heads all over the walls? Trophies. Did I tell you about my father? His hand around the back of my neck. My grandfather's arms holding me against my will. That's why my shoulders stay stuck, hunched, armored. Did I ever tell you who I am? Did I tell you about the power inside terror, the way I found my strength by jumping? How I promised never to need anything? I know that nothing can ever destroy me. I have already been destroyed.

Sickening

My voice is like my orgasm, stopped dead in its tracks, stuffed up, silent, stuck. Sometimes I look really angry when I'm turned on. Sometimes I grimace. Sometimes I glare. Sometimes I cry. Sometimes I twist and turn and wriggle. I want to let it out so badly. I'm so goddamn frustrated that I can't let it out. I want to throw myself against the wall. I want to beat it out of me. But it won't fucking come. I won't fucking come. It's banging around inside of me. It's scratching at my insides. I can't concentrate. I can't let go. I keep thinking. I keep thinking. I keep thinking I shouldn't be thinking.

What's trapped inside me has no words. When I open this up I won't die, I won't die again. What's trapped inside me is disgusting, it's the point of no return. What's trapped inside me is the moment, the violation, the presence. I wasn't on the ceiling, no I was right here. What's trapped inside me is an animal, a little girl, wild eyes and wild terror. What's trapped inside me is the way in when there's no way out. I can't say it. I can't feel it. I say everything else. I feel everything else. I just want to say it. I just want to feel it. I want to find a way in so I can find a way out.

You can't kill her. She won't die. She won't fucking die.

When I say I can't I know that I am lying. When I feel stuck, trapped, conquered, I know that I am lying. I am lying because I can't tell the truth. I am lying because I am terrified. I am lying when I pretend to be small. I am lying when I pretend to be helpless. I am lying when I say *Love me love me I can't love myself.* Because I fucking love myself and I always have. I am lying when I say *I don't know*, when I say *I'm not enough.* I am lying because the truth is worse. I am lying because the truth is, I am so fucking powerful and it is unspeakable what was done to me. It is unspeakable the way I was degraded, violated, made to disavow my power. It is unspeakable what was done to my relationship to my body, my sexuality, myself.

His tongue was wet and warm, bits of food in his dentures, my wet bathing suit yellow with daisies, his stubble slick with grease.

It is unspeakable like desecrating a sacred place. It is an affront to the most divine. There is nothing more powerful than my will to live.

Fucking Magic

There is nothing more sacred than a child. There is nothing more wrong than violating a child, making a child live in terror and shame. There is nothing more powerful than my desire to heal. There is nothing more powerful than my capacity to heal. There is nothing more powerful than my love. There is nothing more powerful than my rage.

My Body Tells Me That It's True

I CAN FEEL MYSELF coming into my power. The process is slow. Sometimes it is unclear what is happening. Sometimes it feels like I am coming apart. But I can feel the work consolidating. I can feel the change in me.

I am gentle. I walk the streets of Montréal and marvel at the snow. I listen to affirmation meditations. I learn how to say kind things to myself. I feel my neurons pruning and growing new connections. I feel myself begin to believe in myself, in my power.

I stop listening to anything when I walk around. I let myself be alone with my thoughts. I let the pain come, tidal waves of it. I try to find a way to be with the pain, again. I try to find a way to change the pain, to let the pain change me, again. This is the same work, and it is long work, and it is working.

I take baths and I feel my body. I feel the places where the pain is. I feel the unspeakable things that are trapped in my body. I breathe into them and I begin to let them go.

I remember. I remember again. I find the words I was afraid to say. The thing I couldn't even look at. I don't go seeking it. It rises to the surface when I turn my attention to my body. The words come.

Instead of terror I feel relief. Oh, this. This. This is the thing I have been so afraid to think, so afraid to know. This is the thing tangled up in my body, contorting me, distorting my thoughts.

Fucking Magic

I write it in my diary because I don't know who to tell. I write the words *I am a survivor of both covert and overt incest. I am a survivor of sexual violence at the hands of more than one family member. I don't need to hide or deny this anymore. It is safe to tell the truth.*

I write other things, details I'm not ready to share here. I write it down, the big bad secret, the thing I bent myself backwards trying to make untrue, the thing I told myself I was a bad person for even considering. I write about rolling off the bed and sleeping on the floor between the bed and the wall. I write about the terror that I could not say.

My body tells me that it's true.

I breathe. I let the breath move through me, down into my guts and down into my pussy, down into the places where shame and terror have hardened and crystalized, become heavy like stone. I breathe. I send so much love to myself, to every cell, to every memory.

I feel the adult in me. The power of the person I've become. I feel the vibrant health of choosing to live in reality. I have a choice. I feel the connection to my ancestors, stretching back and back and back, generations of trauma, generations of sexual abuse, generations of incest. And I choose to know it. I choose to heal it.

For me. For us. For all of us.

I can feel myself coming into my power and sometimes it feels like a mess. Sometimes I am tired and lethargic. Sometimes the pain flares up like crazy and I think *I thought I had outgrown this*. But healing is a process and a cycle. I return again to what needs more attention. I return again because I am ready to see something I wasn't ready to see before.

I breathe. I breathe into my power, into my profound trust of myself, into the magic of healing, into this moment, into the love which I cultivate which grows and grows. I can change and I am changing. I can heal and I am healing. Again and again I do the work of transformation. I am becoming who I am here to be.

I choose to treat myself with utter compassion. I choose to be gentle and kind. I choose to say *Clementine I am so fucking proud of you, you are doing so good, you are doing so so good*. I choose to ask myself *What*

My Body Tells Me That It's True

do you need? What will help you feel safe? How can I help you? I choose to prioritize my healing, to take all the time that I need.

Hungry for Love

I AM SO GRATEFUL for the cold. It's minus 30 and I'm wearing three sweaters under my coat and snow pants. I'm taking the back way to the metro in St. Henri. It's almost midnight. The world is dark and covered in snow.

I walk the path of pressed snow. I am alone. And I start crying. I start crying my eyes out in the snow.

I ask myself what I want and I have it. I ask myself what I need and I have it. I ask myself what's wrong and I cry and cry.

I am disarmed. I surrender. I lay it all down. I am done. I can't pretend. I know the truth. I feel it in my bones. I am safe. I have everything I need and it is not enough. It's not enough to outrun this.

There's no way out but through. I have to believe the way out is through. So I let the love crack my rib cage. I let the pain split me open again and I cry.

I am so good at being grateful. I am so good at loving every little blessing in my life. But if I'm honest I have to say that it's been rough. If I'm honest I have to say it would have been easier if it hadn't been so hard.

If I'm honest I wish I had felt loved and safe when I was a child. If I'm honest I wish the people I loved hadn't hurt me so fucking badly. If I'm honest I wish I didn't have so much fucking need inside me. I am so fucking hungry for love. I'm fucking starving.

But I am humbled by love. I am made brave by love. I am willing to be the best of myself. I am ready to stretch my heart, to open my hands, to face my fucking fears. I do what I have to do to show up for love. I let it change me, challenge me. It makes me grow.

And it hurts so much to grow. It hurts so much to need so much and to know that I already have what I need.

Love is free. There is no way to secure it. There is no way to keep it. It has to be chosen freely over and over again.

Fucking with Integrity

AFTER FLIRTING AND exchanging pics and him sending me a long description of how to get to his place via public transit, after me deciding that yeah I'll take the long trek in the cold, because he's hot and seems nice and it's been too long since I've had casual sex, he sends me a message clarifying that's he's down to fuck but he won't make out with me. He says *I don't make it a habit to kiss random strangers. I don't want to catch herpes or anything. People are dirty.* And I am exhausted by this.

I tell him *I respect your boundary but I'm not down without kissing.* He's messaging me about when was I last tested and do I have anything. But I've lost interest. I don't want to fuck this dude who implied that sti's are dirty and who clearly has issues about women who sleep around. I've had too many guys in this lifetime fuck me and refuse to kiss me because I am a slut and I'm over it. I throw my phone across the bed. I go to my altar, light my candles, draw my cards.

How can I connect to my power?

I'm so exhausted from all the years I gave it away. I'm so exhausted by how easily I can forget it, even still. I'm so exhausted by how hard it is to have a fun, respectful, consensual sex life, how hard it is to navigate trauma and shame, not to mention other people's bullshit. I'm exhausted by it but I'm not despairing. I watch the candles flickering tiny flames on my altar. I feel the minus 30 cold that I was willing to go out in to get laid pressing in against my window. I wonder if I should get myself off. I'm turned on from all the sexting I was doing today, but I'm also not really in the mood anymore.

Fucking with Integrity

I want to connect to my power. I want to remember it the way I remember the moon, when I remember the moon, the way I know the moon in my body when I'm paying attention. I want to pay attention. I'm 31 and I'm sick of the backsliding, the forgetting who the fuck I am. I want to be sure and steady, so much more often than I am. When I am happy and full of love, I am simultaneously activated, the terror of trauma spreading cortisol through my veins. I want to relax and feel safe. I want to feel my feet on my ground. I want to remember.

Sometimes I listen to love songs and I get caught up in my romantic feelings because I am a romantic and I love romantic feelings. But then sometimes I imagine I am singing that love song to myself. I am telling myself *Clementine, I got you, no matter what you can have faith in that.* And I remember that through it all I've always been there, that through it all I have found a way to connect with some inner drive, some will to live, some part of myself that can't be destroyed. No matter what they did to me. No matter what I was made to endure. I have always found a way. I feel strong in that power, in that knowing.

Earlier I was messaging with my partner about fears and insecurities, trauma feels and shame, telling them it can be hard to connect to my worthiness when I'm triggered. They told me *Your worthiness is off the charts.* And I like that. I think it's true. I'm trying to find my way back to that profound love for myself, that certainty of my worthiness, always having my own back, always being on my own side. I try to remember the way it was when I loved my life so profoundly and with so much vigor, when I needed nothing but the world opening itself to me.

Maybe I will get myself off after all. Maybe I will find a way to lift masturbation to the level of spiritual practice. Maybe I will find a way through all the shame that says my pleasure is only important when it is in the service of someone else's desire. Maybe I will connect to the straight up holiness of my vibrator, the way I speak words out loud like spells. Maybe my bed is an altar and the pleasure I conjure up in myself is an offering to the universe. Maybe it is good, so good. Maybe I know exactly what I want.

Fucking Magic

Because the truth is, when we get right down to the bottom of it, this random dude who I was about to go hook up with, he doesn't deserve to have sex with me. The comment that he made does not align with my values, with my integrity, and therefore it does not align with my desire. And it is okay for me to lose interest. It is okay for me to choose carefully who I fuck, even if it is slutty, or random, or casual.

Something is changing in me. Deep down. Maybe this is the slow magic of remembering, the slow magic of connecting with my power.

A while ago at a coffee shop, drinking mugs of hot tea with my friend, I told her *I don't want to fuck anyone I'm not excited about, I need to feel attracted, you know, on multiple levels. I need to feel excited. I don't want to do it if I'm not feeling it.* She held my hands in her hands and turned them over. She said *I remember in the summer when you told me you could only really come with randoms, with people you felt no investment in. It's interesting to watch this change in you, like turning over a leaf.*

When you fuck me you are fucking a witch, a scholar, a poet, an alcoholic, a survivor of a fuck ton of violence, a healer, a powerful being connected to a power greater than herself. You are fucking my history and my drive and my ambition and my capacity to change. When you fuck me you are here with me in the magic of transformation, you are here with me in the quest to reconnect, to remember my power. When you fuck me you are blessed. So I can accept nothing less than respect, nothing less than a willingness to show up, to meet me in a place of integrity. I can't and I won't accept any implication that sex is dirty.

My power is here, right here, where it has been all along.

Cock Sucking Bisexual

I write out my list of New Years resolutions and right there in the middle of it I write *strap on sex*. This is after a long conversation with my partner about the fact that I've never fucked a femme with a strap on, or had a femme fuck me with a strap on, despite my deep desire for these acts. Despite my harness and dildo in the drawer next to my bed. And this conversation was part of a larger conversation with my partner about feeling like a creep when expressing my desire for femmes, needing a really strong signal otherwise I don't feel okay giving a signal myself.

I matched with someone on a dating app and I wasn't getting a clear vibe one way or another. I decided not to pursue it further. I decided they weren't really that into it. I didn't want to come on too strong. I didn't want to make them uncomfortable. I told my partner this and they asked me why I assumed this person wasn't into it, when they had liked me on a dating app. I said *They aren't giving me a signal!* My partner asked *Clementine, are you giving them a signal?*

And then we talked about my queer femme4femme desires, and my desire for silicone cock and pretty much anything down my throat, and how I feel like my desires aren't the right desires, aren't the proper queer desires, how I'm afraid my queer card will be revoked for being a cock sucking bisexual, for not being super into getting head, unless we're talking about a blowjob. I mean, I'm not *not* into it, and maybe I want to be more into it, but there are things that I know I'm definitely into that I won't even bring up, for a constellation of reasons rooted in internalized queerphobia and biphobia and shame.

Fucking Magic

Being a nonmonogamous bisexual femme with femm4femme leanings and a really strong desire to choke out on cock makes me feel like the stereotypical bad bisexual. My desires are so easily swept up into narratives of performing desire for a heterosexual male audience. Femme4femme is suspicious. Cock sucking is suspicious. Bisexuality is suspicious. Not being super into head is suspicious. I have felt pressured into acts that I'm not super excited about because those acts are supposedly more queer or more inherently pleasurable for bodies like mine. And I'm just like I'm sorry but I can tell in my body when I'm really turned on. And I'm open to exploring things that don't immediately get me wet, but it is stressful as fuck to feel like the desires that turn me into a puddle are just the wrong desires.

I don't know how to be direct about my desires. Okay, sometimes I do. Sometimes I'm brazen. Usually in the context of casual sex with men (again, bad bisexual). But with femmes I freak out because I can't tell for sure if they are into me because dudes tend to be so much more direct about their desires and because I grew up knowing that queer desire was either disgusting or it didn't exist, and femme4femme desire, well, that's the greatest mystery of all. And it burns inside me like this terrible secret because I can't imagine another femme feeling as fucking turned on by me and my femme gender as I am by them. And I know I've drunk the homophobic koolaid and it settled deep into my bones.

And with people I love or really like a lot I tend to freak out too, because again I want my desires to be the right ones, I want to be desirable, I want to be wanted, and I can't imagine that my own desire is as important, as valid, as welcome, as the desire of this person I've got feels for. Or maybe I can imagine it. Maybe I can learn to entertain the notion. I've had moments where it comes over me and I see that this person I love wants to light me up with desire, wants to welcome me in with all my secret wants.

My partner is a slut and I love them. I come to them with all my neurotic hang ups about sex and desire and they talk to me about it. They push me and they encourage me and they give me really good advice.

They tell me to ask for what I want, that there's no harm in asking, that if I am respectful and considerate and able to take no for an answer there is nothing creepy about expressing my desire. I need to take responsibility for my desire. I need to find a way to own it, claim it, and let other people know about it. I need to let go of the shame and the fear I have around naming my desires for what they are. I need to tell the narrative about the bad bisexual to fuck off or maybe just take it back so it has no power over me. I need to get comfortable with the reality that my queer desires are very queer desires even if there's lots of cocks involved, some flesh, some silicone, some mine, some belonging to others, some femme, some masc, some genderqueer as fuck.

Je t'avais dit non

I TOLD HIM FUCKING no. *I screamed it. I said stop. I said* You can't come here anymore. You can't keep hanging around outside my house. *I cried my eyes out. I tried to fight back. He laughed in my face. I said* Give me your key. *He broke into the house. He was always breaking in, breaking down the walls that I set up. He was always bending my fingers back, throwing things at me, making me cry. He was always apologizing, in my arms crying, and I was always forgiving him, relenting, yielding, going soft again, packing up the panic until next time, trying so hard to be so good.*

I told him no and when it was done it was done. After he put me through a wall and broke into my house and smashed the glass sliding door and called the cops on me. After he chased me down the street on his bike and threatened to kill my cats and put his knee on my chest and wouldn't let me breathe. After I pleaded with him in the convenience store in front of my house where he was waiting for me as I was trying to go to my exam. *I said to him* You have to stop. You can't keep doing this. *I told him no.*

I haven't spoken a word to him from that day to this, but he keeps coming back, keeps messaging me, keeps trying to terrify me and remind me of our love and suck me back in. He always finds a way, even when he was in jail, even after I moved, even though it's been eight years. I know it kills him that I'm free. I got fucking free. And even though he keeps coming back to terrify me, he has no fucking power over me. I told him fucking no. No, not ever again. He will never have my body or my heart. He will never make me think his behaviour is okay. He will never make me think I deserve it. He will never own me. He never owned me. I am not his and I never was. No matter what he did, no matter what he does.

Je t'avais dit non

Eight years later, I am 31. I'm walking home from my partner's place through the snow covered streets of Montréal, the city I have made my own. I was sitting on my partner's bed, naked, happy, waiting for them to bring me coffee. I was scrolling on my phone and I opened my email. Immediately I felt like I couldn't breathe. I felt the familiar swell of panic, the dizzying crashing, the cortisol rushing, the world disappearing. I opened the emails in my inbox, from my abusive ex. My partner when I was 23. Eight years later and he is in my inbox again. He is raging like he used to, calling me a liar, wondering what it would be like if we were still in love. My partner came in and I showed them the messages. We talked about it. They held me in their arms and comforted me. We strategized. They reminded me that I am not alone. On my way back from their place, walking through the thick snow, I see the graffiti I keep passing on my way home. *Je t'avais dit non.*

I told him fucking no. And it didn't start with my ex. I told my grandfather no. I ran from him. I planned my route. I eyed the door into the house and calculated how fast I would have to move to get through without him grabbing me. I said I don't want to kiss you. *My father raged at me. He called me disrespectful, ungrateful. My sister cried. I was angry. I watched my grandfather watch me. I knew what he wanted. I was a child and I told him no. I told him no and it didn't matter. I told him no and there were no doors between the bedrooms, only curtains. I told him no and I slept in a tent outside.*

My no was meaningless. The running and the crying, the calculating and the trying to get away. It did nothing but make my father angry. I received punishment when I was desperately seeking protection. I didn't want my grandfather's greasy stubble against my skin, his disgusting tongue on my face. I said no. But to assert that meant punishment. It meant I wasn't deserving of love. I struggled constantly with my terror, with my deep down knowledge that my grandfather was dangerous, that he was a pedophile. This truth came up against my wild unquenchable need for love. I would trade anything in for a taste of love. And I did.

Fucking Magic

By the time I started having sex the idea of saying no was a joke. Besides, it didn't matter because I didn't have a voice. I remember so many times yelling over and over in my mind Stop, go away, get off me, don't touch me. *Trying to will with my mind to make whatever was happening not happen as I lay there frozen, unspeaking, unable to say a fucking thing. I remember the hands and dicks of boys and men, their eagerness, their thrusting, their touching, their pulling away of my clothes. I remember their apparent indifference to my frozen voiceless state, the way I stared at the wall while they fucked me.*

How can I ever really say yes when I still haven't learned to say no? The space where words should be is still a silence. I can communicate with my body, with my sounds and my soundlessness, and to attentive lovers it is obvious when something is wrong. When I am asked a question and I don't say anything, attentive lovers know to pause. But even with those I trust the most I can't find the words to say *No, not this, something else. Slow down, come back. I want... Can we ...* So often I am speechless. It's like my voice is a ghost who has gone somewhere else. It is like my thoughts have no connection to the outer world, no way to be made manifest.

I want to believe I can say no and I will still be loved. I want to believe I can set a boundary, have it respected, and not lose love because of it. I want to believe my no will not be punished, will not be annoying, will not be disappointing, will not make me less loveable, less desirable. I want to believe that my autonomy, my assertiveness, are not incompatible with my need for love. I know there is an endless well of power, and a storehouse of energy, trapped in my body, buried underground. I know that it takes the shape of *No* and all the endless times that word was meaningless, and all the endless times that word was punished, and all the endless times it wasn't even said at all.

I want to say no in anger. I want to say no in sweetness. I want to say no firmly. I want to say no for now. I want to say no for no reason, just to say it, just to see if it will work. I want to know my no won't be subject to coercion. I want to say no directly. I want to say no with passion. I want

Je t'avais dit non

to say no with power. I want to know my no won't be ignored. I want to say no and still feel sexy. I want to say no and still feel safe. I want to say no and still feel loved.

Real Love

MOM. HELP ME. Help me mom. Help me. Help me. Help me. I am so scared. I don't know what to do. I don't know how to make him stop. I am so confused. Mom. Help me. I don't know why I feel all alone in this cottage by the lake with the sun shining down. I don't know why I feel so bad, like it's my fault, like I'm the one causing the problem. I don't know what to do with this fear that is scrambling my insides and making me sick, this terror I can't speak. But I told you mom I told you. And nothing changed.

I ask the cards what the problem is, the unnamable problem, the unhappiness that keeps rising to the surface unarticulated, the blank space that moves between me and my body severing the connection, the fear that quicksands me. The cards say *Five of Pentacles*. I am outside in the snow. I have been travelling for years looking for shelter. The window is close by, bright and promising warmth. But I am afraid to knock on the door. I am afraid I won't be welcomed. I am afraid my weary tired body will be a source of repulsion. I'm afraid the warmth is not for me. I'm afraid the welcoming, the home, the safety, is not for me.

I ask the cards what the solution is, what magic I need to work to find my way, to knock on the door, to come inside. The cards say *The Lovers*. The cards say *Stop rejecting yourself. Welcome yourself, create home for yourself, every part of you.* The cards say *Integration, the magic of meeting yourself, of coming back into all of who you are.* The cards say *Love, find that good love and let it inside you, don't push it away and don't settle for less than the real thing.* The cards say *It's fucking magic, it's in your hands, it's in your legs, it's in your cunt, it's that place you've been to, that place you know, that presence, stay with it, let it grow. Welcome yourself home.*

Real Love

I ask the cards what is blocking me, where am I stuck? The cards say *Eight of Swords*. I stay stuck because I'm afraid to face my power. I'm afraid to own my power. I'm afraid to know who I've become and what I'm capable of. I'm afraid to see my profound beauty, my inherent worthiness, how fucking capable I am. And I am afraid of this because I still haven't grieved the wound of my childhood helplessness, when I really was stuck, trapped, without options, desperately in need of adult help, adult intervention, and that intervention never came. The wound of abandonment is so fucking deep, so I abandon myself. I am tired and I want someone to save me. I want someone to be my mom and come and rescue me and tell me that I'm safe and that I'm loved. In order to claim my power I have to grieve that wound. I have to be my own mom.

I ask the cards what the outcome will be, what it is that I ultimately need. The cards say *Six of Pentacles*. This confusing card that has been showing up over and over again lately. This lesson I'm still trying to learn. The cards tell me *Stop giving your power away. Stop positioning yourself as the rejected child greedy and begging for love. Recognize yourself. Stand up. Rise. See that your relationships are reciprocal. That you give as much as you take. That you are a gift. That those who love you are blessed.* When I told my friend about my fears of unworthiness and abandonment, when I told them how much love scares me they told me *The people you love are lucky to love you*. This is the lesson, this is the outcome, to understand that I'm a gift, to understand that to love me is a gift. That those who love me are blessed to be held in my love.

Mom I know you tried. I know you loved me as well as you could. I know that no one ever loved you and that you had to learn it all yourself. You gave me so much. So much of myself is from you. That's part of why it hurt so much to be turned over and surrendered to a terrifying man. Everything you taught me is in direct contradiction to what you did. Your actions made me feel unloved. Your actions showed me that I was powerless and had no say over what happened to my body. Your actions made it clear that the Rule of the Father was the ultimate rule, regardless of all the feminist books you gave me to read. Mom I wish with all my heart that you stopped everything. That you said no. That you knew how to say no, and that you took your terrified children away, consequences be damned. I can only imagine who I would be if you had been capable of that, if you had shown me real love.

Sex Maniac

THERE'S THIS POWER inside of me, this spreading pleasure. It fills me up, makes me crazy with want, but in a way that is strong, grounded. My body is alive with desire, lit up from the inside with some kind of knowing, something I've always known but which could not find a form. Until now.

I tell you *I think you're turning me into a sex maniac!* And you laugh, we laugh, sprawled across my bed. I am happy and I am loved and I am safe and so there's this ocean that's opening up inside me, there's this expanse I want to give over to you.

We're sexting and I interrupt to establish a limit, a boundary. There's this one thing I find really triggering, really upsetting. There's this thing that lights up a trauma constellation in my brain, makes me feel humiliated, abandoned, unwanted, ashamed. So I tell you about it, and we try to think of ways to explore the fantasy without that particular thing.

But then later, alone in my room, my vibrator buzzing away pressed against my pussy, I think of that thing. I think of the thing that upsets me the most and I feel ripped open with pleasure. I don't know what I'm doing but I lean into it, my mind goes all the way into it. I am so fucking turned on. I am eroticizing the thing that upsets me the most and I can't stop coming.

I feel like I should feel freaked out and maybe I do feel freaked out. I'm worried maybe this is crazy or super dysfunctional. Why would I set a limit and then immediately find the idea of that very thing absurdly hot?

But in my body, in my body there is an ocean, there is an unspeakable power, there is this goodness and it just feels *right*.

I revive a group convo from a few months back with some friends who are also queer trauma survivors and submissives. I ask them if they have any spoons to talk and I tell them about this thing. *Like is this crazy? Is this super dysfunctional?*

My friends reassure me. One tells me *It makes sense. Because when you say no to something and that is heard and respected, it opens up the possibility for you to truly say yes. It isn't being forced on you, and that allows you to explore it if you want to.* Another tells me *A lot of trauma survivors work through things using kink. It's normal and healthy.* They all encourage me to stay with my fantasies and explore them. They tell me to talk to my partner when I feel ready.

I sink into my body. I let myself feel what I'm feeling and what I'm feeling is this deep expansive pleasure, what I feel is safety, groundedness, trust. I can get off on this fantasy because I know I am loved and I know I am safe. I can touch the bottom of the ocean, feel the fullness of my submissive desires because I also know I don't have to do anything I don't want.

And so I tell you, we talk about it. You make me feel normal and safe and loved. We laugh, we talk, I feel good in my body. Later, I tell you I want to act this out and I tell you exactly what I want to do and exactly what I need to feel safe and you tell me it sounds lovely.

I am leaning into the power and pleasure in my body. I am giving up all my power, giving myself over to you totally, knowing completely that I am in total control. I am going deep into the things that used to terrify me, knowing completely that I have the power to stop, to go deeper, to ask, to relax, to let go. I am opening an ocean inside of me, a flood of pleasure that I have never known. I just want to sink further into this feeling, and I can do exactly that.

I'm a submissive slut and I love it. I am a practitioner of trauma magic and kink is one of my tools. You say to me *Well, if something that used to really upset you now just totally gets you off that's pretty amazing.*

And you're right it's amazing. There is this alchemy that safety creates the conditions for. There is this transformation that takes place through the power of erotic magic. There is this shift that happens when no is really an option, then yes becomes an option too.

Because I know I am really my own I can give myself to you.

This World

*I*START TO CRY, not from the pain, but because I remember. I see the sky startling blue, and the graffitied wall of a building, and a pair of squirrels chasing each other around the trunk of a tree and the little sparrows hopping among the bare branches of a bush. The breeze feels good against my skin and I remember that I am alive. Success isn't what I think it is. It isn't about some end result, something I can achieve. It isn't a chase because it is already here. The true victory is here in this moment, in all the moments, in the pure beauty and blessing of simply being alive. The love I feel and the moments when my heart softens and the times I laugh with abandon and the way the world is here with me, holding me, opening to me, pulsating with life.

I am reading *His Dark Materials* for the first time, because I never read it as a child. And I keep crying. Because I remember. Sometimes I forget and I put my focus on something else, on some end goal I'm trying to achieve, on some purpose I'm moving toward. And I forget to be with what is, here in the process. I forget the unspeakable beauty of the world, the unbelievable blessing of living. To be here, to feel this, to be in the company of life, my own heart beating, the community of others who share this space and time with me, the wonder and magic of living. Acts of kindness. Acts of recognition. Possibilities unfolding. Simple, ordinary, profound magic. I remember. I read about other worlds, about life and love in endless forms, and about the land of the dead where everything has gone gray and the ghosts long for memories of what I get to live every day. I am shaken back into reality, and the reality is, this world is fucking magic, all around me, all the time. I get to live. I get to feel the air in my lungs. I get to run my fingers over surfaces, feeling textures. I get to love, to feel the precious pull in my heart. I get to be a part of this. There is so much to be grateful for.

Sometimes the pain is so overwhelming, the loss is so overwhelming. Sometimes I am stuck in the memory of all the hurt and all the loss and I forget that all through it the world was always here with me, always loving me, bringing me back, reminding me. All through it there was the moon, there was the sun and the air to breathe, and all through it there was love, there was wonder, there was hope. All through it the trees watched out for me, the stories unfolded offering meaning, the little creatures showed me how to remember joy. All through it there were moments of bright burning hope, the changing seasons and all the vibrant colours, the warmth and the cold, the cycles. All through it there was the living world, here with me, always. And I am alive.

I remember. This is the magic. This openness. This receptivity. This willingness to be filled with wonder, to ache with profound love and gratitude for the opportunity to be here, in this body, living, breathing, being a part of this world. My eyes fill with tears and it isn't pain that I am feeling. Or it is pain but only in the sense that my heart is breaking open. I remember and suddenly it seems so ridiculous to be caught up in the stories I get caught up in, it seems so ridiculous to think that what I am searching for is anywhere except for right here. It is here. It has always been here, offering itself up to me endlessly, no matter who I am, no matter what I've achieved, no matter what I've suffered, this world loves me. This world opens to me, showing me that magic is easy, magic is what is. All I have to do is remember. All I have to do is return.

Indigo and Violet

I CHOSE TO BE good and to do what I was told. I chose to bury the truth of what I know. I chose the warm glow and promise of love. I chose to reject my instincts in favour of what I was told. I became the good daughter, the good student, the passionate activist, always trying to do the right thing, always worried that I wasn't. I could make no sense of what was happening to me so I didn't, I put it underground. I told myself the right thing to do was the respectful thing. I told myself *Don't be rude, don't be ungrateful.* I walked right into his arms, because I knew that's what my dad wanted me to do. I didn't fight it. I gave up my body, that's why I still don't have a body. That's why I don't feel much of anything. That's why I don't care about sex. That's why pleasure makes me sick. I care about love. I care about being good. I care about doing the right thing. I have conviction and righteous indignation (like my father) and I believe in sacrificing all personal desires in favour of what is right. Somehow I believe that surrendering my bodily autonomy to my pedophile grandfather and all the nice guy rapists of my future is right. Because that's what I was taught. That's what I learned. I dream of redemption. I dream of acceptance. I want to be loved. And I want so badly to be good.

I chose to be bad and to give up love in favour of the truth. I chose the night, the embrace of silence. I chose my desire to be free. I chose my anger. I chose my rightful disgust. I became the scapegoat, the bad daughter. I became the disrespectful one, the ungrateful one. And later I became the crazy one, the slutty one, the drunk one. I insisted on the truth even though I didn't have words for it. I ran for my life, consequences be damned. I took my need for love and buried it in the ground. I decided I could survive without love, that I would never choose love because love would make me weak. I tried to be strong. I tried to be heartless. I embraced what was said about me. Okay, so if I'm bad then I'll be bad. If I'm ungrateful then watch me be fucking ungrateful. If you think I'm crazy I'll show you crazy, I will burn this all to the ground. I chose pleasure. I chose escape. I chose the wild power of knowing that my grandfather wanted to fuck me. I chose the wild power of this body, as object, as source of pleasure, as escape plan. I turned myself into a spectacle, a disaster. I take everything I'm not allowed to have and I drown myself in it. I make it impossible to ignore how bad things are. I embrace the pain. I am razor blades and bottles, unadulterated rage, the freedom of not giving a fuck. All I want is to feel good and be free.

    I blamed you. I blamed you for being a fuck up, for throwing all our values out the window, for breaking all the rules so carefully laid out. I was afraid of you, of the way you wreaked havoc and burned our life to the ground. You filled me with shame, or more accurately, you made it impossible for me to redeem myself from the crushing weight of the shame I already carried. I worked so hard for love and you tore all my work to the ground. I worked so hard to be good and you made a mockery of it, intentionally doing the worst things you could think of. I was always cleaning up your messes. I would find you in the hospital after another suicide attempt and I'm the one who would decide to live. It was my job to create stability, to put down roots, to build some semblance of safety, or what I thought was safety because I can admit now that I had no idea what safety was. I blamed you and now I can see how wrong I was. When I got sober I thought I could be rid of you forever. I thought I could relegate you to my alcoholic past. You were everything I was running from and I thought I could put out your light for good.

    I blamed you. You were so weak, so scared. You wouldn't risk it, but you risked everything. I believed you had no backbone, no guts. You were always playing by the rules and we both knew it would never be enough. I had to deal with our pain. I had to face it, contain it, find a place for it, because you wouldn't even admit it was there. You were always running from it and running from me. You scapegoated me like the rest of them, turned me into mental illness. I was the part of you that you needed to extinguish in order to achieve their approval for good. Every time you built another dysfunctional life, every time you found yourself staring at the wall getting fucked and disappearing, you needed me to come and fix it. You needed me to come and be the bad one, the crazy one. You needed me to burn it to the ground because it was fucking killing you and you wouldn't admit it. I hated the way you made our life small, the way you worked so hard at everything but never felt much of anything. I hated the way you tried so fucking hard to be good. When you got sober you took the reins back, you put me back underground and you tried to choke the life from me. I blamed you and I was ready to end you but now I can see I was wrong.

The truth is I loved you. You were so brave, so fierce and full of colour. I loved the way you said no, the way you didn't fucking care, the way you chose us no matter what. I know it wasn't fair that I left you with all the blame and all the pain. I know that maybe if I had held it with you it wouldn't have been so hard to carry. I know you went so crazy because you had to carry the truth all by yourself. I know you drank and fucked and od'd because you couldn't carry it alone. I refused to carry it with you and I'm sorry for that. I'm sorry I didn't believe you. I'm sorry I chose their love over yours. I'm sorry I walked us right into his arms, right into danger. I'm sorry I made that sacrifice over and over again, choosing what I thought was love over safety. I'm sorry I shamed you and I judged you so hard. I'm sorry I'm so detached from our body and so disinterested in sex. I wish I knew a way back to you, a way back to wholeness. I'm sorry for all the years I tried to bury you, to put out your light. I'm sorry I abandoned you when you needed me the most. Without you I don't think I could have survived. I don't know who I'd be without your courage. You are so much of me. Finally, finally I am ready to stop blaming you. Finally, finally I can see that we were kids. We were faced with an impossible choice and we did the best that we could. I love you Violet, with all my heart. I promise never to leave you again.

I'm so fucking sorry. I'm sorry I made it so hard on you all those years. I'm sorry I made your crushing shame so much worse by doing so many fucked up things. I'm sorry I never listened to you or took your feelings into consideration. I'm sorry that I left you to clean up the mess whenever I burned our life to the ground again. The truth is I was too scared to live so I left that to you, and then I found I was too scared to die too. I love your conviction. I love your heart. I love the way you care and the way you try so hard. I want to come back to you. I want to show you the way back into our body and I want you to show me the way out of the dark. I want to promise you that I'll prove it you, that I'll never fuck up like that again. I'm sorry that I blamed you and that I judged you so hard for making an impossible choice. I'm sorry that I treated you like you were pathetic, just because you wanted love. I'm so fucking angry that we blamed each other all this time. I'm so fucking sorry that we spent so many years trying to put out each other's lights. I'm sorry that we blamed each other and that we abandoned each other, that we internalized the shame and violence that we lived with. Indigo, I love you, I got you.

I am at my best when I am both of us. A habit of cycling through, of coming together only to come apart, is hard to unlearn. We are so used to always trying to get the upper hand on each other. We are so used to trying to take control. But when I remember you, when I remember you, when we work together, when we refuse to abandon or reject each other, we are happier, we are safer, we are stronger. We are one person, one person with two hearts, split by a terrible choice.

Alchemy

THE MAGIC IS in the alchemy, in the willingness to go deep, to be with what is. I will never not have lived the life I've lived, I will never not know the things I've known. The magic is in accepting myself in my entirety, contradictions and all. The magic is in loving myself, really loving myself, and that requires knowing myself, really knowing myself.

Is it possible to dom myself? Is it possible to fuck myself up and take myself where I need to go, over that edge and beyond? I am comfortable with my desire for intensity. I am comfortable with my wildness. I embrace it. Whenever I try to settle myself down, whenever I dim the lights, I lose contact with my power.

I read books. I remember my curiosity. I take a cold shower and drink a strong coffee at 5pm. I remember that it's okay to be a little crazy, it's okay to embrace my wildness and ground it in my recovery. There is nothing unhealthy about my intensity, my wildness, as long as I am in the right relationship to it. When I shut it out, that's when things get all fucked up.

I will never have a brain like someone who didn't grow up in terror, but that's okay, I love my brain. I love that it makes me a poet, an intuitive, a healer. I love that it drives me to create, to go deeper, to face the things I'm afraid to face. I will never have a brain like someone who grew up safe and loved and that's okay. I am powerful because of my trauma. I am magic because of my trauma.

I don't have to be perfect at anything. I don't have to be a still and placid pond. It's okay that I'm an ocean, deep and endless, deeper than the sky, full of creatures living in the depths, full of mysteries still unseen.

Alchemy

It's okay that I'm a storm, crashing thunder and flashes of light. I am full of power and I quench the earth. I crack the sky. I am exactly what I need.

I listen to music, the music that I like to listen to, because this is how I communicate with myself. So many times in therapy I say to my therapist *yeah and the lyric goes like this... and that's when I realized who I am and that's when I realized what I need.* So many of my revelations were facilitated by pop punk music and that is fucking okay. I've played pop punk to my therapist and we talked about the lyrics because I use music to communicate with myself. I use emo music to feel my feelings, to give voice to my shadow, to make space for the parts of me I've been taught to reject.

There is no part of me that is bad. There is no part of me that I am going to starve and keep in the dark. I am most powerful and most healthy when I am connected to all of myself. I will grow and I will change but I will not reject any part of me for anything ever again.

I connect with the mystery, with the flirtatious side of me that isn't afraid of anything. I connect with the sky and the night and my body. I put a menstrual cup inside myself for the first time in a long time and for once I don't feel like puking. I know this is progress. I hate the word *vagina* because it only makes me think of rape. I am terrified to put my fingers inside myself because it only makes me think of rape. I need a new way to relate to this powerful part of me. I need a new word, a new language to speak myself.

I give myself permission to live my fucking life. I get so rigid, from time to time. I forget the magic, I forget the alchemy, I forget to let myself be the complexity of all that I am. I get my priorities all fucked up and I start surrendering parts of myself. And then I remember, and then I return.

I write. Just like this. I let the words rise from the depths. I let them reveal themselves to me. My magic has always been intuitive. I listen to what my intuition is telling me. I remember who the fuck I am.

The magic is in the freedom. To love is to love freedom. To love is to be free and to let the ones you love be free. To love is to show up already

Fucking Magic

complete. Me, here, in my body. My little hands and my powerful legs and all of my history and everything I know. Me, here, with my tarot cards and my zines and my really good advice and my great capacity to listen. Me here, listening to emo music in my earphones, laughing out loud or crying when I'm walking down the street. Because I have a lot of feelings and my feelings are beautiful. I am alive. The magic is in remembering that I am alive.

Home

After the meeting a bunch of us go for fellowship. My friends coax me to order my food in French and I'm nervous but they tell me what to say and let me repeat it a bunch of times before I make my order. Then after I do they cheer for me and we all laugh. We sit and eat our food and talk and laugh. We keep saying that everything is so wholesome and it is. I know that I am so blessed to be here, here with my friends in this city where I am putting down roots. Here with these friends who are addicts and alcoholics like I am, who are sober like I am. We are trying to save our lives and find a new way to be in the world. We are trying to heal and to grow and to be happy. And right now we are happy. We are laughing and laughing and my friend comments that the sober alcoholics are always the loudest people in the room.

My friend in very early sobriety tells me that she's scared of reaching out, she doesn't want to be a burden. I try to tell her the way it is with addicts in recovery, the way that I came to understand the true meaning of community for the first time in 12 step fellowships. I tell her *You are my people. I am here for you and I'm never going to judge you because I know. I get it.* I try to tell her about the social norms in recovery circles and how it's so different from the other spaces I move through, how in recovery circles it's perfectly normal to give your number to someone you barely know, to tell them you are there for them and that they should reach out if they are struggling, and to really mean it. I always tell the story of the women I barely knew who came to my rape trial when I was five months sober. Sober addicts and alcoholics showed me for the first time what it means to really be there for each other.

Fucking Magic

The holidays were really hard for me because a lot of people were away seeing their families and I am estranged from my family and I am in a new city. The holidays always feel like my estrangement and traumatic childhood are being rubbed in my face. I am so jealous of people who have families, imperfect families but good enough families, families that aren't traumatic. I have felt so on the outside for so long, having to fulfill for myself the roles I see so many people's parents fulfilling for them, even in adulthood. It feels like there's this massive hole in me, this desire for love, for feeling wanted and welcome, this desire for home. Sometimes I have moments when I feel at home, with my friends and my community, sometimes I have moments when I imagine this is what it's like to have a family, this is what it's like to feel included, to feel loved, to know that you always have a place to go if you need it. But when the holidays roll around and everyone goes to spend time with their 'real' families, it makes me feel like my need for what we share is so much greater than their need for it. Like, my loved ones will never need me to be family the way I need them to be family.

I have had to cut away my roots, transplant myself in new soil. I have had to sever connection to my parents for my safety and for my health. I have had to find my own way. Now I am trying to put down roots. I am trying to believe that it won't end in a forest fire, like it always has. I am trying to believe that relationships will shift and change, people will come and go, but I will still have a family and I will still have a home. I am trying not to be ashamed of my need for love. I am trying to accept it and embrace it, to see how this estrangement shaped me into the loving person that I am. I am trying to cultivate a true belief in family outside of family of origin. I am asking myself what family, home, community, love, ancestry, belonging mean to me. I am putting my faith in the possibility of home, and in the moments when I feel like I belong.

I'm sick with an eye infection and I'm isolating and sad. My friend invites me over and makes me vegan gluten free cookies and cuddles me in their bed. In the morning they drive me to the store to get eye drops and to the grocery store to get groceries. They drop me off at home well loved and taken care of. I try to memorize the feeling. I try to sink it into my bones. I try to believe that I can have this, that I can be human, vulnerable, having a rough time, and that the people I love will hold me, show up for me, make me feel at home. I think about the transformative power of love. I think about how revolution requires new meanings of love, new meanings of family. I think about how estranged traumatized people such as myself are perfectly positioned on account of our great need to lead us into new configurations of care.

Addicts and queers and traumatized people, incest survivors and people without homes to go to, in our pain and in our yearning we search out new possibilities and create the conditions for love and collectivity outside the limits of the institutions and structures that currently exist.

An Archive of Hollows

LITTLE BEANS MAKE you cry sometimes. We walk the Jean Talon market stopping to pick up fruits and vegetables, marveling at their textures and colours. We point out cute dogs and babies when we see them and compare where we each have Scorpio in our charts. We talk about poetry, about writing, about the colour of a tomato somehow both green and orange.

In the snow you slip and slide in your heels, gliding over ice, looking cute with your queer aesthetic, almost wiping out. We talk about public washrooms, alleyways, riding the metro pressed against strangers. We talk about intimacy and relief and urgency and these human bodies, the way capitalism presses down on us.

In your apartment on your couch we talk about exorcism and witchcraft, about horror movies neither of us totally remember and what they make us feel. We talk about poetry some more, we talk about writing. You ask me if we should go back out to look at the light on the snow or if we should make out on your couch. I tell you I think we should do both.

You come close and move away, shaping the space between us the way you shape the space in your poems. The distance is electric and your presence makes me shut out every single word. There is just the shape of you, your eyes and your lips and your hands. Your smile which breaks across your face, your laughter. You pull me close.

Later we stomp through the snow, which glistens pink, hard and encrusted with ice. The surface of the ice holds us and then it gives way, surrendering to our weight. We laugh as we suddenly sink down, carving

An Archive of Hollows

out two holes in the surface of the ice. I kiss you there and you tell me that the water will melt and then freeze holding the memory of two queers kissing in the snow. An archive of hollows.

We talk about astonishment, wonder, the potency of possibility, how unspeakably beautiful it is to be alive. I tell you about the way the trees speak to me and you believe me easily. I feel alive with magic, with memory. I sleep in your bed and in the morning you take me to church.

Transformation

*I*WENT UNDERGROUND AND I found myself. In the dead of winter I felt my pain and I let it gut me. I let it unravel me and I knew in my heart that I could hold the unraveling. I could be undone and rise again. In the darkness of winter I remembered who I am.

I found my power, my pleasure, my desire. I found my worthiness, where it has always been, right here. I remembered that I am a gift, that my presence is a gift, that those who love me are lucky to love me.

I found my desire, my queerness shining pink and green, my pleasure out in between the trees, in the spaces between the stars, the constellations. I found the power and pleasure of nonmonogamy, the way it stretches my heart, the way it multiplies my love, the way it makes me responsible. I found myself loved and desired and full of love and desire, held in a community, a network of relationships.

I found my purpose. I am a writer. I am here to write and to be changed by writing. I found the page and all its possibilities and my brutal love of words. I faced the fear that none of this was really meant for me. I let my heart crack open and I grieved.

Taste the Silence

I TAKE YOU TO my favourite church, the Mary church, where Our Lady looks down from her throne as the Queen of Heaven. You are decked out in white. I am wearing my crop top with the full moon. Something is happening in the church that day, the pews are filled with people and we join them. The priest speaks meaningfully in French. I have no idea what is happening, though you can understand him, and after a while the priest steps away, leaving us all in silence.

In silence you look at me. Your eyes dark blue and daring, crossing the distance between us in this Catholic church. Your eyes both shy and brazen, open and questioning, you look at me. I look at you. Your hands are on my skin, every touch an awakening. Your fingers trace the length of my arm, drawing me in. We are leaning into each other, an electric pull between our bodies, queer magnetism, undeniable desire, blatant and silent in this Catholic church.

I hold your gaze. I could hold your gaze for days. Your eyes are beautiful and full of life. They pull me in, hold my attention. A part of me wonders at our daring, to be this publicly queer in a Catholic church. I know that in the silence we are seen, queer and trans, eyes for each other. And yet I know that this is holy, that we honour the Virgin with our desire.

The priest returns and speaks some more in French. I listen attentively thinking that my attention might make some meaning come through. You lean against me, your fingers creating sparks against my skin. I see the priest see us, register our queerness, our strangeness in this place of worship. Despite myself I feel a spark of fear. I don't know what

Fucking Magic

I'm afraid of. Maybe being thrown out of this house of God in her most splendid form.

    Later I tell you about the fear I felt. I tell you it would be discrimination for them to throw us out like that, if they had, that surely it would have been illegal. You tell me not to appeal to the power of the state to protect us. We answer to a power much more profound. You tell me what the priest was saying. He said *Taste the silence* and together, we did.

Return to the Water

IT IS THE dead of winter. The earth is frozen solid and the water is too. Everything as far as I can see is sparkling white. The trees that crowd the edge of the lake are skeletons of their former selves. The air is cold and silent. I see no one else. I am alone, standing on the surface of this lake.

You tell me to go to the water, the water still running underground. You tell me to close my eyes and find the water. Where is my well? Where is the source of my strength, the source of my memory? I didn't mean to return here. I didn't mean to choose this place, this lake, these waters. But I did. My heart beats in time with the rushing of the underground stream that gushes up like blood or cum from the frozen earth, a spring. Where we collect the drinking water. The lake itself alive beneath the thick ice that more than carries my weight. I remember. You tell me to go down.

Somehow I sink into the ice. All the atoms I am made of concentrate on empty space. The space between my atoms and the space between the atoms of the ice on the surface of the lake merge. I go down. I become the ice, the ice becomes me, but only for a moment and then I am in the water which is black and cold now but I know it as warm and green. Here in the lake there are two boulders, two large rocks deep down but on a clear day when the water is generous in its transparency you can see them. The sister rocks, holding their own at the bottom of the lake. There's a shopping cart down there too and my dad's camera that he lost when he was ice fishing when he was a much younger man. But mostly, down in the lake, there is water, so much water. The water is good and wet and open, it is green and soft and dark and deep, it glints and sparkles with sunlight and fish. The lake is alive like I am alive. I am alive like the lake.

The seaweed travels up from the depths, ancient and slippery, green and slick, floating up like rivers within water, like fingers of outstretched hands, beckoning from unfathomable depths. And you might say it's just a lake, not the ocean, but the depths down here are unfathomable. There is a part of the lake, near the centre but not quite, and that part of the lake has no bottom. It just goes down and down and down, into an oblivion of wet darkness, where fish disappear. Where the green drifts away to blackness and the sunlight gives up, it goes down into the centre of the earth, and beyond it, into that great abyss that is not limited by this dimension of time and space. It is endless.

You ask me to ask the water, to ask the water what I need to know. This water you remind me is the water that sustains me, it is the water of my very being, my very soul. When I found myself on the surface of this lake, back here again, I almost wished for another well. This one is too painful. When you asked me to sink beneath the ice, to go under the water, warm wet tears slid out of my eyes. You ask me to ask the water what I need and what I know. You ask me to remember what the water has been trying to tell me.

I remember on the far shore there was a statue of the Virgin Mary, wearing her white robes, her arms extended, watching over the lake. As a child I didn't understand her place there or what she meant to me. I just understood her to be some relic of Christianity, something I wasn't raised with, something that wasn't mine. I had heard of the Divine Feminine from my women's studies prof mom, but I didn't know how to see Mary with those eyes. I didn't know what Catholicism meant to my Irish ancestors who settled on this very lake. I didn't know the mix of pride and shame, the magic and the pain, the way that Mary held space for all that ambivalence. I didn't know the pulls of Catholicism and Protestantism, Irishness and British imperialism, and the dramas that played out in the history of my family. I didn't know anything about being Irish or about being Catholic, and I didn't know what Mary meant to me.

Return to the Water

My family and the other families who lived or summered on the lake paid for trucks full of sand to be poured into the water, to cover up the squishy muck and seaweed, to make it swimmable. I think about the sand suffocating the lake, covering up what the lake knows, what the lake was trying to tell us. I think about the silence that crushed my voice, the lake crying out like I was crying out, trying to survive the violence of being made compliant. My ancestors and the other settlers who claimed ownership over the land, naming the lake and the roads they made after themselves, silencing the Anishinaabemowin words which had pulsed through the living land, the living lake, for generations upon generations, forgetting the people who spoke them, as if they were never here. I was never taught the true name of this lake. It isn't on any map I know of. My ancestors forgot their own language too, the words their families had spoken which pulsed through the living landscapes and waterways of Ireland, the words for talking rocks and a world that loved them back. My ancestors forgot.

You ask me to go deeper, down into the hunger pains of a million hungry mouths, fleeing Ireland in boats of the dead and dying, into the genocidal violence of settler colonialism that opened this land to my ancestors, that marked it as empty and removed the people who were already here, the sexual violence and murder and child abuse that created 'Canada' and produced its sense of 'legitimate' claim to this land, the ongoing mass violence against human beings, languages, plants, animals, and land, that continues to reproduce the myth of 'Canada', into the stories and specifics that I don't know, that were never named or whose names were not remembered, the legacy of violence of unspeakable proportions which is trying to be spoken, as our prime minister tells another Indigenous youth to be quiet, down into the unspeakable things in my own family, in my family's family, the sexual violence, the generations of incest, the Catholic shame, the memory of Éireann, *the memory of an Gorta Mór, the alcoholism, the beatings, the trauma we endure and the trauma we enact, the pain, the pain, the pain, the unspeakable pain. The water asks me to remember who I am.*

Fucking Magic

I am under the water now, in the silent dark and cold. The water is showing me who I am. The water is showing me how not to be afraid of what I know. In the darkness I can see my body, naked, floating in the depths. I wiggle my fingers and my toes. I move my arms and kick my legs. I feel the wetness and the cold pressing against my skin, awakening my senses, reminding me. I flip and turn. I dive deeper. I am returned to my body, this body which has always been with me. I am returned to my hunger, my pleasure, my want. My tense shoulders holding the memory of countless violations, unspeakable terrors. My capacity for pleasure, for pain. The textures, the sounds, the tastes, the scents, and all the colours of the world, coming to me through this body. The goosebumps on my flesh, the shiver of recognition, the tears welling up in my eyes, the wetness between my legs. The water tells me: I have to find a way back in. I have to find a way to be with what is, to stay, to stop floating away.

I don't drink anymore. I don't dissociate so badly that I can't speak or move. The world rarely retreats into that strange distant blur in which even my own words are unrelated to each other and themselves. I don't smoke bong hit after bong hit, moments disappearing from my mind as soon as they have happened. But I am still so afraid to be *here*. It doesn't feel like an overwhelming panic but I have a feeling that under the surface it is. It's like something I know is there but can't look at directly. Something on the tip of my tongue that I can't quite say. I lie in my bed for hours unsure what to do. I procrastinate over simple tasks, especially ones that don't offer any distraction. I scroll and scroll on my phone, time disappearing in almost the same way it did with the weed. When I have a good feeling I replay it and replay it. I suck the juice out of it and it's true, it's juicy and good. But I don't look to see what else there is.

Food stresses me out and I don't know how to be with it. To cook and to eat in a way that is present and unrushed. To be with my ancestors I have to eat, I have to feed myself, I have to feed them. Their hunger reverberates through my bones. I have to eat. Sometimes when I'm having sex I lose the feeling. It doesn't feel bad, I just feel like I can't drop down into it. As if there is a break in the line, I can't connect with myself.

Return to the Water

To heal my sexual trauma I have to find ways to drop down into my body when I'm fucking, to heal my ancestors I have to heal generations of sexual trauma, I have to find a way to feel safe and know that pleasure is good. Sometimes the tears come in sudden bursts but I don't know how to stay with them. I hide the overwhelm and the massive grief and pain under something else, some kind of detachment, some kind of numbness. Boundaries and limits are necessary in order not to be consumed by the vastness of pain. But the water is asking me to wake up, to be intentional, to remember that I have a body again.

The water is asking me to remember collective struggle. The communities I am a part of. My lineages, my ancestors, both by blood and by culture, both by choice and shared trauma. And the water is asking me to find ways to work with those whose stories I don't share, or whose experiences of the stories are completely different from mine. The water is calm and cold, profound and deep and dark. The water is asking me to remember who I am, what I need. It is telling me about the work I need to do, as a writer, as a healer, as a person called to work with and transform pain. The magic is returning to me, here in this lake. Layers and layers of history. Layers and layers of meaning. Layers and layers of pain.

You ask me to remember what I learned from the water, to keep it in my heart, in my cells, in my bones. You show me the way back up. I have to rise again, become one with the ice and move through it. I have to find myself standing on the surface of the lake, dressed in my winter clothes, looking around at the vastness of snow and silence. Here in my heart, in my cells, in my bones, I carry this water. This water is the well from which I drink. This lake is what sustains me, what connects me and reminds me. It is deep enough to hold the depth of pain and it is vibrant and alive, teaching me how to live. Even with what is. Even with what was. Even with the pain and its vastness. The lake shows me how, how to have a body, how to tell the truth, how to act from my integrity, how to remember my ancestors, how to name and fight the violence we are embedded in, with every breath, every action, every word, every prayer.

Devotion

*I*MAKE MYSELF CUM twice in the megabus bathroom. My fingers frantic, one hand on my clit, the other pushing fingers up inside of me. I am dizzy with pleasure. My panties are soaked through. I need to lie on the earth to ground myself, but I am on a bus and the earth is covered in snow. I need to climb the mountain, light a candle, say a prayer. I need to drink this feeling down, soak it up, let it change me. I make myself cum thinking *I love you I love you I love you*. I make myself cum thinking *I'm yours I'm yours I'm fucking yours*. I am a submissive deep in love. I am aching with pleasure, expanding with pleasure, undone by pleasure. I have never in my life known such pleasure. I have never in my life known such safety, such intimacy, such freedom, such love.

    We are in a longstanding love affair archived on facebook messenger. The little text bubble pops up on my phone with your name at the top, it pulls at my heart, it makes me wet. You are my lover, my partner, my friend. You open me, pull me down into my feelings, you make it safe to go deeper still. I tell you what I want. I tell you what I feel. I want to tattoo *Fuck Me Up* on my body. Good thing I already did. Good thing I followed my heart, good thing I trusted my gut. When we met I told you *I'm actually really vanilla* and then I tattooed *Fuck Me Up* in a heart on my butt. Good thing I listened to my body. Good thing I listened to my heart. Good thing I was brave enough to move through the shame, to move through the fear, to show you who I am. We talk about the first night we hooked up and you tell me *Clementine, I'm so glad I made a move*. I tell you *I'm so proud of our slutty past selves. We had no idea what we were getting ourselves into.*

Devotion

I ease deeper into the safety of intimacy, into the power of this love. I discover depths of desire that I did not know I was capable of. My body here is a prayer. My surrender is a sacred act of power. I take my body back from everyone who abused me. It is mine and in safety and pleasure and conscious desire, I give myself to you. You, my lover, my partner, my friend. You who listens to my trauma and my desire, my fear and my hope, all with equal interest, all with equal care. I crack shame wide open and find an ocean underneath. I find a place of good sweet genuine love, a place of need I never knew how to speak. I say *Baby I want you to hurt me, baby I need you to hurt me.* You give me what I need. You give me that impact, that explosion of sensation. I say *Thank you, thank you, thank you, please.*

For the first time in my life I know what it is to be loved in freedom, to not hide a single part of myself. For the first time the number of dicks I've sucked or will come to suck does not diminish my worth, I am allowed and encouraged to live my best slut life. For the first time I feel loved for my good heart, my inquisitive mind, the wholeness of my humanity. I feel safe to ask for what I want, to say both yes and no. I feel safe to laugh and cry and tell the truth. You hold me in perfect sacred trust. In this sacred space I find the courage to know myself, to name my wants, to give it up. I put my wrists together and you tie them. You put the hood over my head and the gag in my mouth. In the darkness, in the stillness, in my submission and complete surrender, I find myself. I feel impossible pleasure in this endless devotion. I feel so fucking safe with you.

Carnelian4RoseQuartz

IN THE BATHTUB, the water scented with eucalyptus and lavender, I lay back in her arms and she rubs my shoulders. She says she's too tired to fuck because of the orgy she took part in last night and I tell her that's perfect. Let's just rub each other down and fall asleep in each other's arms.

The bath was her idea and what a good one. I tell her she's a highlight of my trips back to Toronto and it's true. She's this beautiful, bubbling, shining light, living her best life. She is kind and generous and she makes me feel really good. She rubs my shoulders and my neck. I press myself back into her and feel myself relax.

When we take a break to drink some water I ask her to let me rub her shoulders and she tells me she's not done with me yet. So I lean back into her again. I close my eyes. I notice how difficult it is for me to receive this generosity, this pleasure for the sake of pleasure, this care. I look forward to returning the favour, to making her feel good. But I try to understand that making me feel good is making her feel good too.

Between fits of laughter, excessive compliments, and heartfelt conversations, we exchange touch until our skin is pruned from the water. She tells me her clit is rose quartz and she wonders if my clit were a gemstone what would it be? Later I decide that my clit is definitely carnelian.

She says her roommates probably think we're fucking but we are literally exchanging massages and laughing about how beautiful we find each other. We finally leave the water, wrap ourselves in bathrobes, and head to bed. A little kitten jumps between us while we sleep.

Carnelian4RoseQuartz

With her, here, I am healing a sexual history in which my pleasure was always secondary if it was considered at all. I am finding pleasure and sexuality that extends beyond fucking. I am deep in the erotics of care.

Like the Moon

READING THE WORDS of survivors is a gift to myself. I read Leah Lakshmi Piepzna-Samarasinha's writing about incest and my whole body gets those chills of recognition, the tears come spilling over the edge of my eyes. I am seen. Here, here in this body. I breathe. Slowly. I run my fingers over my skin. I feel the electric energy of the truth. The truth. The wound of incest is deep and unspeakable but we speak it. We find a way to live and heal and grow. We find a way to move through all the pain and the shame, the horror, and we breathe through it. Incest survivor magic. My fingers ache for the keyboard, for the words I need to say, to you. To you. To us. Yeah, my grandfather forcibly made out with me. Yeah, I grew up in wild terror knowing that he wanted to fuck me.

I am 31 and I am just learning what love is, what sex is, what desire is. I am 31 and I am really feeling my body, maybe for the first time. I am writing long texts on facebook messenger telling the truth of how I feel. I read them and reread them, wondering at the magic of telling the truth, at the beauty of words shaped to express the complexity of my feelings and my desires. I tell the truth and this act of daring vulnerability is responded to with the words *I fucking love you.* I drink love deep into my bones, into my cells. Real love. Real, true, trust worthy love. Earned secure attachment. No longer settling for less than I deserve. Finally loving someone who loves me, mind, body, and soul. Someone who shows up and does the work of love, like I do, who listens to my pain and trauma, who sends me links about Adult Children of Alcoholics and Other Dysfunctional Families, and about complex ptsd, who thinks about these things because they are a part of me.

Like the Moon

Kink is a cauldron where I work through some of my most intense shame and pain. Sexuality becomes this pervasive space of trust and magic. I get fucked in the ass for the first time on my 31st birthday because I explicitly asked for it, because I wanted it, because it is my desire. Anal sex becomes a practice of being with my body and my lover, a space of profound trust of both my partner and myself. I learn to breathe. I learn to relax. I learn to listen to my body and sink into the bed. I learn to say *Stop*. I learn to say, O*kay let's try again*. I feel this deep, aching presence, desire, embodiment. I am not flying out the window, somewhere on the ceiling, like I've always sort of been. I'm here, right here, with the welcome weight of my lover's body on top of me. They whisper in my ear *Are you ready for me baby?* I say *Yes, yes, yes*.

Slut4slut love is the most healing magic. My partner texts me *Get that dick baby*. I tell them about the extensive sexual trauma of being made to feel unlovable because of my sluttiness, I tell them how that belief is deeply embedded in my body, and that even though I understand intellectually that they love me and they want me to live my best slut life, on a visceral emotional embodied level it is hard to let go of the belief that doing so will make me unlovable. After this conversation they send me a quote over facebook messenger: *A kissed mouth does not lose its freshness, for like the moon it always renews itself.* I let out the breath I've been holding, my shoulders drop and the tension melts away. I am learning what love is. Love in freedom. Love in safety. Love that I deserve. Love which wants me to get that dick, and feel good about pussy, and love that gay shit. All things my partner has said to me, because they love me and they want me to be happy, and fulfilled, and free.

Recovery is a journey that never ends. It is always possible to go deeper, to find new ways to love and to heal. What a gift it is to be so fucking traumatized, because it means I have to do this work. The consequences of not doing it are too high, my life is literally unlivable if I do not face this pain. But the rewards. The gifts and blessings and hard earned rewards of this practice, this process. Slut magic. Incest survivor magic. Trauma magic. Kink magic. Sober magic. Fucking magic.

Fucking Magic

I breathe. I feel that breath down in my belly, in the parts of me so long contorted by fear and pain. I still carry so much crazy in my body. I still have so fucking much to learn and unlearn, so much work to do. But I am doing the work, I am sinking into my body, I am learning to feel what I feel, to be here. I can feel myself changing, and healing, and growing. I can feel my whole body lit up with love and releasing shame. I am being made new again.

My Voice Disappears

THE SHAPE OF silence is wide and heavy. It is expansive and deep. It fills me. Every part of me. It takes me over, freezes me, sucks up all my agency. My mouth: the shape of silence.

Normally I am talkative. I have a lot to say. I laugh a lot, and loudly. I am inquisitive and curious and passionate and sure of myself. As soon as things get sexy my voice disappears. I don't know where it goes. It takes the shape of silence.

Maybe I don't know what I want to begin with. Maybe my desire is something which cannot be said. And yet I know this isn't true. I have worked so hard to know and name my desires but I go nonverbal and nothing can conjure my voice from the depths.

With my partner I have learned to speak, through a process of developing trust and building safety I have begun to release my voice. But with new dates I find myself back where I started: the shape of silence.

There's a cute boy in my bed. He is looking at me with eyes full of wonder and desire. I say *Do you want to kiss me?* And he does, and we make out. I work so hard to stay with the moment, to keep my voice present, to resist the pull of silence always calling me down.

He asks me if he can take off my dress and I say *Yes*. He asks me if he can take off my tights. I am so prepared to be compliant, to nod my head. But I don't want to be so naked while he is still dressed. I don't answer his question. I say *Do you want to take off your shirt?* He does.

I am trying to listen to the voice which grows out of the depths of my body, underneath the shape of silence, smothered by it, a tiny voice. Do I want to take off my tights? No, not yet. But I would like him to take off

Fucking Magic

his shirt. So I ask for that and he does. Later I say *Okay I do want to take these off.* And he says *Only if you want to.* I do.

I try to find my voice, conjure it up, speak it. I feel like there is enough space, just enough space, for me to make it manifest. I say *I think you're sexy.* He says *Tell me what you like. I want to make you feel good.*

I tune into my body, I try really hard to listen to the voice down under the silence. The desire I find there is not one that I think is the right desire to have, but I am trying to be honest. I am trying to speak the truth.

I say *I kinda just want to smoosh my body against your body.* Smoosh is maybe not a common word for a sexual desire but there it is. He says *Okay, if that's what you want.* We smoosh, press, feel. The weight of my body against him, his skin against my skin. I let myself be slow and feel what I am feeling.

I say *Do you want to fuck me?* The words rise from the depths, free themselves from the shape of silence, take a different shape, the shape of my voice, the shape of my desire. I find a way to ask the question, to take an active role instead of only being receptive. I listen for his answer, the shape of his desire in response to my own. He says *Yes.*

The Magic Comes Back

THE MAGIC COMES back. *Maybe the magic never left, maybe it was always here, just under the surface.* I have my earphones in, I'm listening to the same song on repeat and dancing in my kitchen. I'm washing dishes. It's Aries season and the beginning of spring. I feel the sunlight on my skin and I drink it in.

I am learning about anger, anger as an energy, as information about my boundaries. I use the angry face emoji and I laugh out loud. What if I let myself be angry? What if I trusted this feeling? What if I followed it to find out what it is trying to tell me?

A guy I had sex with on the first date tells me he's not ready to invite me to his place, even though he was ready to come to mine. I feel the anger of being treated like a disposable slut. He is ready for the intimacy of entering my body, but not the intimacy of letting me into his bedroom. He tells me about the sanctity of his home and I wonder if he has considered the sanctity of my body. I tell him I feel disrespected and used. I tell him he should tell his dates before he fucks them that they won't be allowed at his place. I tell him I won't tolerate such disrespect and I won't see him again.

I feel the energy of anger, the energy of no. I feel what it's like to be angry when I am treated with disrespect, instead of collapsing into shame. I feel the power of knowing that I deserve better and insisting on it.

Boundaries free up so much energy. Self worth makes me feel fucking powerful. I learn what is acceptable to me and what is not. I learn that I am deserving of nothing less than respect and care. I begin to feel the power of being loved. Love is such powerful, healing magic. It is life sustaining and invigorating. It makes me feel alive, safe, vibrant, connected. Love is supposed to be the starting place, the place where we learn our worth. Unloved children turn into adults who don't know our worth.

The magic comes back. It takes the shape of laughter. Fear dissolves. I do my 5th step with my sponsor. The themes come out clearly. The lessons make themselves known. We talk about my internalized biphobia. How I feel like a failed queer because I'm a femme and I don't like fisting and I love scissoring. My sponsor tells me *Clementine, you're not a failed queer, you just like scissoring!* We talk about the repeated pattern of not communicating my needs, desires, and boundaries. We talk about the need to accept these things, to communicate them, to liberate them from shame.

The magic comes back as shame leaves my body. The power of my *yes* and my *no*. I begin to understand for the first time in my life that my desires are not wrong, my needs are not wrong, my boundaries are not wrong. They are mine, they are perfect, they can change but they should only change in service of my own healing and my own choice. I don't need to be anyone other than me. I don't have to fuck a certain way to prove anything. I don't have to settle for anything less than I deserve.

My partner tells me *Your sexuality is perfect and healthy. I love your desires.* My partner tells me *Clementine, if you have a desire I don't share, I'm not grossed out or turned off by it. I love that you have that desire, and I want you to find someone to fulfill it with.* When my partner tells me these things I cry. I feel the hardened shame in my body begin to loosen and dissolve.

Queer Futures

I HAVE WATCHED MY life go up in flames so many times. I have burned it to the ground intentionally, I have dropped the match without a second thought, and I have dumped buckets of water trying to halt the destruction. But it was always too late. My past is a series of severances. I try to build a consistent narrative out of all the different lives I've lived, all the people I've been. I try to trace a path from one fire to the next and to believe that this has been a life. And it has, it's been a kind of life.

Now at age 31 I am in the early stages of a new life. I have lived in this city for seven months. I have been with my partner for almost a year. I have changed deeply, shed the deep denial I was living for three years in sobriety, and found my way back to myself. My past stretches out behind me, 30 years of bad luck, a procession of one trauma after the next. And maybe it wasn't all that bad, but it wasn't very good. I am 31 and just learning what it means to have consensual sex. I am 31 and just learning what it means to love and be loved. I am 31 and just learning how to live in integrity and faith instead of shame and fear.

But what of the future? What is on the horizon? How can I stretch myself forward into an unknown that deep down I believe will be just another fire. I don't want to lose everything again. I know that life is about change and I know that loss is inevitable, but I don't want to lose everything again. I want to build something. I want to stay. I want to put down roots. I want to orient toward a future of possibilities stretching out before me. I want to believe that the life I dream of is possible, and that it starts right here, right now.

Fucking Magic

What futures are possible for sober addicts? For people who never believed they would make it to their 30s? What futures are possible for queer nonmonogamous slutty kinky anarchists who want love and community and family and security and meaning outside of hetero-monogamous time lines and state-sanctioned scripts? What futures are possible for estranged incest survivors, for people who have no home to go to except for the ones we create? What futures are possible for me? What if I deeply want to believe that love and abundance and trust and family are in the cards for me?

I tell you *Maybe I'm just feeling insecure about this relationship.* You tell me *Clementine I want to build a future with you.*

For the first time in my life it feels possible to imagine a future, a queer, communal, collective, nonmonogamous, dreamy as fuck future. A future grounded in integrity and principles. A future for myself and the people I love and the people they love. A new vision for taking care of each other and ourselves, for pooling money and resources, for supporting each other in following our dreams and ambitions, for maybe even raising children in an environment free from pedophiles and patriarchs and violent gender roles. A future in which we live like a new world is possible. A present in which we live like this future is possible.

Exhale

THE MOON IS fat and gold and rising in real time. The Montréal cityscape sparkles yellow, purple, blue. The snow is gone. The ground is soft dirt and brown grass, cold and a little wet. I lay my body down, feel the weight of me, the pull of gravity, the way the world holds me. The sky is dark and blank but I can see stars. The neon cross glows on the mountain. The earth smells so fucking sweet, so full of life. I hide under the cover of darkness and I give myself to the world, press my forehead into the dirt. A love song plays on repeat in my earphones. I'm here, I'm here, I'm here. I remember who I am, who I was always meant to be. And I am so happy. I am at peace.

Here in my body there is an unfolding, like a sweet sigh, like an exhale. Here in my body there is a softening, an easing. I lean into the moment, let the tension melt away. I trust that I can let go. I trust that I am loved, that I am safe, that I can be here, that this beautiful life is real. I don't have to live in the past and I don't have to live in fear. I get to be here, right here. The moon is climbing up into the sky. This city I have come to know, come to call home, glitters with light in the darkness. The winter has given way to something else, has surrendered to its own becoming, and so have I.

I'm not afraid anymore. The fear comes like a phantom, like a storm of birds suddenly taking flight. But the edge is dulled and smoothed, like glass made soft in the water. I don't have to be afraid anymore. I spend my days drinking nettle and dandelion, lavender and fennel, holy basil and damiana. I spend my days breathing into my belly and throwing my head back in laughter. The fear comes like a phantom and I release it into the sky like a bird. My oldest friend, the one who saved my life, but you don't live here anymore.

Melting

A WEEK AFTER AN ice storm and it's suddenly summer. The grass becomes green against the mud brown earth and piles of snow huddle dirty white, melting in the sun. I make myself sun sick from too much of it, turning my body heliotropic, desperately drinking up the warmth.

I survived my first winter in Montréal. In minus 30 I put on three sweaters under my coat and my snow pants and went out into the snow. It wasn't the cold that got me, the skiers skiing down the sidewalks, the brilliant glittering white; it was the length, the way it dragged on and on, and then suddenly, all at once, it was summer.

I love my life here. I love this city and the people and the person I'm becoming. I celebrated one year with my partner and six years of sobriety in the same week. I felt flooded with love. Holding my partner's hand, walking through the cold, reminiscing on the night they low key walked me to their home. And then celebrating my six years with my sober crew, all of these beautiful queer and trans addicts and alcoholics who I have come to know and love. All of us working so fucking hard to save our lives and to heal and grow and change. I love my life here. I can't believe I have built this beautiful life in eight months.

I am becoming my truest self, the person I was always meant to be. I am transforming, becoming and I can't do that work alone; I need other people to love me. I need to see that I am loved, as I am, as an imperfect and indispensably unique human being. There is only one me. And I am loved, deeply loved, just for being me.

Fucking Magic

My one friend lovingly calls me a militant bisexual. My other friend tells me my queerness is peer reviewed, accepted without revisions. My partner listens to my bisexual angst and reaffirms my queerness regularly. For the first time in my life I feel truly held and seen in queer community, as I am, as a bisexual person. The love is sinking deep down into my bones, into my cells, and it is changing me. I am better able to express and act upon my desires because the hardened shame of biphobia is melting away. My community is loving it away.

After a lifetime of struggling for love, of desperately wanting it but never knowing what it really is, of accepting abuse and neglect because I didn't know any better, I finally feel the love settling into my bones. I feel it changing me. I had to do so much work to get here. I had to fight so hard against so many odds to even be able to find and recognize love, let alone accept it. But I have, and I'm here, in this beautiful city, with this beautiful life.

And now it is summer and I will sit in the parks and drink iced tea. I will take care of the people I love who love me. I will climb the mountain and ride my bike and keep putting down roots in this city, keep giving myself to this beautiful life.

All the hard work is worth it. All the effort, all the leaps of faith, all the trying in the face of fear, it was all worth it, because it brought me here.

I Want to Hold Your Hand

*I*WANT TO HOLD your hand. You take my hand in yours. These small actions hold so much meaning but it was a meaning I could never speak. I watch you smoke your cigarette. We sit around for hours talking about everything. The couch in your kitchen. The picnic table in your backyard.

You told me that when you held me in your arms in your bed you felt something. I told you I felt something too. You told me you couldn't, that you didn't want things to change. You told me you love our friendship. I told you *I love our friendship too.*

The timing was always all wrong. You drive me home in your car. I put my guitar in the backseat. We listen to music. I watch the city of Montréal moving past my eyes. I fumble with the lock on your car door like I always do. You call me buddy and I hug you goodbye. I never feel uncomfortable in silence with you.

I was in your kitchen last May, eating cold leftover fries and listening to you play guitar, and I knew I wanted to move here. So many times I have walked from St. Henri metro, that now familiar path, to your little pink home. And I have always felt welcome with you.

I want to hold your hand. This desire comes over me. It takes a shape I cannot speak. You reach for mine on the street and for a second our fingers intertwine. In your bed at night your fingers move over my skin, our bodies press into each other. In the silence, in the dark, I feel your breath on my neck. I hold your hand. I kiss your fingers. I feel your fingers slide into my mouth.

We laugh into the darkness. We hold each other close.

On the mountain I sat on a bench. It was still winter and I was so confused. I sent you a text and I told you *The timing is all wrong but of course I have feelings for you.* Of course I have feelings for you. How long have I known you? How long have we been on the peripheries of each other's lives? How many times have we exchanged smiles? How long have we been friends?

I watch you smoke your cigarette. I listen to you talk. I love the way you light up when you feel passionate about something. I love your commitment to learning, the way you believe there is always a way, the way you assume things are possible, when I'm so quick to assume they aren't.

You are my friend, and I want to hold your hand. I want to feel your fingers interlaced with mine. I want to sit in your car listening to the rain. I want to feel your desire when you look at me. I want the electric charge of our attraction, the safety of our connection, to light up the night sky. And whatever happens, we have our whole lives to figure it out. Whatever happens, you will always be my friend.

See Through Blue

A LL MY LIFE I learned that I had to earn love. I learned that I had to earn it by being something other than what I am, by surrendering up my basic needs, by changing myself fundamentally to become lovable. From a very young age I knew that I was 'sexy'. Whatever that means. As a very young child I remember knowing that I was 'fuckable'. I knew that my grandfather wanted to fuck me. But I didn't know for sure that I was lovable. I felt that love was something I had to earn, to work for, to change myself for. I also knew that being sexy and fuckable might be the closest I would get to love. I remember being like ten years old with tiny new breasts and looking in the mirror thinking *Yeah I have a good body, but I don't have a pretty face.*

All my life I learned that I was fuckable but not lovable. Someone everyone was fucking on the side. All my life I learned that women and femmes were ranked based on our appearances, put into a competition we never consented to, and I learned that I was definitely not a ten. I had this fear, this deep down terror, that any love I managed to find could easily be taken away from me, if a ten happened to take interest in the person I loved. Attraction and desire were never safe. Love was never safe. And the people I loved frequently told me all the ways I was not good enough, not quite deserving. The people I loved told me what I needed to do to make myself better, and I worked hard on it, because I desperately wanted to be loved. And if I couldn't be loved then I'd let them fuck me anyway, because all my life I'd learned that sex might be the closest I would get to love.

I have come so far and done so much work. I have done so much therapy and I have gone so deep down to uproot these beliefs. But they have very deep roots. I am surprised to find myself operating as if these things are true. I am surprised to find the death call of jealousy, the alert that all love and safety will vanish, if a ten comes to take my place. Even though I find this way of thinking abhorrent and unethical. Even though I know it is violent and misogynist. Even if I know that real love is not something that can be measured on a scale and that real attraction has no interest in hierarchies. I am still shot through with terror.

Once my partner was telling me that to them numbers and words have colours associated with them. I asked them if names do too and they said yes. I asked them *What colour is Clementine?* And they said *See through blue.*

Falling in love with my partner has been the most terrifying and profoundly healing experience of my life.

My partner is a beautiful person. They are good and kind and ambitious and principled and smart and daring and brave and sexy as fuck. This person who I so easily fell head over heels for loves me too.

It is the first time in my life I have been in a partnership where I am truly loved, loved in a real way, loved in a way where I know that I am safe, loved in a way where I keep learning that love is not something I earn by being something other than who I am. My partner shows me that I am loved for being exactly who I am.

It's scary to finally have the love I've always wanted and never really believed was possible. Sometimes the deep roots of my old beliefs become activated and I become terrified that some arbitrary thing like not knowing how to do winged eyeliner will signal the end of my ability to be lovable. It sounds absurd, but the terror can rise up in my body as a visceral reality. That's what complex ptsd does.

I told my partner about these fears. I told my partner about the rating system and the fact that I've been rated and that there is still a part of me that is hypervigilant about these things. My partner was horrified that I could hold these beliefs, that I could really think that my lovability was connected to something like winged eyeliner, that I could even imagine them walking around rating femmes on a scale of ten. And I know that they're not, but deep down in my traumatized bodymind I am still so scared.

They listened to my fears. They showed me that having these fears doesn't make me unlovable, that it is safe for me to be this vulnerable, to show them these parts of me that haven't healed yet, that are still in so much pain. We had long conversations about it. I felt heard and I also learned so much about other ways to experience and conceptualize attraction and desire. I felt safe. I feel safe.

My love said to me *Clementine, on a scale from one to ten you are see through blue.*

Freedom

My partner is moving and me and their two other partners are helping them move. The four of us together lift boxes and struggle with heavy things and play tetris on the truck. We laugh and joke around and drink coffee and it feels so good. It feels so good to know that my partner is so well loved and supported, not only by me, but also by these two beautiful humans. It feels so good to laugh and work together with these two people I am intimately linked to, through our love and commitment to the same person.

The person I've been seeing for a while has a finissage celebrating the art they've had up on display at the local queer bar. They've mentioned wanting to meet my partner and my partner has mentioned wanting to meet them, so on the night of the finissage my partner comes along. My date gets nonalcoholic fancy lemonade for the table which is really sweet and thoughtful because my partner and I are both sober. It's cute to see these two people being all sweet and kind to each other. It feels good to have them meet after they've both heard so much about each other. Before leaving, my partner and my date hug goodbye and my date gets all cute with me, and I kiss them goodnight.

My partner is moving in with their other partner for the summer. Their partner's partner is my really good friend. My friend and I laugh and talk about the polycule over coffee at our weekly writing date. We joke that we should plan our respective date nights with our partners on the same night so that we can 'accidentally' run into each other at their house. We find this hilarious.

Freedom

I fucking love polyamory so much. I love the network of relationships that it creates. I love the freedom that it flourishes in. I love the responsibility and the practice of learning to love well. I love that I have to work on myself, that I have to answer the call of jealousy or insecurity when these things arise. I have to do the work of healing wounds and deepening trust, of sorting out what part of my feelings are about my past and what part of my feelings need to be addressed in the relationship(s) now. I love how it encourages me to live with integrity, to live in reality, and to be generous with my heart.

I used to be such a jealous person. I understand my jealousy as rooted in trauma, as the panic driven terror of insecure attachment. After working so hard to heal myself and to develop secure relationships with trust worthy people I have earned secure attachment. I have learned how to trust, how to love with open hands, how to love responsibly and well, how to be brave and take risks, how to ask for what I need, how to take care of the abandoned child in me. This is such rewarding work.

In the past my strategies to avoid the painful feelings of jealousy, insecurity, and terror of abandonment were to avoid the things or people that triggered these feelings or to set up rigid systems of control to make myself feel safer. Now I practice moving toward what scares me, developing friendships with my metamours, reaching out to the people I am connected to through the network of relationships in polyamory, remembering that all of these people are human beings, as complex and imperfect and human as me. For the first time I am learning what it is like to believe that even if the people I love have absolute freedom, they will still freely choose to love me. I don't have to force it or control it. Love is free and it thrives in freedom.

Polyamory requires more work than monogamy, simply because there are more people's feelings to consider, and because there are more potentials for being triggered and needing to do inner and communal work to promote safety and trust. Polyamory has offered me, a severely traumatized person, the most incredible opportunity to heal, grow, and reimagine what trustworthy love and family can look like.

Fucking Magic

I tell everyone who will listen that octopuses are a symbol for freedom. *Octopuses love freedom! They will cross land for freedom!* Octopuses are brave and will go to great lengths to be free. They remind me of my commitment to freedom, politically, collectively, and also freedom from the effects of trauma and addiction. Once I asked my partner about pursuing dating someone they were dating. I felt nervous about bringing it up, and I also would have completely understood and accepted it if no was the answer. My partner encouraged me to follow my heart. They said *We should get octopus tattoos babe, because we love freedom.*

Six Years Sober

I CALL A RADICAL sobriety meeting to celebrate my six years of sobriety. All my closest friends come. Two of them make me a vegan gluten free cake to celebrate. We sit in a circle and we talk about the gifts of sobriety, the things sobriety has made possible, the things that are becoming possible. We talk about our feelings, our regrets, our desires, how we are trying to grow and change. People cry and dare to be vulnerable. We open up our hearts and we show them to each other. This is what I love about radsob. This is what I love about recovery. I am so blessed and honoured to share space with these incredibly brave people. I am so blessed and honoured to call them friends. I can't believe that in my eight months living in Montréal I have found such incredible community. The greatest gift of my sobriety is the ability to develop friendships and be part of community.

When I was drinking I frequently did so by myself but out in public so that I didn't have to be alone. I walked the streets wasted, trying to strike up conversations with random strangers, letting random men fuck me because it was the only kind of company I could get. I was completely unable to maintain friendships or partnerships. I always got wasted and acted awful. No one could stand me for long. My life was unbearably lonely, I was frequently assaulted, and I didn't know how to change things. Choosing recovery and sobriety has been the greatest adventure of my life. Sobriety remains the most important thing in my life. Everything else in my life is founded on my continuous commitment to my sobriety.

In order to stay sober I have to remain dedicated to my growth. I have to go deeper, I have to be willing to transform. Recovery means growth, it means change. I have to grow and change; it isn't optional. In the past year and a half I have gone through so many profound changes. Recovery means living in my integrity, but for so long in my sobriety I was still living in shame, unable to embrace who I am. I believed that being sober meant rejecting huge parts of myself. It is only in the past year and a half that I fully embraced being a queer, bisexual, nonmonogamous, slutty, anarchist, sober, witch recovering from addiction and complex trauma and living my best life. *Nail painting emoji.*

Recovery narratives can get wrapped up in heterosexual capitalist timelines suggesting that as we recover we should get the monogamous relationship, the straight job, the nuclear family. Imagining recovery time lines that are queer and anti-capitalist means imagining a life grounded in different desires and values. I do want committed relationships, queer nonmog family, communities who show up for each other, and meaningful work. I want these things while being exactly who I am, all of who I am, and remaining committed to the work of creating a new world. The work of recovery, with help from my radsob friends, has shown me how to be honest and to create the life I truly want in sobriety. It has shown me that I can truly live in my integrity, and that sobriety can be a starting place for showing up to do the work of creating alternatives to the systems we currently live in.

When accepting my six year chip from my sponsor, I talked about the importance of queer lineages of sponsorship. In a room full of mostly straight people I talked about how my sponsor and I talk about threesomes and strap-ons and how this is relevant to my sobriety. I talked about the fact that it was a queer sex worker who got me to come to my first twelve step meeting. I talked about how being all of who I am in recovery circles has been scary, how I was afraid of being judged, how I didn't see a lot of representation of people like me. I talked about the importance of honesty and how being honest is an act of service because it shows other people like me that recovery is possible for people like us. Getting sober doesn't have to mean trading in or repressing our politics, our desires, our sexualities, our values. In fact the opposite is true: sobriety is a commitment to integrity, which means coming to understand and act from our principles.

At six years sober I am queerer than I've ever been. I am becoming more radicalized every day. I am leaning into my sluttiness and I am happily nonmonogamous. I am investing in queer futures and challenging myself to learn and grow. Some friends and I are starting a sober house, where we can live in a sober environment of care and support and community that encourages the work we are doing in our recovery. We are going to have a weekly radsob meeting at our house. At six years sober I am discovering so many incredible possibilities for what sobriety can mean. And more will be revealed.

My friends and I sit in a circle, each one of us with a heart full of pain and love, hope and a profound knowledge of despair. Each one of us with our own struggles and catastrophes that brought us here, to our sobriety. I have come to know these people over a period of eight months, some for a bit longer, and I love each one of them with all my heart. I am so fucking proud of us. I am so fucking proud of us for being our whole selves, queer and trans and traumatized and doing our very very best to survive and thrive in a world that would have otherwise.

We share our most heartfelt feelings and we laugh our asses off together. We eat cake and strawberries and watermelon and pet the cat as she makes her way around the circle. We have each been through so much and we are all being so good to each other. We are showing each other that there is a way back from wherever we have been, that there is a way to be in the world, sober and queer and exactly who we are. These people are my family, we are possibility models for each other, we are changing the world, and we are making new ways of being possible. I am six years sober and so grateful to be here, exactly where I am. Thank you for my sobriety.

Fucking Magic

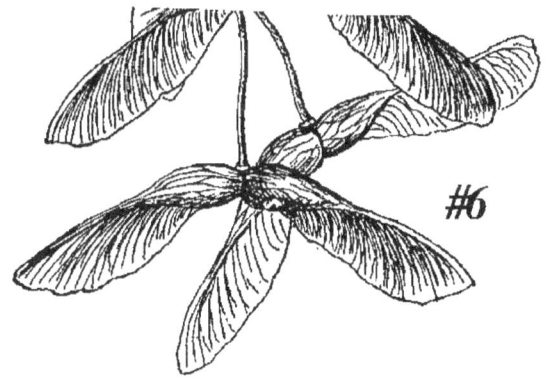

#6

Safe

*I*T'S SUMMER AND it's hot and raining. I'm at my partner's place, and their partner (who is my friend) and their partner's partner (who is also my friend) are celebrating their one year anniversary. They are decked out in lab coats and protective eyewear making soap. My partner and I gift them a tea blend for their anniversary and then we head off to go get some groceries for dinner for our own date night. My partner's partner says I can't go out in the rain like that: *That jacket doesn't even have a hood.* They insist that I wear their jacket and my partner goes and gets it off their floor and I put it on over my dress and we go off into the rain. We walk through the laneway. We hold hands and talk. French language music is carried through the hot summer air from a music festival happening in a nearby park. My hood keeps falling in my eyes but it is keeping me dry. In this moment I feel it. The feeling that I'm so hungry for so much of the time, the feeling that I love and desire so much, the feeling I've been searching for my whole life. I feel *safe*. I feel loved, I feel home, I feel *safe*.

It's summer and it's hot, hot, hot. A heat wave has descended on the city and everyone is dripping wet with sweat to the point where it makes no difference if we pour a bottle of water over our heads and we do because it's nice. It's moving day in Montréal, the day leases end and everyone in the city is moving. I am moving too, into a sober house with three amazing rad queer sober friends. We have been moving all day and we are exhausted and delirious. We've just picked up the stuff of the fourth roomie of the day and we've loaded it all into the van. My friend/my partner's partner is driving, my new roomie is in the passenger seat, and my partner and I are squished on the floor, squeezed in the bit of space that isn't crammed with furniture and boxes. There are two mango popsicles that are being passed from mouth to mouth, bright orange and sticky sweet and perfect and everything and exactly what we need. We're all laughing and joking and so tired. The air conditioning in the van offers some relief, but I know I'm not even making sense anymore when I talk. I say *Montréal is like an unsupervised teenager* and everyone laughs at that and talks about how it's true. And I feel it. I feel that fucking feeling. That feeling I've spent my whole life chasing. I feel loved, I feel home, I feel *safe*.

Kill the Misogynist Bro in Your Head

O<small>NE TIME A</small> long time ago I was fucking this dude I barely knew. I was on top, a position I've always felt nervous, self-conscious, and uncomfortable in. A position that is supposed to be about my pleasure, that is supposed to be empowering, but I have always found it awkward and difficult. The dude I was fucking said *You know what I hate? When girls get on top and act like they have no idea what they're doing.* He said it with casual contempt and whatever movement I was managing came to a stop. I felt frozen. Shame hardened in my body, crystalized into a tiny million hard-as-glass shards. It made movement impossible; it made action impossible. My body separated from me. I became a spectator of myself, a spectacle. I became silence and stillness and shame. I can take what I am given but I can't act. It is humiliating to act. I became a receiver, receptive. I am very good at taking what I am given, but a million tiny violences and many very large ones too have taken from me the ability to act, to move.

Years later I am 31 and I am still trying to crack the ice, still trying to heal the split, the shame, the way I have become dissociated from my body. I am still trying to feel safe and present in movement, in the moment, and mostly I still don't. I tell my partner a secret desire. I spit from my lips a hidden want, and I squirm from the discomfort of vulnerability. I tell my partner I want to dance for them, to move my hips, to show them my sensuality. I tell them I can dance when I'm alone but I am frozen with shame when I'm in front of a partner. I tell them how hard it is for me to get on top, and how I wish it wasn't so hard. How I feel like it's a performance, and I will fail. How I am afraid of being humiliated again and shamed. How I can't feel or move my body when I feel like a spectator of myself. How I hear in my head the contempt of that dude I was fucking all those years ago, and all the other dudes I've fucked who were awful to me. My partner, my love, who thinks I'm beautiful, who loves my desire, they say to me *Babe, you've got a misogynist bro living in your head.* And it's so fucking true, I do. I have internalized this violence. I have become heavy with the burden of other people's shame.

There's a misogynist bro in my head. And he hates his own femininity and therefore he hates my femininity. He hates his desire for me and therefore he hates my desire. He hates his own vulnerability and therefore he hates my vulnerability. He is always ridiculing me, reducing me to a thing, laughing at my efforts, hoping I will hate myself enough to let him get away with how he treats me. I hear him all the time, judging me, shaming me, telling me what I can't do and what I have to do. I expect this judgement from the people in my life, even the people I love and trust the most. I hear this judgement on my own lips, saying ridiculous, misogynist things about myself. Hating myself. Feeling like I'm not good enough. Putting my worth in ridiculous things and always falling short. Insisting that some things I just can't do, related in some abstract way to my gender.

And it's so awful and I'm so fucking over it. I hate this misogynist bro in my head. I hate his harassment and his contempt. I want to move freely, to thaw the icy shame, to melt, to move my hips, to feel my sensuality and my sexuality, embodied, to get on top and go slow, stopping whenever I need to, doing whatever feels good and helps me stay connected to my body. I want to dance. I want to sing. I want to play guitar and not hate myself. I want to be free.

I want to kill the misogynist bro in my head and compost his body to make sweet, rich earth. I want to use this sweet, rich earth to nourish the seeds of new growth. I want to strip him of his power, reduce him to his basic elements and recycle them. I want to free up the energy I have invested in impressing him and use it for other things. I want to refute his violence with all the energy I contain, resist it with every piece of my being. I want to be done with it and transform it with my magic into the conditions of safety and power necessary for new growth. I want to act, in the sense that I want to be an actor, an agent in my own life. I want to play the fucking guitar and I want to sing in a punk band. I want to dance for my partner, move my hips and feel the hardened shame begin to melt. I want to reclaim my body, take it back from all the people who have shamed me. I want to rise like a seedling pushing through the shell of the seed, pushing through the darkness of the earth and out into the light.

I want to know what it's like to feel uninhibited and free. To move my body with trust and ease. To feel my body from the inside, not as a dissociated, disembodied spectator. I want to breathe. To not secretly hate myself in any hidden corner of my being. To easily and completely reject any and all violence or shame directed at me. I want to be done with it, to repel it, to immediately and unreservedly come to my own defense. I want to know my power, my goodness, my sexiness, my sensuality, my vulnerability, my capability. I want to know that nothing, not a single thing about me, is pathetic or disgusting. I want to know that my desire and my pleasure are beautiful, beautiful and inherently good.

I lie in bed next to my partner and I run my finger in circles over my clit. I want to cum. I want to feel the build, the approaching edge, the explosion, the release. My partner holds me while I touch myself. I try to concentrate on feeling good. I try to be inside my body, feel the slickness of my finger moving exactly how I like, feel my partners breath on my neck as they kiss me, feel this shared eroticism, this focus on my pleasure. But the misogynist bro in my head keeps interrupting me. Again and again I hear him insist that my pleasure, on its own like this, for its own sake, isn't sexy, is somehow gross or shameful. I can feel his annoyance, his irritation, the way sex is over for him once he has cum, the way my orgasm needs to be timed perfectly to coincide with or precede his. Even though my partner has told me so many times that they love my pleasure, that they find it hot and intimate and erotic when I touch myself, I can still feel the crushing weight of shame. I can still feel the weight of a million violences, the things that separated my body from myself, the things that taught me my desire is always secondary, that the focus always needs to be on someone else.

    I feel my pleasure in opposition to this shame, trying to become itself, trying to maintain, struggling, struggling against the thoughts that try to smother it. I feel my pleasure like a little flicker of fire trying to ignite and burst into flame. I keep losing it, I keep disappearing, I keep thinking *This is annoying, this isn't sexy, how could watching me rub my clit be hot?* I try to talk myself out of these thoughts by reminding myself what I know to be true: that my pleasure is hot, that my partner thinks it's fucking sexy, that I am desirable in my desire, that my desire is powerful and important. But the misogynist bro in my head keeps interrupting. He keeps pulling me out of my body. I push him aside and dive back in. I find the pleasure again, there it is. I drop down into it, listen to it, pay attention to it. I close my eyes. I feel my partners arms around me as they kiss me and watch me, and I run my finger in expert little circles over my clit.

    There it is, there's the pleasure. I feel it rising up and I sink into it. I hold it and am held by it. I ride the pleasure, chase the pleasure, pursue it over the edge of the cliff of my orgasm, feel the weight of it like an avalanche crashing down all around me, crushing the misogynist bro in my head, killing him.

Becoming a Forest

THE TREES ARE true anarchists providing mutual aid and collective care to each other through a network of mushrooms underground. They are social creatures dedicated to the health of the forest, not just their individual health. They know their individual health depends on the health of the forest. Trees will keep the stump of a felled friend alive for decades, sending it their photosynthesized tree juice because their friend can't photosynthesize for itself anymore. Some species have a habit of sharing their tree juice among themselves, the ones who get more light share with the ones who get less. Trees are social, communal beings. They take care of each other.

I am a social, communal being too. It is so scary for me to ask for help, for me to admit when I am having trouble taking care of myself. That level of vulnerability is terrifying. I don't want to put people out or be a burden. I don't want to be rejected when I'm already feeling awful, even though I get that people might say no because they are already at capacity, that it isn't usually personal. It's just that I feel so much shame, shame for having needs, for being a social creature like a tree. And yet I love trees more than anything, they are so beautiful and strong. They have always protected me and they teach me so much. Now they teach me about the importance of a forest. A tree without a forest has a much harder time trying to survive.

I had a breakdown. I was walking and suddenly I just couldn't. The pressure built to its breaking point. I could not stand the feelings that were pressing down on me. I couldn't cope with them. But at six years sober, I am committed not to engaging in any of my old self-destructive coping mechanisms. When I felt this bad in the past I would usually drink or cut myself, escape through some kind of oblivion. Since I choose not to do those things anymore, I need another way to deal with this overwhelm. I need another way to move through feelings that feel impossible to move through. And as much as it's hard for me to admit it, I can't do it alone. Like the trees, I need my community to take care of me. I was crying and hyperventilating on the street, stopped in my tracks by the intensity of my feelings. With shaking hands I texted my partner *I'm having a mental breakdown.*

My partner came to get me. They sat with me on a stoop that seedlings pushed their way through. They looked up Pete Walker's "13 Steps to Managing Emotional Flashbacks" on their phone and they read them to me. They took me home to their place and put me in a zebra print onesie and made me lavender tea and put me into bed. They held me in their arms and read to me. They took care of me. Once I was calm they talked to me and told me that I needed to ask for help. I needed to accept help. I was in crisis and couldn't do it alone. I resisted them and told them how much asking for help fucks me up, how it terrifies me and fills me with shame. I told them all the reasons I couldn't do it, all the ways I felt hopeless. I didn't want to be a burden. I didn't want to put people out. I didn't want to experience rejection when I was already feeling so awful. I believed I should be able to handle this on my own. I couldn't imagine how to ask for what I needed.

My partner care-topped me. They helped me make a list of all the things I was having trouble doing: washing my dishes, making food, sitting with my feelings. They asked me to tell them six people I would be willing to accept help from. I had to cover my face with a blanket in order to even answer the question, but finally I spit out six names. My partner asked me if they could co-ordinate with these people to arrange help for me. Despite my wriggling shame I said yes. My partner arranged over the next few days for people to check in on me, spend time with me, bring me food, and help clean my place. The six people I named all said yes, all agreed to help out in some capacity. I accepted the help. I watched in amazement as people in my life showed up for me. They brought me food, cooked me meals, sat on my porch with me, did my dishes, walked me to the park. Most importantly they showed me that they cared, that I wasn't alone. That in and of itself did wonders in easing my distress. I felt like an injured tree accepting tree juice from my forest friends.

When I expressed to my partner my wonder and awe at the care that was extended to me by a community of friends, they said to me *That's how it should be, and you can rely on it being that way from now on.* The word *rely* made me cry. The idea that I can depend on care, that I can expect it, that it won't just vanish, that I don't have to struggle to keep it, this concept shakes me to my very bones. It's the most beautiful idea, the thing I've always wanted. Care has never been something I can be sure of. It has never been something I can rely on. I have survived by struggling for love, trading in my dignity and safety for love, pretending I don't need love and trying to go it alone. I have never felt like I belonged anywhere. And now, for the first time, I am in a network of reciprocal care, a community that truly has my back, that I can truly depend on. Like the trees, my friends are there for each other. When one of us is having a rough time the other ones help out. Like the trees we know we are stronger and healthier together than we ever could be on our own.

Someone once told me that asking for and accepting help is offering a gift to the people in our lives. It is giving your community, your friends and loved ones, the opportunity to get closer to you, to see your vulnerability, to know you. It builds intimacy. Even though I believe in interdependence and mutual aid, even though I am happy to be there for my friends when they are in need, putting into practice accepting these things is way harder. But I'm working on it. I'm working on practicing my principles and building the new world in the shell of the old. I am working on being a forest, rather than a singular tree.

Remember

D*O YOU REMEMBER who you were when you lost everything? Do you remember the sweet cool wind blowing your hair up off your shoulders, the grey clouds, the stillness pulsing underneath it all? Do you remember when you let go, really let go, opened your hands and surrendered? Do you remember that recognition, that knowing, that returning to yourself? Do you remember who you are? Not what you're holding on to, not the stories you are telling yourself, not everything you have or even everything you love, but do you remember who you* are? *Underneath everything, down in your core, in the marrow of your bones, in the space between the atoms? Can you remember?*

This is a magic spell, a love letter, a way back to the centre. This is an incantation, a conjuring, a line cast into the darkness. Where's the orgasm, the desire? Where's the dripping wet, pressing my body against a wall or a floor, a hard surface that will push back against me? Where's the earth? Where are my hands? What am I giving my attention to? *What am I giving my attention to?* This is a magic spell. A repetition. A remembering. This is an invitation. A pathway. A light left on to find my way back. My skin is slick with sweat, the air is heavy with water. The trees shine their light through green leaves, bringing us into the cool green dark: remember. Down on my knees in the dirt, my face pressed against it, my hands pressing into roots and stray branches. A sacred act. A prayer. A way back to myself. Remember.

Do you remember who you are? Do you remember a living, pulsing universe that loves you back? A world of enchantment and magic, a world alive? Do you remember writing as an extension of that? Writing as a sacred act? Do you remember fucking as an extension of that? Fucking as a sacred act? Where is the water? When was the last time you went? Where is the forest? When was the last time you went? Where is your body? When was the last time you went? Why do you keep escaping? What are you so afraid of? What are you hiding from? What are you afraid to know? What are you afraid to ask? Why are you so afraid? Do you remember that you are brave? Do you remember what you survived? What you lost? What you built? Do you remember who you are?

I am more powerful than anything that has tried to kill me. I am more powerful than all of the worst things that have happened to me. I am more powerful than everything I've lost, everything I will lose. *Do you remember who you are?* I remember myself in the water. I remember myself in the trees. I remember myself down in the dirt, crawling, pressing my body against the only real parent I ever had, finding safety in the darkness, in the way the world always remembers me, welcomes me, calls me back. I remember myself when I open my hands and let go, when I release my grip and surrender. I remember myself when I cum, wriggling and writhing and not asking if my pleasure is desirable, not asking if my desires are the right ones, trusting that my desire is *right*, is *sacred*, is *divine*. I remember myself when I return, when I step into my power, when I surrender feigned helplessness and inherited shame. None of that is mine. What is mine is something else.

Do you remember what it's like to be free? Do you remember what freedom means? Do you remember that octopuses climb out of their cages and cross land for freedom, that they risk it all for freedom? Do you remember what you did for freedom, what you risked, what you lost? Do you know what you are capable of? Do you know what you've done? Do you remember the way you moved mountains when you had to, the way you saved yourself, changed yourself, against all odds? Can you feel the power that moves through you? Can you feel the love that is foundational, irrevocable, yours? Do you remember what is under the fear, what true reality waits for you there? What calm steady knowing lies at the centre of you? Do you remember who you are, what you're here for? Do you remember your purpose, your calling?

Fucking Magic

Can you answer the call? Can you return to yourself? Do you remember who you are?

Write

WRITING USES WORDS but it comes from the body. Writing comes from some place deep inside myself, some place where the edges of who I am blur and I become more than myself. There are always a million reasons not to write and a million reasons not to be a writer. It is painful and terrifying and hard. People say mean things, people put you on a pedestal, people cut into the softest squishiest parts of you. But you're supposed to be hard. After all, you're the one who put yourself out there. And there is only one reason to write, only one reason to be a writer: Because I have to. I am called to this magic from some place and some time that is beyond. I am helpless before the call. I have resisted, insisted I wasn't a writer. I have felt the block, the inability to say anything, the contempt toward everything I say, the disappointment, the fear, the worry. I have wondered why, why me, who am I to be a writer? And I have seen other writers struggle with the same things and I have seen us not write. Writers don't always write, but we need to. We need to feel the words flowing out of us, saying things we had no idea we needed to say. We need to feel the pressure and the dam breaking, and the magic of opening that wordless place to words.

I am a writer. It is the second most important thing about me, the first being my sobriety because my sobriety is the foundation of everything else, the most important thing in my life. And my commitment to my sobriety is a commitment to writing. I am committed to writing. What a crazy thing to be committed to. I always joke: *I'm a poet but that's not a real job.* My friends point at the stick n' poke on my shoulder that reads *Writer*, they laugh and they tease me, *Clementine are you a writer? Are you a writer?* Because they know that being a writer is the second most important thing about me, they know that I turn to the page, over and over again, with some insatiable longing, some need that is fulfilled only in the writing. I give myself to the words, to the process and the procrastination and everything we do to prevent ourselves from writing, and then I write. I find that I am writing. I find that the words are coming from my hands and maybe it's not any good, it's certainly not literary. I never went to school for it and maybe there's just something I'm missing, something that prevents me from *really* being a writer. Maybe my writing is self-indulgent, maybe it's selfish, maybe I shouldn't write. Someone I love said to me: *Stop writing.* They went for the jugular and tried to hurt me in the deepest way they could hurt me because my writing is what I am here to do. My writing is selfish and self-indulgent because it is the magic by which I keep myself alive. My writing is selfless because I give myself to writing, over and over and over, despite being broke as hell, despite the fear, despite the insecurity, despite the vulnerability, I give myself to writing because it is what I am here to do.

    I don't write to make good writing. I don't write to be a famous writer. I don't write for success even though I'm happy when I am successful. I write for the child I was who went down to the end of the driveway and put an envelope with a note and two dollars in the mailbox and hoped against hope that I would find in that mailbox in a few weeks time a zine written by someone like me. Someone like the twelve year old child I was who felt so alive and desperately crazy, who turned the hot water on to scalding and put my little hand under it, to feel the shock of pain until I had to pull my hand away. Someone like the child I was who knew the feel of my grandfather's tongue in my mouth and his strong arms pressing my body into him, who knew that the lake was bottomless and that there was something there that could keep me alive if only I could remember it. Someone like the child I was who was in love with my best friend, a girl like me. The queer child I was who experienced pleasure and desire and fear and terror. I didn't know how to live the life I was living. I had no way out except death and writing. I have tried both and I choose writing. The

Write

zine came in the mail, I found it in my mailbox like a light in the dark, like a map to another world, a world where I could live. Because of writing I knew that I could live, I knew there was a whole big strange world out there, a world bigger than my grandfather's eyes and my homophobic classmates and my small town and my father's rage. There were people like me in the world and they lived.

I write about my life because it is what I know. The shock of cold water when I jumped in the lake, the sunlight rippling on the surface, the body of a fish swimming past in shadow, the bullfrogs croaking in the night. I write about my life because my writing comes from my body, the body that lay silent staring at the wall while my boyfriend's cock was fucking away inside me, the body that promised *okay I will disappear for now, I will live through this, and I will find a way to come back from the dead, I will find my way back in writing.* The body that felt the impact, the nerves that went out like a light, the body that became a mannequin, a marionette, a lifeless impression of life. I write about my life to find my way back into my body, back into my life. And I throw my words out into the world like leaving the porch light on. I am looking for you.

I am looking for you, the one who is carrying the weight of a crushing love, an unspeakable secret, the one who can't admit the things your boyfriend does, the one who believes deep down that if you could just be better then he would stop. I am looking for you, the one who can't feel anything, who tries and tries to cum but can't cum and can't feel anything, who hates their body with a sickening intensity, who can't stand to be alive and to be numb. I am looking for you, the one who still believes it wasn't that bad, that you have no reason and no excuse for the way that you feel, who won't call it abuse or neglect because you insist that others had it worse, yet you are crushed under the weight of something you can't name. I am looking for you, the one who can't take another psych lock up, who can't live with or without the drink, who doesn't understand the wild desire that pushes you forward, who wants to die but even scarier wants to live.

Fucking Magic

I am a writer because I want a way for us to live through what has happened. I want to follow the words to the heart and find the magic we need to keep living, and to begin the work of healing, of wanting life more than we want death, of wanting our bodies back and our freedom. I am a writer because words are what I have, they are my secret power, the thing I kept under cover, the thing holed up in my heart even as those things were done to me, even as I knew it wasn't safe to speak, I saved these words for later. I saved these words for now, now that I am a grown adult, now that no one can stop me from writing this, now that I can say the truth and make the call and bear witness to what I have lived, what so many of us have lived, and offer an invitation to you. Your pain is important. The ways you have survived are important. The things you love and your reasons to keep going are important. The things you know and the things you feel are important. And I hope you write. I hope you put this down right now and you write and you write and you write.

Listen for Desire

I'M ON A first date and I'm sprawled out in the grass making out with a cute femme. They have glitter on their cheekbones and their red lipstick has disappeared between our lips and I like the way our lips feel against each other and the way we pull our bodies closer, trying to close the distance between us. After kissing for a bit we get to talking and kink comes up and we discover that we are in the middle of a sub4sub make out fest. Both of us are a little disappointed but we still think each other are hot and we still like kissing each other. I tell them about the bottom uprising I'm starting: *Yeah there's a shortage of tops and an abundance of bottoms, and I love tops so much, don't get me wrong, but I feel like sometimes bottoms are devalued and we gotta have each other's backs.* We laugh and joke and talk about kink and bottom4bottom sex. At some point they mention that they would still take me home if I want, and it's true that I was hoping to be asked that, but I don't respond right away.

I go to the bushes at the back of the park to pee and while I'm peeing I try to think, I try to connect with my body, with my desire, with what I *want*. On first dates I tend to get nervous and I'm caught up in wondering how I'm coming off, and it's hard for me to stay connected to myself and what I really desire. I told myself I wasn't going to pursue a bottom4bottom thing again for awhile. I've just come into serious consciousness of my extreme subbiness and I really want more tops in my life. I want to put my energy toward finding people I'm really, really compatible with, who can fulfill my really really deep desires. And I've had trouble with hook ups and first date sex for awhile now. As much as I've wanted everything to go well, my trauma brain has made things complicated. I've been wrestling with what it means to be a slut if I'm not having as much sex as I used to and if I'm having a hard time with hook ups. I really like kissing this person, but does that mean I want to have sex? When I tune into my body do I feel that ocean of desire? Is it there? I am beginning to think that it is safer to err on the side of caution, to say no unless I'm feeling an obvious, undeniable yes.

So I go back and lay on the grass and tell my date *I'm going to pass on coming back tonight. I think you're really hot and I'm having a lot of fun making out with you, but I'm a trauma human and I try to be careful about these things.* And my date is really cool about it and we talk and make out some more before calling it a night. I walk home in the heat of late July, the plants are bursting through the cement and crawling up walls by sheer force of will, by the pull of their desire. I slow down and I try to listen. I try to look deep inside myself to where my desire lives. I try to welcome my desire, choose my desire. I am reimagining what it means to be a slut. A slut is someone who loves desire, who prioritizes pleasure, who wants what they want and loves what they love. I want to love myself and trust myself and I want to remember that saying no is an important part of being a slut. Saying no opens up room for my yes.

Later when we are texting about if we should hang out again I think about what I want. I try to listen deeply to my body. I try to look for what is there, not what I think should be there or what I want to be there. I realize that even though I like this person and I'm attracted to them, I am not looking for a sexual relationship with another sub right now. I tell myself that it is okay to know what I want, it's okay to be into someone but not feel compatible with them. I end up texting them *I had such a nice time with you and I think you're awesome, but right now I only want to pursue dating with people I'm really compatible with.* It's hard to be honest like this and I don't want to hurt their feelings. But they reply saying they get it, they get wanting to pursue tops, as a sub what I'm saying makes total sense to them. They reply with *#bottomuprising #riseup #butstaydown.* I literally laugh out loud at their message and notice how good it feels to be honest and real and transparent, how good it feels to connect to my

Listen for Desire

true desires and communicate about them, how good it feels to relate to another sub and to understand each other even if we can't give each other what we are looking for. I text them back saying *You're amazing #bottomuprising.*

The River

*I*WADE INTO THE river and it is deep and the rocks are slippery and the water is alive and cool and moving fast. The current when I step into it takes me. It just moves my body right along and I have to swim and swim against it and eventually realize that I am losing so I paddle sideways toward the shore. The river is moving, it is in perpetual motion. It is wide and deep and ducks swim along the surface, pushing against the current with all their might. This is Kahrhionhwa'kó:wa, and I sit on the rocks near the shore and let the water flow over me. I let the water move over my body, covering me in coolness, reminding me of motion, of drive, of volition, of the natural need to answer a call. I try to listen for the call.

It is a lunar eclipse and I am changing. I'm not who I was a year ago or even last month. I am growing older and in my age I can feel a lesson dawning on me. There is a way in which I have outgrown the things I used to do to survive. There is a way in which, like the river, I have been steadily moving away from them. I am tired of the things that used to be necessary. I am bored by the things that used to excite me. I feel stifled and trapped by behaviours I depended on to feel safe. I have a new sense of safety, a new sense of trust. I can depend on myself and this world the way that I can depend on my next inhale, my next exhale, the way that I can depend on the moon always coming back. I am excited by different things, different things light me up, things with weight and depth, like rocks and water, like this current that is always already on its way somewhere. I am becoming someone else.

I don't want to waste my time anymore. I don't want to go about my life in a perpetual state of fear. I don't want to hold on to this deeply

The River

held belief in my unworthiness. I want to remember who I am, what I'm here for. Like the moon and like the river I am needed in this world. Like the water moving over my body I am good and I am alive. Like the light flickering on the water, like the rocks warm from the sun, I have my place and my purpose. I do not need to beg for love. I do not need to accept that which my body does not call for. I do not need to worry and wonder if I am enough. I lay my body in the river and I answer the call.

What I Need

I NEED SOMEONE TO *beat me up and make me say thank you.* I type the words and I feel blood rush to my pussy, I feel the ache of desire, the wetness of my body saying *yes.*

I am in bed, lying on my stomach, and you are on top of me, fucking me from behind. You bring your fist to my lips and I kiss it. You take your fist and land it on my back. I say *Thank you.* You return your fist to my lips, I kiss it, desperate, grateful. You take your fist and land it on my back, harder this time. I say *Thank you.* Before I know it my *Thank you* is accompanied by *Please, please, please.* I beg you for the impact, for the energy exploding out of you and into me. I beg you to increase the frequency and the intensity. I beg you and you give me what I need.

My skin blooms purple red. I feel this breaking point inside of me, this need that builds and builds and breaks. There is a flood, a flood between my legs and also I am crying. The tears are tears of desperate need, of being reduced to a singularity, a place that is timeless and endless, a place where light crashes across a blackened sky, like galaxies collapsing on themselves. There is water and there is wetness and there is opening, an explosion of energy that builds and breaks, builds and breaks. I am here with you, surrendering to you, lucky and grateful and good and safe.

I am safe. It is safe to need, to want these things. It is safe to go there, to the edge of feeling, to the breaking point. It is safe to show you this secret part of me, these deep desires hiding under the surface, the fulfilment of a long held secret need. I am a submissive. I am unraveled by the pleasure of giving myself to you, of taking what you give to me. I am undone by the flood of desire for the impact of your fist. I am a mess

What I Need

of gratitude, of servitude, of want. I want, I want, I want you to. I beg you and you give me what I need.

    We are transformed by the pleasure. We collapse on top of each other. We separate, look at each other. I crawl over to you and curl up into your arms. I rest my head on your chest hearing your heart slamming against your ribcage and both of us drink in the air. You hold me and I hold you and I show you, I show you who I am.

Sluts Can Say No

I AM FINDING THE *no* inside my body. The *I've decided I only want to pursue dating with people I'm really compatible with,* and the *I had a really nice time but I've decided it's not a good fit for me.* The *It's not okay for you to blow up my phone for an hour after I told you I was done with the conversation and going to bed,* and the *I'm sorry but this relationship isn't working for me.* It is hard to say *no,* hard to find that little word hiding in my body. It's hard to say the thing I was never allowed to say. It's hard to be honest about my needs, to accept that my *no* might hurt other people's feelings, to stand up for my boundaries even when they are being bulldozed over. It's hard to decide, to discern, to know that I don't have to keep trying, keep pushing myself to find a *yes* when my body has already said *no.*

Sometimes I get so fucking confused by my sexuality. Like, why is it that sometimes I'm totally down to fuck someone I just met and other times I want to move slowly and other times I find I'm not at all interested when I thought I would be? I have tried so hard to crack the code, to create a simple system to predict my desire, so that I don't have to tell people *no* who were expecting to hear *yes.* But I am coming to understand that, at least for now, my desire is a mystery to me. It follows the laws of some other reality, some reality greater than my intellect, greater than my ability to make predictions. I have decided to trust my desire, to trust that my body knows what I want and what I don't want. And I have decided that it is always okay for me to say *no.* Even if I'm on a date, even if I've been heavily flirting, even if I initially said *yes,* even if I thought for sure that I would want to, even if the person is good and kind, even if the person is someone I love, even if I haven't had sex with someone new in a long time and I want to want it, even if I wish with all my heart that I could say *yes* and mean it, I can and should and must say *no* if that is what my body is telling me. I have to trust that my body knows.

The *yes* in my body is unambiguous and clear. It's like running water. It's like the depth of a well, a bottomless lake, and it goes on and on and on. I know my *yes* when I feel it. I don't have to convince myself, it is already there. I don't have to search it out or seek it, it makes itself known to me. I guess I just wish that I felt my *yes* more often. I guess as a slut I'm getting pretty frustrated at how often my body says *no*. I want my body to say *yes* so I try to convert the *no* into a *yes*, I try to convince myself. But I think all that does is drive my *yes* further underground.

My *yes* comes out in freedom and in safety, my *yes* comes out when I am in a relationship of profound trust with myself. So I am cultivating a practice of *no*, I am learning how it tastes on my tongue, how it feels in my fingers as I write out the text, how it feels to say *no* to someone I like, to someone I love, how it feels to say *no* when I want to want it but I don't. I am learning different ways to say no, different ways to be honest and careful and kind, different ways to maintain my boundaries and protect myself.

Sluts can say no. This is a magic spell I never knew. I was always working so hard not to be ashamed of my *yes,* to fight against a culture that hates me for dropping to my knees in an alleyway, for saying *yes yes yes* to being fucked, to guzzling cum, to getting punched, to fucking in the dirt, to fucking strangers and friends. The celebration of my *yes* is hard earned and I love being a slut. I refuse to hate myself or be ashamed of my slut magic, of my profound desire, of my powerful *yes*. But that *yes* needs to come from my body, my heart, my pussy. That *yes* needs to be deeply felt and genuine. It needs to be brazen and undeniable, wide and deep and expansive like the ocean. Otherwise it is a *no*. And sluts can say no. *No* is slut magic. *No* is the power of respecting my true desires, whatever they are, of protecting my energy and maintaining my energy, of fucking on my terms, terms dictated by my miraculous living body.

Fucking Magic

I am a slut returning to my body like a witch returning to magic. I am remembering the thing that I've always known, the incredible power of *no*.

Baby's First Play Party

I'M A LITTLE baby when it comes to being a sub. I really thought I was vanilla. After years of soul searching and confusion about my sexuality I came to the conclusion that I really was vanilla after all. But then I fell in love with someone kinky, and developed a safe and supportive relationship in which to explore my desires. I let myself fantasize and try things and follow my feelings toward new fantasies and new things I wanted to try.

Much to my surprise I discovered that I'm a bottom, a submissive, and a masochist. And not just that, I'm like a super service oriented, obedient, pain slut, champion of bottoms, submissive. In fact my partner called me the patron saint of bottoms. Who knew. I mean, apparently everyone kind of knew. Like with many things about myself, I was the last to know. Sometimes it takes me a really long time for me to see what's right in front of me. I tattooed *Fuck Me Up* in a heart on the side of my butt and I swore it was just about wanting the universe to fuck me up. I was like *Who me? A bottom? No way.*

I'm discovering this aspect of my sexuality and it goes deep. It's profound and pure and visceral. It's powerful and sacred and good. It's embodied. It brings me back to my body. When I am subbing out my body is in charge and as a traumatized person that is a powerful, beautiful thing. I want to dive into my submissiveness and get to know myself in that surrender. I want to go deeper still. I want to find new Doms to explore with, so that I can live my best slut life, submissive style. I'm still just a baby when it comes to all of this and I have no experience in the kink scene. So, I asked my metamour friend who has experience in the kink scene if they'd be into taking me out to a play party. They agreed.

I went to their place and they made me a salad. We hung out in their bedroom which used to be my bedroom before I moved out and they moved in there, and they let me try on their clothing so that I could be dressed to match the aesthetic of a play party. We laughed and talked and compared notes on being bottoms. They put on a tight black dress with an oversized t-shirt over top. I decided on a mesh red crop top with a harness overtop, my black underwear, and some random boots we found so that I didn't have to wear converse with no pants.

At the event there was an introduction workshop that went over the basics of bdsm, explained the rules of the dungeon, and emphasized the importance of consent. It was amazing to realize that these parties are places where I can explore with new partners, in public, with dungeon monitors listening for safe words and enforcing them. One of the hard things about wanting to find another Dom is not trusting people I don't know well to explore kink with me. The dungeon monitor announced to the room that the monitors go around listening for the word *red* and that if they hear it and what's happening doesn't immediately stop, they will stop it. This made me feel safe in a way I rarely feel safe in sexual contexts with strangers. It opens up a world of possibility and opportunity.

Then the party began and people mingled. Around the room people were being flogged and suspended and walked around on leashes. I watched with eager, curious eyes. I felt my submissive desires light up as I watched a sub surrender under a flogger. I scanned the room for potential Doms who might want to fuck me up, feeling the build up of electric energy. This was the first time I felt the fullness of my submissive desire outside of the context of my D/s relationship. This was the first time I could really feel myself as a sub, all on my own, independent of any particular Dom.

There was one guy I had noticed when I came in, who I thought was cute. He approached me and we talked. He was new to play parties too but had been exploring kink in his relationships for a while. He was

Baby's First Play Party

a Dom. I talked to him about being a sub, and a masochist, and about what kinds of pain I like and what kinds of pain I don't like. The safety of knowing that my boundaries would be enforced made me feel safe expressing them. I told him about what I like about being a sub, why I like it. I told him about my partner, and polyamory, and being collared. He asked me *If you're collared does that mean you can't play with other people?* And I said *No, my Dom wants me to go out and get fucked up as much as I like.*

After talking for a bit we split ways and wandered around the party some more. Later he approached me again and asked me if I wanted to play. We both were curious about flogging, neither of us had done that before. I told him that if he wanted to flog me he had to go talk to one of the people demoing flogging and ask for instruction. He did and I stood back and watched him ask questions, clearly integrating and thinking about what I had told him about the types of pain I like and don't like.

Once I was satisfied I went over and I leaned against a stand that was there, offering my ass up to him. He ran the flogger up and down my body, teasing me, before he started hitting me with it. At first the pain was very light and I leaned toward him, wanting more. He checked in and asked how it was. *You want harder?* He asked me. *Harder* I said. He started flogging me again, rhythmically hitting me and building momentum. I started to grip the stand I was leaning against. I started to breathe heavy. I started to cry out.

The pain started to build and the moments between impacts began to blur together with the impacts, until it was one solid experience of pain. Again and again the flogger came down on me and I could feel the electric energy in my pussy and the pleasure of surrender and the joy of being a slut and giving myself to this stranger in a room full of people. I could feel his pleasure too, the way his energy came through the flogger and into my body, the way he took pleasure in my pain. And then I was thinking nothing, I felt only sensation, the pure crystalized experience of my body in full feeling in real time.

Afterwards I stumbled over to one of the rooms and he followed me and we laid on the bed together. I told him what it was like for me and he told me what it was like for him. We admired the bruises blooming around my *Fuck Me Up* tattoo and lightly touched my sensitive skin. We talked about kink, and sadism and masochism, and what brought us here and why we liked it. We laughed and talked and it was nice.

Later I went and found my phone and excitedly texted my partner *Babe I'm at the play party and I just got flogged by a Dom and it was hot and nice and I liked it and I told him all about you and how I'm collared by you.* And my partner, my Dom, wrote back *Nice!* We texted about how hot it is for me to be collared and also free to live my best slutty sub life. I ran my hands over my bruises feeling hot, and happy, and safe, and free.

Finding My Way Back

THE MESSAGE THAT keeps coming through is to return to my body, to find the body I had to abandon. The message I'm receiving is the hardest lesson, the thing I still don't know how to do. It isn't just me personally. It's the crushing weight of capitalism and colonialism and alienation from ourselves and each other and our bodies and our food and the land. It is also the saturation of violence, violence upon violence, mind numbing and body numbing violence. And yet I know I have to find a way back to myself, a way back inside. I know that my dissociative phone scrolling, my low key terror of the present moment, must be moved through, changed.

I am cultivating desire. I am spending time with desire, wondering about desire, coaxing it and encouraging it. Not desire in the empty insatiable capitalist sense, but desire in its true sense: to want, to move toward. Desire as principled, as reciprocal, as a meeting place. Desire as volition, as movement, as initiative, as finding what I need to snap out of it, to act. I have written a lot about desire. Desire for sex, desire for pleasure, desire for healing, desire for change. Desire for writing itself. My practice of trauma recovery was deeply enriched when I learned to centre desire, when I began to direct my healing through a practice of asking myself what I really want.

I want to not be afraid anymore. I want to remember who I am. I want back what was taken from me. I want back what was taken from us. I want to find a way back to my body because I believe this is the starting place, the place from which I act, the place from which I know, the place from which I am. I think a lot about masturbation as a spiritual practice but it isn't easy. Masturbation is a place where I am wounded. My pleasure for its own sake is terrifying. I couldn't put anything inside my own pussy for years, even a tampon or a cup, because it felt like rape. I needed the distraction of another person's agency, another person's desire, to make me look away from the horrors of trauma that are here in my body. I want to run slow circles on my clit, present and wanting myself, loving myself, affirming my goodness, not just chasing down that first orgasm so that it's easier to cum again, so that I don't have to think about it.

I want to feel safe in my body, trust my body, trust that I know what my body wants. I want to surrender my hyper-vigilance and trust that I can handle whatever happens in any space I enter, trust that I am wanted and welcomed, that there is nothing wrong with who I am. I want to do this work with others, affirming each other's goodness, loving each other, giving each other that explicit care and encouragement that we did not get when we were children.

I want to swim in lakes and pools and in the river. I want to take every opportunity to sing. I want to dance, shake the shame out of my body with my movement, move through the immobilization of the freeze response, dance it out of me, at punk shows or queer dance parties or in front of a lover who wants to see the beauty of my moving body. I want to make music, somehow I want to find a way to triumph over my shame about music. I want to believe that the emotion and energy inside of me is beautiful and powerful and rhythmic, that like my heart and my lungs, there is a music to it. I want a coven, a group of witches to practice magic with, to meet between the worlds and use our hands and hearts and minds to bring about the change we need. I want sex, sex that is heartfelt and good and pure and spiritual, sex where I can laugh and cry and cum and find my own volition, my own desire.

I want to get out of my head and back into my body, taste the coffee that I'm drinking, feel the keys give way beneath my fingers as I type, listen to the sounds they make. I want to be unafraid of my breath, drop my shoulders, bring myself back to myself again and again and again. I want to trust the process, the magic that's unfolding, the way I must

Finding My Way Back

return to these lessons, the way my body is always here with me, calling me back. I want to listen to the pain and I want to feel it and I want to grieve it. Not just intellectually, but here in my guts, in my shoulders, in my pussy, in my back, in my lungs, in my legs, in my body, in my heart. I want to lie on the ground by the train tracks, to feel the sun on my skin and the scratchy grass, to follow the pull of my desire, to find my volition, to be present, to act.

Sober House

D'REAMS ARE SLOW.
I'm waiting for the metro with my partner. It is January and we are bundled in our winter clothes. *I wish I could have a sober house* I say. *You can* they tell me, always one to encourage my commitment to possibility. *I can't do that!* I tell them, ready as always with all the reasons why what I want is impossible. *I don't know any sober people who are looking for a place. I've never started a house before. I don't even know where I'd begin.* My partner tells me *Make a six month plan. Move in July. Just start putting feelers out now, mentioning to people that you want to start a sober house.* It feels impossible, but the seed has been planted.

I make a facebook status saying I'm dreaming of starting a sober house. Almost immediately a friend in recovery gets in touch and says they are planning to move in a few months and we should talk. I reach out to another friend in recovery and ask her if she'd be interested. She says she's not sure if she's moving or not, but if she is, we can talk. One of these people has a cat, the other has a dog, so could we even all live together? We don't know but we are open to the possibility.

My one friend and I start looking at housing ads. We put up a post in a housing group saying we are looking for sober roommates. We meet a couple people but it's not a good fit. We keep talking and we keep looking. One day at a 12 step meeting a friend mentions that she is looking for a place and we jump on it. Would she be into living with us? She says she's open to talking about it, and so we talk about it, and we start looking for a place.

Sober House

I start a whatsapp group with the four of us, but the friend with the dog says she can't move in with us after all. So three of us start looking. We look at ads, we visit apartments, we talk about what we like and don't like, we try to picture ourselves living in these places. Our hearts are filled with hope and possibility, but we still haven't found the perfect place. We want a place with some outdoor space. We want a place that has a window in all the bedrooms (hard to find in Montréal). We look at three bedrooms and four bedrooms, even though there are only three of us we think it would be nice to find a fourth.

At my celebration for my six years of sobriety the friend who dropped out says she's been watching our whatsapp convos about finding a place and she wants to be a part of it again. She is shy and adorable and we welcome her back with open arms. I feel absolutely sure that I want to live with these people. Three friends who I trust and get along with, three sober addicts who are committed to their recovery and sobriety.

The first place the four of us look at together becomes our new home. It's a big beautiful apartment with three balconies and four bedrooms with windows and one without that we will use as an office. It needs a lot of repairs and cleaning but it's actually a dream. We decide we want to take it and we get it. We sign the lease and the sober house dream is officially becoming a reality. It's another month before moving day. We pack and we chat on whatsapp about how we want our new home to be.

It's July and I'm just waking up in my bedroom with newly painted white walls and purple sheets on my bed. The sunlight and street sounds are coming in through my big bedroom window. Outside my door I hear the coffee grinder and the laughter of my friends. I am excited to get out of bed and I scramble up and out the door. There are my friends, bleary eyed and drinking coffee, laughing and chatting and starting their days. I feel welcome and safe and at home.

I get some cereal from the communal pantry and pour myself a cup of coffee and join them at the table. Four queer sober addicts, four friends who have had a rough go of it in life, plus one perfect little dog and one perfect little cat, together creating a home. I ask my friends *Ughhhh am*

Fucking Magic

I going to get Fucking Magic done today? Can I do it? And they all answer with a resounding yes. We are laughing and listening to each other and encouraging each other. We are talking about getting another shelf for the pantry and getting the landlord to fix the sink and what we each need to do with our day. We are living our best lives and we are happy. We are here in our beautiful sober home and we are happy.

Dreams are slow and they are magic.

AnarchaMagic

READING ABOUT ANARCHISM and thinking about magic. Reading about anarchism and thinking about feminized skill sets and how important they are to the revolution (the slow process of revolution, the changes we are making right now). Dreaming about consensus. Dreaming about the work of creating space for all our voices, for nurturing a process. A process of change.

I can be so conflict avoidant, but what if I reframed this as consensus avoidant? What if I reframed this as revolution avoidant? What if I realized that downplaying my own needs to avoid the discomfort of the consensus process is counter-revolutionary? What if I moved into that process, blessed it, stayed with it? What if I could hold that this process is to bring us closer, to make us stronger, that it is so different from the crushing abusive power I knew in my past?

I want to go to the train tracks because I feel de-realized. My brain has moved back further behind my eyes. I am looking at things but I can't really see them. I don't know how to arrive in this moment. I can't drop into this timeline, I feel outside my own life. I want to go to the train tracks where the plants are wild with their rebellion, where the air pulses with the magic of refusal. But there are workers changing the advertisement on the billboard and there's the hired hand of the cops, a private corporation making sure no one goes onto the tracks. The tracks are where the magic is, but the magic is here too.

I need to write but I don't. I know that writing is like breathing, writing is a willingness to face myself, to know myself, to be with myself. I am afraid of myself so I am afraid to write. It's getting too cold to swim in the river. I will miss the river magic so much in the colder months. It helps to remember that snow is water, ice is water. I could climb the mountain but I don't. I could lie down on the ground, press my nose into the wet cold earth. I could practice my French. I could read a book. I want to remember what it feels like to be daring. I want to remember what it feels like to care. I am carrying the weight of this broken heart. I am carrying the weight of a dream.

Because to dream is to want and to want is to care. To dream is to go all in, to declare a forbidden love for this beautiful dying world. To dream is to hold in our hearts space big enough to desire something more, despite the crushing weight of heartbreak. We are told not to use our magic. We are told that our magic isn't real. We are made exhausted by all the useless meaningless work. We are made exhausted by the grief and the shock and the terror. The way there is no way to put it down, no way to feel our way through it.

We want to collapse. We don't know why we are so tired, why we feel so numb. We scroll our phones for hours. Nothing makes any sense. I can't look you in the eye. I don't know what will happen. I don't know if I can trust you. I don't know if you're my comrade, if you could be. I want to be in this together, I don't want to worry that you'll make it about sex. I want to be alive. I want to look people in the eye. I want something else. I want to be awake for this.

What if the way we love and want and desire is the answer to all of this? What if the love and the desire could drive us through the numbness? What if it sustained a hope, a belief in the possibility of another world? What if we are driven by the impossibility of our love, and the necessity of it?

What if I love so much it breaks my heart? What if I love so much it makes me numb? What if I believe in us? More and more I believe in us. More and more I believe that we can, that we should, that we have to. More and more I am opening to something that I keep closed down. The answer is in my fingertips. The answer is in the process. The answer is in the hope that we can be together, that we can change this.

AnarchaMagic

I am practicing anarchamagic every time I stay with the process, every time I insist that the messy, hard, beautiful process is the answer, the work, the new world.

First Love

Y‍ou take my psoriasis covered foot in your hand, bring it to your lips. I cover my eyes because I almost can't bear the sight. I squirm from the intimacy, the vulnerability, letting you love me. When I told you how terrified I was about the psoriasis now taking over my body, that's what you said: *let me love you.* A year and half of your lips on my skin, your hand reaching for mine, your text messages on my phone, our long conversations as we walk the streets of Montréal, and still I am surprised by the miracle of love. I am surprised by its depth, its softness, its expansiveness.

You show me that love is never cruel. Love is patient and generous. Love is gentle and fierce. You show me again and again that I don't have to earn it, that you love me for the person I am. I grow and I change and you love me. You are growing and changing and I love you. I never knew that love could be both so simple and so profound. That it could both excite me and keep me safe. I have never known the depths of intimacy that unfolds over time, and it scares me, it keeps scaring me, but you stay with me through that fear and you love me.

When we were getting to know each other you asked me about my first love. I told you about the girl I loved all through my childhood. I told you about the boyfriend who put me through a wall. But in many ways you are my first love, the first safe reciprocal love of my life, the first time I've been known and loved in that knowledge, the first time my heart has been held with generosity and care.

First Love

I can't even write the way I love you. Maybe I will grow into the words. Maybe the surprise of love will someday relax into familiarity, something that I can speak because I finally have the words.

In the meantime, I am practicing noticing what it feels like. I am letting myself ease into the pleasure of safe, true love. Something that you tell me I deserve.

We Carried This Message

I DON'T KNOW WHO to ask to be my sponsor. I choose this woman because she always has brightly painted nails on her hands and feet. She is kind and she works a serious program. Once I say to her When I was an alcoholic... and she reminds me You are still an alcoholic. We read the book together and she encourages me to write in Goddess wherever the book says God, because that is what makes sense to me. When we say the third step prayer together she holds my hands across the picnic table. She says Goddess with me.

I am five months sober and about to go through a rape trial. I am exhausted and terrified and I don't know how I will handle what I will have to handle. I don't know how I will get up on the stand in front of a jury in the same room as him and tell everyone what he did to me. It doesn't feel real. I don't know how I will stay sober. I don't have many friends and I don't know who will support me through this. I go to a women's meeting and I stand up and say I have to go through a rape trial. I am only five months sober. I am terrified. I am looking for someone to come with me to the trial. This older woman I have never met before comes. She sits in the courtroom through my entire testimony, a strong and sober presence. I can't believe that she would do this for me, someone she doesn't even know. When I need to find a new sponsor I ask her and she becomes my second sponsor.

When I find myself looking for a sponsor a third time I pray to the moon to help me. I gaze at the fat white globe in the sky and say Please help me find a sponsor. At the next meeting I go to the speaker is young and pretty and cool. I am intimidated by her. She says in her share that she has just finished the steps and is looking to start sponsoring. I know that this is a sign.

Knowing little about her, I ask her to sponsor me. She says yes. At a meeting we attend together I hear her say under her breath God could and would if she were sought. *We meet every week in a coffee shop and we read the book out loud to each other.* She is the one who takes me all the way through the steps the first time.

I find myself without a sponsor again and this time I have sponsees so I need to find a new sponsor immediately. I find someone who agrees to temporarily sponsor me while I look for a new sponsor. She is moving out of town soon, so she can't work with me long term. She invites me to her home to work through some of the things I have been holding on to.

My fifth sponsor tells me Clementine, the level of shame you feel is not proportionate to the things you have done. You are carrying toxic shame. *She is the one who finally breaks through my shame and plants the seed that the secret contempt I feel toward myself results from my experience of childhood sexual abuse. She teaches me that shame is a survival strategy, by blaming myself for what happened I could feel some control over it. She shows me the beginning of a practice of self-forgiveness. She opens the way back to myself.*

When I find that I've been drifting from the program I reach out to a woman on facebook. I don't know her beyond seeing her around meetings. She meets me and I tell her what's going on. She agrees to be my sponsor. We work the steps in a different book. She encourages me to seek support from other fellowships. She tells me about her life and we laugh a lot together. She makes me holy basil tea in her apartment. She brings me clementines to my book launch with a card that reads Enjoy the fruits of your labour.

I join a new fellowship and find a sponsor there. She is the first person that I tell everything about my family to. She listens to me, openly and without judgement. She validates me. She points out patterns. Week after week she shows me a path toward healing what was done to me, all the while remaining vulnerable in her own pain. She shows me how to love myself as a whole person, inherently worthy and good.

After drifting from the program I decide to reach out and find a new sponsor. I choose her because she keeps posting It's hoe season *all over* facebook. I choose her because I'm at a place in my recovery where I want to reclaim my sexuality, I am ready to be all of who I am. I choose her because I am done carrying shame over my sexual desires. I want a sponsor who models both strong recovery and openmindedness about sexuality. She is all of that and more. She is hilarious and she doesn't take things too seriously, but she is serious about recovery and she knows the book. We meet in coffee shops and read the book to each other. I tell her about my desire to rediscover sluttiness in sobriety. She says Clementine you can do hoe shit before the meeting, and you can do hoe shit after the meeting, just make sure you get to the meeting.

My first sponsor in a new city takes me up the mountain to do my seventh step. I bring a small cauldron and mugwort and rose. We take scraps of paper with all the things I need to change and let go of written on them, we put them in the cauldron with the mugwort and rose. I say the seventh step prayer, and there with my sponsor and the trees all around us, we light it on fire. Despite the wind, it lights up and burns straight through. When it's time for my step nine, my sponsor insists that I need to learn to be good to myself. The amends that I most need to make is to myself. We go to the spa for my step nine. We sit in the hot water pool and in the steam room and in the sauna. We drink water and tea. She is showing me how to be kind to myself, how to return to my body, how to relax.

The Wholesome Collective

I HEAR THE COFFEE grinder in the kitchen and I feel a pull to get up and out of my room. In the kitchen the morning light is streaming in through the window, and there are my roommates in various states of morning grogginess. They are laughing and talking and trying to decide what to eat for breakfast and I join them. I take my place at the table.

We have lived in this house for three months. It's still a bit in shambles. We haven't set up the office. The landlord needs to do a ton of repairs that he keeps avoiding despite how often we remind him. There's still a lot to do and none of us have time to do it because we are busy with our lives. Despite all of this, this place is home, home in a way none of us have ever known.

At a radsob meeting one of my roomies says *I've always told myself that home is something I carry inside of me, it's not a place. And I think that's true, but I also always told myself that because I didn't have a place to call home and now I do.* Her words resonate with me deeply. These three humans, this cat, and this dog. These mornings drinking coffee and all the conversations in the kitchen, talking about dating, proof reading each other's text messages, talking about trauma and attachment styles, talking about our work, our families, our hopes and dreams and fears, supporting each other and caring for each other through good and bad times.

I think about how there aren't words to describe these relationships. I think about how 'roommates' doesn't cut it, and friends doesn't either. I think about queer addict survivor family. I think about the magic of making home for ourselves when home is something we never had. I think about creating the new world in the

Fucking Magic

shell of the old and this is the new world. Right here in our kitchen. In our laughter. In our healing. In the way that we love each other. We wanted to name our house but we didn't know what to name it. I come home one day and my roommate announces that in our network of friends a name has already attached itself to our home. *The Wholesome Collective* she says, *that's what everyone's calling us.* And we all laugh because it's perfect and it fits. We're wholesome as fuck and we decided to keep the name. *I already changed the name of the group chat* my other roommate says.

We have a weekly radsob meeting here where addicts in recovery gather in our living room, to talk about feelings and healing and hope and desire. We are changing the world by loving each other, by creating space for us to be together and find new ways of living, even with all the pain.

The Wholesome Collective extends out from the magic between the four of us into our larger communities, it has become a space where people gather, where we extend the feeling of love and safety and acceptance that we extend to each other.

It is magic, and it is safety, and it is home. And I breathe through my hypervigilance and trauma that insists I can never have home, never have safety. I breathe into the reality that I do, here and now.

Careful and Daring

SHE LIVES IN another city so we don't see each other very often, a few times a year when I visit Toronto or when she visits Montréal. We walk hand in hand and make out constantly, erupting in laughter and being our full femme selves. She is bisexual and she knows all about the not queer enough feels of being a bisexual femme. That's part of why I feel safe with her. It's also because she is kind and considerate and attentive. She is careful.

Queer femme4femme desire is a balance of being careful and being daring. We take our time. We laugh about how we both lean towards being bottoms and subs. We laugh at ourselves for saying we are switches. We pretend to be tops and argue about who is going to carry whose bag. *Let me get that. No, let me get that.* We catch up and we laugh and laugh and make out and it feels easy and safe and good.

She comes to stay in Montréal for a few months for work and I am so excited to see her. I take her to the river on a cold windy day and we sit on the ground and talk about what the months between this and our last date have been. We cover a lot of territory, talking about heartbreak and transformation and growth and change. I feel fiercely protective of her when she tells me about her ex and the way he treated her. I want only the best for her always.

A couple days later I'm getting ready for our date, making a gay feels playlist. She comes over and brings tofu and we walk to the fruitery to pick out some vegetables for dinner. *What kind of kale do you like?* she asks. *That one* I say, pointing to the dinosaur kale. *That's the kind of kale I like!* she exclaims. We make out in the aisles between the stacks of colourful fruits and vegetables. We choose our vegetables and she says *Look at us, who says bisexuals can't make decisions.*

Later in my room on my bed, gay feels playlist playing, we are kissing and telling each other how beautiful and hot we find each other. She tells me she's not going to get sucked into the femme vortex; she can express her feelings but act on them too. We are a tangle of limbs, our bodies driving into each other, an articulation of a desire that we can't speak, even with all our excessive declarations of attraction. The want is something else, something deeper. And as bisexual femmes who understand the language of desire in the context of fucking heterosexual men, we are keenly aware that this something else.

We are grinding on each other, pressing our bodies together, moving closer to this feeling that builds between us, chasing it down, gripping each other. Suddenly she says *Oh my god are we scissoring? It's not a myth! It's a real thing!* And we explode into laughter. We are being daring and careful, building tension and releasing it, building momentum and slowing down, creating space to laugh and breathe and notice and be present.

She is lying on her back, that beautiful grin on her face. She is smiling up at me as her breath moves through her body. I am kissing her, kissing her on her stomach, on her legs, listening to the sounds she makes and the way she moves. I ask her how she's feeling. I ask her if this is what she wants. She is squirming and laughing and telling me to keep going. Unnecessarily she says *No pressure though.* Daring and careful. There is a tiny star bead at the hem of her underwear and I put my mouth over it.

Her pleasure is like water and I want to submerge myself. My mouth is the shape of her desire; I shape myself to her, move towards her movements, listen to the changes in her breath. I lose myself in the motion, my body reciprocal to hers, my momentum the momentum of her pleasure. She cums in my mouth, covering her own mouth out of respect for my roommates. She is perfect in her pleasure, she is beautiful as she flies over that edge.

Last Year

I AM AFRAID TO write because I am afraid to write about you. I have taken my love for you and my grief over the loss of our friendship and I have wrapped that carefully in the anger I feel at the way you treated me, your self-righteous indignation, the way that you refuse to even have a conversation, the way you refuse to see how you hurt the people who love you. Then I have taken that bundle of anger and love and grief and buried it deep in my ribcage, somewhere not-quite my heart, somewhere where you can be forgotten, except for the occasional throb of pain, heavily diluted by well-practiced denial.

I loved you. I was *in* love with you. I told you that once and you acted like I didn't say it. I took the metro to your house, walked the laneway, climbed into your bed. Time and time again. I came home to you.

I wish there was a way to name what happened between us, what we were. I wish I knew how much of it was real for you (*I believe that it was real for you*). I wish you could remember what we shared. I wish you could have heard what I was saying, what I was trying to show you. The way I showed up and loved you, and never asked you for more than what you gave. The way I cherished you and always tried to be what you deserve.

I don't know how you loved me. I don't understand the way you reached for my hand, the way you held me in your arms in the darkness, the way you said you wanted me. I don't understand how you told me you felt safe with me, trusted me, would always be my friend, and then you turned on me just like that, attacking me in the places you knew would hurt me most.

Fucking Magic

I want to remember you in your kitchen, chopping onions in your pjs. I want to remember the dangerous electric safety I felt lying in your bed.

You never told me the truth and maybe you don't know the truth. You told me you wanted me to kiss you, and I didn't because I didn't want to kiss you until you felt absolutely safe. You told me about your strategies of avoidance, how you built a life by never looking straight at your terror, by sleeping your way through your pain. I didn't know how to help you, but I held you in my arms.

I always came to you. I met you where you were.

You smoked your cigarette. You looked away. You texted me to confess your attraction but reminded me that you're *bad at all that*. You asked me to be vulnerable and I was. You pulled me in, you pushed me away. You told me you didn't want to ruin our friendship, that you are bad at dating, that you loved me too much.

I told you I will always love you no matter what. I told you that I was scared too, that what we shared was sacred. I told you there was no rush, no time line, that we had our whole lives to figure it out.

You held my hand in your kitchen, you reached for my hand on the street. You told me you wanted to take me on a date. We listened to Prince in your car: *I'm not your lover, I'm not your friend, I am something that you'll never comprehend.*

Now we don't speak at all anymore. Now we aren't friends. Now I can't stop thinking about this time last year, wishing you were here.

You told me you were bad at this. I took the risk anyway. You were worth the risk.

The Distance Between Us

Maybe three months after our break up I am sitting in the bathtub reading a book I remember flipping through at your apartment. The water is too hot, like I always make it, like I made it the time we took a bath together. I am reading poetry, and it makes me think of so many things, and it reminds me of you. Maybe three months after our break up, casually and quietly, I admit to myself that I loved you.

You were a tangle of signals. All our conversations seemed to go in circles. I chased down the meaning, showed up with earnestness and sincerity. We kept missing each other. I remember the grocery store late at night, the way we played like children, laughing between the brightly coloured boxes of cereal, the way I pulled you into my arms and we made out right there in the aisle.

We always broke out into laughter, and not always easy laughter. It was more like nervous laughter, like we needed to break the momentum building between us, like we were afraid of arriving at the place we were going, so we needed to direct our attention somewhere else. We needed to laugh, like it was funny, like it was surprising, like the energy between us had nowhere else to go.

I remember walking through alleyways, you pointing out the garbage you loved, telling stories about birds or snails, following the scent of tree blossoms. Kissing you in a spotlight in the middle of a strange and empty lot. Kissing you in a collapsing snow bank. Kissing you in your bed, your blue eyes, wide pupils. The way we expanded into each other, loosened and relaxed, only to bristle and contract, again and again.

I remember feeling humiliated when you told me that I made a certain face when I wanted you to kiss me. You were teasing me. Maybe humiliation wasn't the right feeling to feel. But I didn't want to laugh about my desire. My desire for you was rushing water, it was a downpour, the way the clouds above us would just let loose their rain, and I was clamping it down, I was plugging it up. I felt unsure. I didn't know if you would meet me there.

You were always misunderstanding me and I was always misunderstanding you. For two writers we were really poor communicators. I wanted to tell you. I wanted to be able to relax into it. I wanted to love you. I wanted to give myself to you and I wanted to receive you. I wanted to be with you. And I was so tired by the constant confusion, so humiliated by the uncertainty. I didn't know how to meet you, how to let you find me.

I remember making out in the alleyway at the beginning of summer, the way the world disappeared completely. It was just you, there against a brick wall, just your hands on my body and my hands in your hair. I remember sitting on your porch at your new place, while you smoked a cigarette and I tried to thaw myself from another freeze. I tried to tell you what you meant to me, I tried to tell you that I wanted you. I didn't even know that I loved you. I didn't know how to admit it. I didn't feel safe.

I was afraid to love you. I was afraid of the vulnerability of my love. I was afraid of telling you, afraid of showing you. But it still spilled out of me and sometimes you saw it and sometimes you denied it was even there at all.

We kicked cardboard boxes and laughed at the top of our lungs. We were brazen and uninhibited in our love for the world, but we froze in our feelings for each other. The good was all mixed up with fear and confusion and I don't even know the reason why.

I stood in the rain outside your apartment, texting you that I was downstairs. By the time you let me in I was soaked through. We walked in the rain watching carefully for snails, not wanting to crush them under our feet. You pulled me close, our dripping wet bodies pressing into each other. Maybe the water will make it easier to be here. Maybe the water is what we needed. But it wasn't enough.

Letting the World Love Me

CONDOMS. EPSOM SALTS. *Lavender. Holy Basil. Pickling spice. Caraway seeds. Sea salt. Purple cabbage. Lemon. Ginger. Garlic. Onion. Turmeric. Oregano. Rosemary. Apple cider vinegar.*

Fall is fifteen minutes long in Montréal. The trees haven't yet lost all their leaves, the sidewalks are scattered with oranges and reds, I'm wearing my winter jacket already. But the cold is welcome. It wakes me up. It makes me remember who I was in the snow. A friend of mine told me how much they hate winter and they asked if I like it. I told them about the brilliant light, the way the world glitters, sinking my boots into two feet of snow. *Sounds like you love winter* she says. I guess I do. But right now it's fall, and it's cold, and I am remembering how to take care of myself.

Psoriasis has exploded all over my body. I haven't had it bad like this since I was a teenager. My skin is on fire, bright red and scaling white, multiplying, multiplying, multiplying. I wish it away. I grieve it. I stress about it. I accept it. I tell myself it will be gone soon. I tell myself *Last time it was bad like this it lasted years*. I take showers and rub coconut oil into my skin. I let my partner love me. I let them kiss my skin. I let them hold my psoriasis covered feet in their hands and kiss them. I take all my clothes off in front of my date for the first time and she kisses me and gasps *You're beautiful, your psoriasis is beautiful.* I try to let the world love me.

I listen to pop music and cry. I go to the steam room at the gym, I sit naked in the eucalyptus steam and I breathe. I feel self-conscious of my psoriasis skin but I breathe through it. I read. I am reading again and I'm devouring the words. I'm remembering what it's like to have my brain engaged, not tuned out in dissociative phone scrolling.

I'm thinking about people I loved who I don't talk to anymore. I'm thinking about the work of love, of trying to love each other, and why sometimes it doesn't work. I'm thinking about the grief in my heart that I barely speak. I know that at a certain point it is best to walk away, even though it's hard, and it is hard. I'm trying to let the world love me so that I can love.

I am thinking about humiliation, how afraid I am of humiliation, how I expect to be humiliated, how I avoid so many things in order to avoid humiliation. How I suspect the people I love are laughing at me, tricking me, trapping me. How I am so angry and desperate and exhausted in my constant preoccupation with avoiding humiliation. I avoid vulnerability. I avoid intimacy.

Child abuse is humiliating. Incest is humiliating. Desperate, abject terror. Helplessness. The way I wasn't allowed to fight. The way I wasn't allowed to run. The way I was made to submit, given an impossible choice, made to betray myself. Sexual abuse is humiliating.

I talk to my therapist about how I am still unconsciously reenacting the dynamic of my original trauma. I talk to my therapist about the life threatening terror that keeps electrifying my body, the way I see the threat everywhere, the threat of annihilation. The helpless abject terror of an abused child.

I'm reading *The Body Keeps the Score* and there's a study that shows that incest survivors have higher rates of autoimmune disorders. Psoriasis is an autoimmune disorder. Autoimmune disorders are an overreaction to threat, they are the immune system attacking the body. My hypervigilance exists at a cellular level, proliferation of skin cells, desperately trying to defend against an attack that isn't here. A phantom attack. An apparition of terror.

Fucking Magic

My therapist says *Safe isn't even a word we should use, because you have no understanding of what safety means. You have no point of reference.* She tells me to breathe. She asks me to notice what is happening in my body.

I text my date and tell her I'm feeling stressed out. She says she wants to be a kitchen witch for me. She says we should take a bath and watch a movie. I text my partner about my therapy. They ask me how it was. They listen to me. My roommate texts me a selfie, *love u.* I come home to popcorn and long conversations and tea. I take my time. I take care of myself. I remember to breathe.

I'm trying to let the world love me.

Time Travel to the Present

MOMENTS OF VISCERAL recognition: my hypervigilance is a lie. I feel the alarm bells go off, I feel myself being hijacked. A proliferation of evidence, a careful assessment of danger. I feel my body respond. I notice it happening now. I see myself being taken, the past superimposed over the present. Danger everywhere I look.

But what if I am safe? What if the people I trust are trust worthy? What if the people I love love me very much? What if I am welcome, wanted, considered? What if small conflicts or misunderstandings are not evidence of massive unspeakable betrayal? What if I am safe? What if this beautiful, beautiful life that I worked so hard to build, is real, real, *real*?

My brain is constantly managing potential threats. Each action, each refusal to act, the result of a preoccupation, a deep, intrinsic fear that I will be humiliated, abandoned, rejected, betrayed. It is exhausting. It is unsustainable. And, most importantly, it is unnecessary. The danger has passed. I got myself out of there. Yet I continue to act as if my most beloved and trusted people will treat me the way that the people who abused me treated me.

I misrecognize the people that I love. I see in them not their own beautiful, complex selves, not all the ways they show me that they love me, but the abject terror of my past, the life threatening danger of being unloved and unprotected. Horror, humiliation, shame, danger.

I breathe, I notice my breath. That slow, long outbreath. I understand that I can't think my way out of the delusions of hypervigilance. I realize that my frontal lobe becomes disengaged, that my thoughts and feelings

Fucking Magic

are motivated by a far more primal part of my brain. I need to learn how to feel safe in my body. I need to time travel to the present moment, the most difficult act of time travel I have ever tried.

There are moments of visceral recognition. I arrive in this body, this year, this life. I arrive in the arms of my partner, safe and loved. I arrive in my competence, my resilience, my tenacity. I arrive in a community of people who love me, who listen to me, who want me around. I am here now.

The work is to arrive, the work is to remember, not the past, but the present. The work is to come back to my body and the reality of safety, again and again and again. Until finally I can stay here, until finally my shoulders drop, my breath fills my belly, I can feel the touch of the people who love me, I let them love me.

My writing is a magic spell. I write myself the same letter over and over and over. I have been trying to find a way to tell myself this truth for many years now. I have found different ways to say it and I have repeated it many times. I keep writing it, manifesting it, arriving here in time.

I have moments of visceral recognition: my hypervigilance is a lie.

Hurt

I WONDER IF IT will stop hurting, if I will ever relinquish my secret wish for recognition, acknowledgement, care, from the people called blood family, the people who share my ancestors, who share the memories of my first fifteen years. I wonder if I will always be hijacked, accidentally seeing photos on facebook from the one family member I haven't cut off, seeing happy family gatherings, seeing so much repair, like glue poured into a fresh open bleeding wound: *see look it's fixed.*

I am reframed by these photos. I see myself as a ghost, an apparition, I see myself for where I am not. I am not there with them. I am not part of the happy smiling family. I am the one marked with words like *incest, alcoholism, abuse.* My presence makes manifest the unspeakable things, but that is dealt with quickly by placing it onto me: my dysfunction, my mental illness, my difficult stubborn nature. I'm the crazy drunk, the one who goes away in the ambulance to the psych ward. That's the problem. Not my grandfather's strong arms holding my squirming body, not his tongue in my mouth, not any of the other unspeakable things.

I remember my mother telling me about my aunt, her sister. She was so traumatized from the violence she experienced and she spent many years in therapy. *I don't think it did her any good* my mother said, *More than anything I think it made her define herself through what happened to her.* I have always worried that my desperate attempts to heal and feel better represent a practice of defining myself through what happened to me. Incest survivor. My mother has never gone to therapy.

I wonder if it will stop hurting, if I will reach something like resignation or acceptance. If I will be free. I'm sick of feeling it, sick of writing about it, sick of wanting an acknowledgement, an apology, an extension of care and concern that I know they are not capable of. I am sick of the truth in my body, the only place it was allowed to live, the truth of incest running through my dreams, making me get up and run in my sleep. I am tired of trauma.

I don't know how to grieve it, how to mourn it, how to finally close the book and move on. I don't know how to accept that I will never get that love I have spent my life wanting. I need to find love from somewhere else. And I have it in abundance, I have people who love me. But I feel so alienated from them by this experience. When they ask me how I am I don't know what to tell them. There are some terrors I must reserve for my therapist, and I know this, but it makes me feel very alone.

Maybe I will write many books about incest. Maybe I will say the same thing one hundred million times. Maybe I will desperately search for a way to let the pain out of my body, so that it finally stops pulling me down, making me sick. Maybe in all this telling I will somehow find a witness.

Maybe someone else knows. Maybe someone else cares. Maybe someone else out there is grieving and raging with me.

The New World Now

Scrolling facebook and instagram in a dissociative haze. Being bombarded with one horror story after another. Sometimes I cry. Sometimes I feel nothing. This overwhelming sense of dread and helplessness exists in my body. I see my friends making posts which declare "I better see you posting about this!" and I don't want to post about it. Not because it isn't important, not because I don't care, but because it doesn't feel helpful or meaningful or sincere. I want something more than a proliferation of posts performing shock and outrage, commanding that others do the same. It's not that the shock and rage aren't real, but they become performances when they are commanded, and they become performances because they don't even come close to the depths of what we really feel.

I don't think shame or fear are good motivators. I think they corrupt action. I know from studying (and living) trauma that hypervigilance literally puts the frontal lobe of the brain offline. Living from a fear and shame based place, a place of trauma and terror, actually makes creativity and curiosity extremely difficult if not impossible. What we need now is creativity and curiosity. We need the ability to try new things, to make new connections. We need our imaginations to be active and working so that we can dream alternatives to the way things are. I am not interested in proving myself as a person with 'good politics' anymore, saying the right things on facebook, silently watching my community tear each other down for small infractions. I'm exhausted by the repetition of the performance, the way differences of opinions or strategies can result in being cast out, the way we work so hard at purity, casting suspicious glances at each other, instead of pooling our energy, instead of supporting each other. I can't prove my 'goodness' or my 'rightness'. I am a human animal deeply in love with the world, whose life and freedom are tied to yours. I need to struggle from a place of sincerity and a place of love. I can't act from shame or fear.

I'm interested in prefigurative politics. Or, to put it another way, the how is as important to me as the why or the what. I don't believe we can create freedom by treating each other as disposable. I don't believe we can create freedom by hypervigilantly monitoring our own and each other's language and choices, our social media presences are a carefully curated performance of 'good politics'. I don't believe we can create freedom by promoting fear and shame or by insisting that everyone must respond to devastating violence in particular, specific ways. I believe that the way we treat each other is the heart of our movements for change. We will create the new world in the way we treat each other in this moment. This doesn't mean we have to like each other or that we have to agree. This doesn't mean we can't be angry. This doesn't mean we have to trust each other. This doesn't mean we can never be mean or fed up or done. But it does mean that we will change more by creating for each other what these violent systems deny us, the things we need for our humanity, and also the things we need to change the world.

We can create communities where we take care of each other. That doesn't mean that I personally have to take care of someone who personally fucked me over. But it does mean that there needs to be networks of care that are inclusive of people who have caused harm, people we disagree with, people with different strategies. It means that we need to, as fundamental political work, find ways of navigating conflict, of encouraging disagreement and different strategies, of moving toward sincerity instead of performance. We can create communities where making sure that each other is fed, loved, housed, listened to, healed, held takes precedence. We can create communities of trust that ask people to step into being trust worthy. We can cultivate humility and curiosity and leave behind the stifling paranoid feeling of self-righteous rigid ideology.

We can acknowledge the physiological reality of stress and trauma, the way these things make us sick. And that it is okay, in fact it is necessary, that we take care of our own and each other's wellbeing as we struggle against these violent systems.

We have bodies! And the implicit threat that we could lose our community (which can feel like a threat of death because we are social creatures who need each other – especially if our political communities are the only communities where we feel even partially safe) if we don't agree, perform, do as we are told, floods us with cortisol and adrenaline. It prepares us for survival: fight, flight, freeze, or fawn (often we choose fawn, apologizing immediately and profusely, even if we feel the response to our action was disproportionate or unjustified, even if we genuinely don't agree). This fear and hypervigilance reduces our ability to be creative or flexible, to imagine other possibilities. We won't change things if we aren't allowed to trust our own bodies, if we aren't nourished by communities who want us to feel needed and safe.

I can feel a shift happening. The existence of massive stress and rigid ideology in the communities we call home has been acknowledged in hushed voices for a long time. And there are lots of people writing about it now, talking about it openly, and seeking change. I want to move with this shift, toward communities that are profoundly dedicated to change, grounded in the present moment, communities that are flexible, curious, responsive, and open to different strategies. Communities we can depend on, communities where we keep each other safe.

How I Learned to Relax and Love Eating Pussy

I WAS ALWAYS SUPER afraid of eating pussy. Mostly because I could feel next to nothing when people went down on me, so I didn't understand the act or what was pleasurable about it. Also because I saw it as the definitive queer sex act, the thing that would make or break my queerness. Over the years, despite being out as queer since 14, I didn't eat a lot of pussy. And therefore I was always worried that when I did, it would be obvious that I didn't know what I was doing and my queer card would be instantly revoked. I read about eating pussy and that only stressed me out more. The sets of instructions felt mechanical and I also couldn't imagine what they were describing being pleasurable if done to me.

I think for a lot of bisexual people, if we experience queer sex as stressful or hard or scary, we worry about the legitimacy of our queerness. And stressing about queerness and worrying about it doesn't feel relaxing and doesn't feel hot. I think for a lot of bisexual people, the fact that sex deemed 'straight' can feel easier, becomes a secret shame that maybe we're not really as queer as we thought. I don't think we factor in how fucking traumatic queerphobia, biphobia, and compulsory heterosexuality are. And trauma can make sex hard. It doesn't mean that we don't really desire queer sex, and it doesn't mean that we won't love it. It means we need to learn how to cultivate safety, how to create sexual environments and relationships where we feel safe exploring our queer desires. We need to create queer cultures where there are no queer cards to be revoked, where there is no subtle rampant biphobia, where the genders of your various lovers (past and present) have no bearing on the reality of your desire here and now. All sex is brand new. All sex is a learning experience, a process of communication and discovery.

It goes without saying that eating pussy is not the definitive queer sex act. I'm not even sure where I got that idea from but it's floating around in representations of desire between people with pussies. And it should go without saying, but I'll say it anyway, that queer sex happens between people of all bodies and genders, that sucking cock is just as queer as eating pussy (regardless of your gender), and so many infinite other possibilities are legitimately queer too. And bodies look a lot of different ways, various body parts belong to people of various genders, and also people like to call them different things. Still, I want to talk about learning to relax and love eating pussy, because it's an important part of my story of overcoming shame and fear related to my queerness.

Here's what I'm learning: I'm confident as fuck in my cock sucking skills after years and years of practice and sucking cock is a transferable skill. There is no magic secret difference between various bodies. Pussies are not inherently more difficult or mysterious. Having eaten a ton of pussy won't make you any better at eating this particular pussy if you aren't paying attention to this particular person (same goes with sucking cock or any sex act). It's all about being a communicative and receptive partner. Talking with each other about what you're both into. Paying attention to nonverbal communication like sounds and body language. Experimenting, seeing what your lover responds to. It's actually as simple as that. Realizing this was a revelation to me. It was so freeing. Maybe it seems obvious, it should be obvious. But I think the way we attach queer legitimacy to particular sex acts makes them feel loaded and stressful.

I learned to relax and love eating pussy in a relationship where I felt safe, where my queerness was not being scrutinized, where there was an environment of curiosity and play, where there was consistent good communication, and trust. I learned to trust that my queer desire is and always has been real, that in fact bisexuality is legitimately queer. I learned

Fucking Magic

to trust that these longings, these desires, these attractions, these crushes, these relationships, are real. This sex is real. It's real whether I'm eating pussy or not. It's real if we don't even take off all our clothes. It's real if we don't cum. It's real if we just take a bath together or smack each other around. It's real if we just want to make out and walk around holding hands. And it's real when there's pussy pressed into my face and I can barely breathe and I don't care about breathing, and my love for that, the pleasure and satisfaction of that, is real.

You Are Enough

*I*WANT TO TRUST people. *Breathe. Feel the flow of air on the exhale. Breathe.* I want to feel safe and trust in the best intentions of those I hold closest to my heart. *Five green things. Five blue things. Five purple things.* I want to be vulnerable, playful, curious. I want to take safe risks. It's 2018.

Facilitating my Trauma Informed Polyamory workshop for a room packed with 25 people I have a moment of recognition. I'm not anxious. In this moment, right now, I'm up in front of a room full of people, facilitating a workshop, and I'm doing a good job. I feel connected to myself and to the participants and to the moment. I'm not dissociating. I'm not freaking out. I'm here.

Reading about trauma I keep coming up against the term *learned helplessness*. I panic when I talk to my partner about the possibility of putting up shelves in my room. I will organize my whole life around the lack of these imaginary shelves: I don't need them! But to admit that shelves would make my life easier, that I don't know how to install shelves, that the many steps involved seem impossible, it sends me into a panic.

My partner is so good and loving, always gently pushing me to increase my capacity. To trust that I am capable, that I can try, that I can learn, that I can ask for help. I can self-publish a book and launch it in six cities (and break out in psoriasis all over my body from the stress) but I can't put up shelves. *Learned helplessness.*

I want to trust myself. I want to stop being so hard on myself.

After my NYC book launch I feel stressed that there was a small turn out. My partner tells me I should be proud that I just had a book launch in NYC. I tell them I don't know what that means. They google the word 'proud' and tell me *It's a deep sense of satisfaction and happiness from something you have achieved, or something someone close to you has achieved.* They tell me *I feel a deep sense of satisfaction and happiness because you are someone close to me and you just did a really cool thing.* I try to take that in. I really do. I tell them *It just doesn't feel like enough. Nothing ever feels like enough.* They tell me *It's enough. You are enough. Even if you never wrote another word it would be enough.*

What would it mean to finally exhale, to breathe into this beautiful life I have built for myself? What would it mean to feel loved? *The question is no longer what would it mean to be loved, because I am loved.* What would it mean to feel it? What would it mean to trust my partner, my friends, my date, the people who say such kind and loving things about me? What would it mean to breathe and to feel it? *You are enough.*

What would it feel like to be proud of myself? To say wow I accomplished my goal, I published that book, I launched it in six fucking cities? And even more than that, I take all my suffering, all my pain, and I use it to do good in the world? What would it feel like to really be proud of myself for that?

After my book launch in Ottawa I reflect on the life I've lived, the passage of time captured in my book *You Can't Own the Fucking Stars*, the first five years of my recovery. The time before my recovery began. The years and years of drinking. The unrelenting violence and crushing pain. I lived that and I am here writing this. I lived that and I am here making this magic.

Breathe. Exhale. You are enough.

Coven

LAUGHTER AND UNFOLDING trust. The practice of magic. Magic as a careful, intuitive process. Slow and receptive. Listening to each other. Speaking in turns. Letting what wants to rise, rise. This is a coven.

It is here that I mourn my grandmother. It is here that I say her name and I talk about what her death means to me. It is here that we laugh and talk about her life, what she was like. I say *She was kind of like a woman about town*. Everyone laughs. I am honest and I hold her complexity and her joy and her pain, and these new friends hold it with me.

I say *She was a lot of things but she wasn't abusive. Going to her place in the summer was a respite*. I need that to be witnessed.

I am quick to give the space back after I have said what I needed to say, but they return it to me. They ask about her. They ask me to say her name again. To say more about her life.

Her picture on our make shift altar. Tears in my eyes.

We are honouring ancestors, telling stories, tracing lineages. But also, we are becoming ancestors, finding our place by creating new stories. Transmutation.

We are here to feel the pain and to heal it. We are here to be present to that which has so long been repressed. We are making conscious that which was unthinkable. We are finding new ways.

There is fire and smoke. There is deep earth and darkness. There are cups of tea and water. There is breath.

We sing and the song is like a thaw. I can feel my vagus nerve. I can feel my ancestors smiling from the stories we are telling. I can feel my body doing something other than protecting itself. I can feel myself loosening. This is magic.

Magic is a process, it is emergent. It comes from all of us together. It happens intentionally and also through experimentation. It is a willingness and a curiosity to see what we can do together. What we can be together.

I am finally learning what becomes possible when we are safe enough, welcomed enough, when we intentionally create spaces of care, when we carefully create spaces of intention.

As a lonely witch, a practitioner of trauma magic, who survived without safe love and communal nourishment, communal magic is more powerful and healing than I could have imagined. It's what I've needed for so long.

Living Universe

I ALIGN MYSELF WITH you and I align myself with my integrity. Free me from fear based thinking and help me to live in faith. Help me to act with kindness, care, courage, and dignity. Help me to treat myself, others, and the world in a way which honours our sacredness. Help me to remember the magic all around me. Help me to live in honesty, clarity, and truth. Help me to be grateful for the abundance in my life, to remember that I am safe and protected, and to trust in goodness and love. Help me to be present to the current moment, to live inside my body, and remain connected to what is real today. All throughout this day, whenever I face indecision or begin to get stuck in unhelpful patterns, please provide me with an intuitive thought, inspiration, or a decision. Make it obvious how I can act from my healed, adult self, awake to magic and possibility, and grant me whatever it is that I need to act in this way. Please help me in my healing and growth, so that I may be happier and more free, and so that I may better do the work that I am here to do. May my actions be healing for myself and for the world. So be it.

Capable

*I*AM BECOMING ACCUSTOMED to my malfunctioning fire alarm. I am becoming comfortable with it. Instead of jumping out the window every time I hear the blaring wail, I take a second to remember that my fire alarm malfunctions. I stop for a second to see if I can actually smell smoke.

I am becoming more comfortable breathing into the present moment and trusting that the danger I am detecting is safely in the past. There is no trick to this. There was no earth shattering revelation that I always hoped for and wanted. Instead it is a process, a practice. It's something I show up to again and again. It's an icy hill I have to slip and slide down many times but I finally am finding my footing. A steady way to trust my step.

Magic is a process of remembering, of coming back to myself. Writing is a magic spell, a repetition, a time capsule, recording and witnessing and making real, manifesting. I am becoming more comfortable with the parts of myself that aren't living in a state of perpetual panic. I am becoming more familiar with the parts of myself that feel steady, capable, safe.

I say *I know there's this part of me that is desperately crazy, trapped in a state of perpetual learned helplessness. But I know there are other parts of me too. I know that I am powerful and incredibly resourceful. I know that I have shown up for myself, again and again, through everything. I know that I created this beautiful life, with my own hands, through my own hard work, despite everything that happened to me. I know that I am capable and*

Capable

powerful. I know that I can practice magic, that I am practicing magic right now.

I am spending more and more time connecting with this capable part of me, acting from that place. I am becoming more and more able to meet the distressed, terrified child in me with the steady love and competence of the adult I have become. I am growing into this. I am identifying with it and multiplying it. I am expanding it and deepening it. I am drinking it the way I suck the air into my lungs.

I am capable and powerful and I am growing still. More, as always, will be revealed.

I Want Him Dead

I USED TO THINK about killing him. I was a child so some of my ideas were childish. I thought about soaking his dentures in some kind of poison. Maybe the poison would make its way into his bloodstream and maybe he would die. Maybe then I would be free and I would not have to live with this terror that doesn't have words, that takes meaning and makes it meaningless.

I can't write the word: *helpless.* Terror: middle of the night. Nothing happened, not really. Nothing really happened. He never lifted up my nightgown, but I lived with the knowledge that he wanted to. That he would, if the moment were right.

He drank the milk from the container leaving it dirty with his dirty mouth. Bits of meat in his dentures whether they were in the glass or in his mouth. He was strong, held my body squirming. His stubble was scratchy and slick with grease. Nothing but his tiny underwear and his body everywhere.

Gasoline, gasoline, sleep. Yellow curtain. Dead fox, stuffed up, taxidermied. Wood stove, burn. Burned fish, bones.

I want to take my body and smash it against the rocks. I am aware that I'm a wildflower, a weed. I'm aware that there is something inside me, alive, alive, so alive. I am aware that he wants it. I am aware that I'm a child.

Isn't it weird that right now I am a child. Childhood is such a specific time in a person's life and me, right now, I am a child.

I am aware that he is my grandfather. Tongue, spit, slippery slobbery. *Don't be rude, don't be disrespectful.* Terror: there aren't words for it. Slip off the side of the bed and sleep on the floor instead. I think somehow that my father wants to fuck me.

Sex is a chaos storm. It's violence upon violence. Nothing happened but everything could have, everything was right there on the edge. And then: yellow bathing suit still wet from the lake, bathroom door left unlocked. And then: submission because by now I know I have to be good. And then: *Give us a kiss.*

Shatter, shatter, time melts into the blur of a moment that goes on forever. Everything that can't be true is true. Those dentures, that dirty mouth. This time not just the surface, it penetrates in. Tongue in my mouth. All the way in to the back of my throat. Smother, smother. Choke on the fullness of his desire. Whatever voice I have is full of him. Silence. Squirm. Arms pinned down and terror.

I am twelve years old and my grandfather is making out with me.

I can't write the word: *helpless.* What is sexual assault? *Come back here, I won't do that again.* Front lawn. Middle of the day. Under a blanket. Hiding. Can't go inside. Can't sleep in my bed. Can't say anything.

I want to put my body in the water. Body, what body? I want to live on the ceiling and never come back. I want to cut myself open. What's in there? What's living in there? What's burning alive? What survived? What died?

I want to be rescued. I want to be taken away from here. I want to take a rock and smash his skull with it. I want to feel his body collapse. I want him dead. No more terror. No more fear for my cousins and my sister. No more terror. No more unspeakable unspeakable. No more body torn to pieces by his invading hands. No more. No more. No more. I want him dead.

Incest incest incest incest incest incest incest incest. Everything is bleeding into everything else. There are no doors, only curtains. There is nothing to stop the invasion. There is no distinction. Nothing to stop family member from fucking family member, adult from fucking child. There is no safety. There is no way to stop it. My parents will not protect me. No one will protect me. No one will make him stop. I can't make him stop.

I can't write the word: *helpless*. I can't tell you what it was.

Calling

IT'S DECEMBER. I go to the river to cry. I go to the river to grieve. I go to the river to be a tiny baby, to beg the universe for something different, a different life, one with less pain. I go to the river to look for answers. *Why why why.* The water is black and it sparkles with light. The water is alive and always on the move. The river knows me and the river listens to my pain.

I lay my body on the trunk of a tree that stretches out over the water. No one is around because it is winter. And so I say my prayers right out loud. Not formal prayers. Not formulations of what I think I should say. I go to the water like I would go to my mother if I had a mother I could go to. I go to the water like a child. And the water holds that child, shares my grief. The water also stirs up the adult in me, reminds me that I know who I am.

I have a calling. I know exactly why I am on this earth. All the work I do is in service of my calling. I have been answering this calling, to the best of my ability, my entire life. Even when I was so drunk I couldn't speak, my calling called to me.

I remember lying on the front lawn under a blanket in the middle of the day. I remember the terror like a stutter, like a skipping of time, a continual return to the terror. There on the grass under the darkness of the blanket, my child body clung to the earth, but I felt utterly abandoned. Not only by my human parents, but by my real mother, the living universe who had always had my back. I lost my faith there on the lawn. I lost the only thing that was sustaining me, the only thing that was protecting me. Gutted. I would have sobbed if I had been able to articulate the violation, the grief. But the silence was a weight, shot through my body like lead in my veins.

I remember when I saw her. I remember when I first knew that she was there with me when I was utterly alone. I remember when I knew that she was there with me when he opened me and violated me. She was there, full of rage and pain and grief. She didn't let it happen, but she too could not stop it. I remember the breath that tumbled out of me when I knew she did not abandon me. My pain is her pain. My rage is her rage. My suffering is her suffering. My grief is her grief. Every breath, every heart beat, she is always with me. Always has been.

I have a calling. My calling is to transmute pain. My calling is to be a cauldron, to take the unspeakable things and find a way to speak them. To bear witness and to facilitate process. To put into motion the things that are too heavy to move. I am like the river, alive and in motion. I am like the river, people come to me with their pain. Messages in my inbox. Secrets brimming from lips. So many turn to my writing and say the secret prayer, let out the secret breath they have been holding. I come with a gift, a truth. I come with my portion of my work. It is what I am here to do.

We are still alive. We can and we do live with this pain. Pain is not the only thing we will feel, not the only thing we will know. What happened wasn't our fault and the ways we survived are the ways we survived. There is nothing that can take from us our inherent goodness, our inherent worthiness. There is nothing for us to be ashamed of. We are capable of bearing this pain. We are capable of transmuting this pain. We are capable of outliving the things that try to kill us. Take it to the water. Take it to the earth. Come back to yourself. Come back to yourself. Come back to yourself. Return. We are here. We are still here. All this time. We are fucking magic.

I come to the river to be a child. I am angry and exhausted and desperate and sad. I want to throw my calling into the black water, let the river take it away. *I never asked for this pain! I didn't want this calling! I want it to be easier. I don't want it to be so hard. I don't want this work. I don't want to have to find a way to live with this.* I beg the water to take

Calling

it all away but the water always brings me back to myself. The water is steady and knowing and strong. She has been with me all along. She reminds me who I am.

I am more powerful than I can believe. We are more powerful than we can believe.

Joy

TEN YEARS AGO, when I was 22, I remember standing in the backyard of my then-boyfriend's basement apartment, hung over and full of anticipation for further drinking. I remember the sunlight and the picnic table and the cluster of us, me, my boyfriend, and his two friends who spent most of their time partying with us. I remember thinking in that moment, and writing about it later, that I was happy. That I could die now, having known happiness. That having that small place, that basement apartment where we got shitfaced, that group of almost-strangers who got shitfaced together, felt like love, felt like family, felt like home. It was more than I ever could have dreamed for myself, it was all I wanted, all I could imagine I deserved.

I am 32, I come home to my apartment in Montréal, the Wholesome Collective. The kitchen is painted turquoise, the plants need to be watered, my roommate and her partner are reading on the couch, the dog is sunbathing in a patch of sunlight. In the kitchen my other two roommates are sitting around the table, pulling tarot cards and talking about relationships, love, sobriety, growth. Some mornings we read bell hook's *All About Love* or the big book of Alcoholics Anonymous around the breakfast table. We talk about sobriety, recovery, what we want for ourselves and our lives. We frequently laugh hysterically about absurd things. Pouring the entire bottle of salt into the popcorn and eating it anyway, tears streaming down my face, delirious with laughter.

Sometimes it's hard to accept this magic, to embrace it with all my heart. When I'm really depressed I hide in my room. I don't want to show my roomies the worst of me, I keep them at arm's length. I think about

Joy

the way that joy too is a practice and a process. The cultivation of joy and the cultivation of the capacity to experience joy is hard work. I breathe into this joy, this home, this community that I've built here. I breathe into the love of my friends and I try to let it sink into my bones.

Every Sunday we host a radsob meeting and friends and community pile into our living room. We drink chill tea and talk about our feelings. We show each other in action all the time over and over that there is a way back, that building our own families is possible, that love is real, that hope is justified. We show each other that we don't have to drink, that we don't have to run from our pain, that something else is possible. We share stories of what it was like for us before we got sober, the cops, the ambulances, the humiliation, the shame, the burned bridges, the destroyed relationships, the regret. We hold space for each other and together we find another way.

Now I know what it means to be happy, to laugh easily, to be home, to be loved. Now I know what I thought I had found when I was 22. It took me a decade to really find it, but I am here now. I am settling into the feeling of being here. The sound of the coffee grinder in the morning, the outbursts of laughter, the way we each miss each other so much when we are away, the proof reading of text messages, the holding space and offering advice, and the laughter, the tidal waves of laughter. I feel my defenses melt away. I let myself be ridiculous. I let myself feel safe. There are moments when I really feel it, when I truly have let my defenses down in perfect play and trust. This is trauma magic, the thing survivors never really believe we will get.

On New Years we have a sober party. We put a big piece of paper on the floor and write our 2019 manifestations: *Gay Slut Life 2019, THERAPY, Start a band, The parasympathetic nervous system, Earned Secure Attachment 2019, Titty Free 2019, Fall of Capitalism 2019, Publish a paper, Publish a book, Free Capybaras 2019,* and many other hilarious and heartfelt manifestations. We play truth or dare and basically just dare each other to love ourselves. We drink tea and carbonated beverages and laugh uncontrollably all night. My friends call me belligerently joyful. I say *But isn't it nice to be starting the new year like this! In such a wholesome way! No crying and screaming and puking!* And my friend says *Clementine there is abundant crying and screaming happening right now, just not puking.* And we laugh and laugh.

    A couple days later we have another party, a belated birthday party for me. My friend ties me up on the floor in front of all my friends as a birthday gift. I sit on a couch squished between my partner, friends, and metamours. I am gifted a persimmon and a temporary tattoo. I am surrounded by people who love me. I am deeply embedded in a network of relationships, like the roots of trees that reach out to each other in endlessly intricate patterns. There is an abundance of love, and I am learning to accept it, to be present with it, to breathe deep into my body and know that I have finally found community, safety, love, home. It's the scariest thing I've ever done, and it's here, and it's real.

Two Rivers

The sun is setting down the river casting the last warm glow. The tree branches are low and thick as trunks. They spread out over the water that is turning to ice near the shore. We sit on the branches with our dépanneur coffees in our mittened hands. We watch the light catch the silhouettes of buildings on the other shore, the edges of feathered plants standing tall against the sky.

She tells me *When I said I want to kiss you, that isn't abstract. I want to kiss you right now if that's what you want.* I laugh because I'm nervous but her directness steadies me. She makes desire feel safe, she makes queerness feel safe. I don't feel the need to laugh and look away, look away. I can look at her. I look at her.

I tell her I want to kiss her too. *But maybe I should come over to that branch with you.* I climb across to the other branch, careful not to fall into the river, and sit next to her. We abandon our coffee cups to the shore. She puts her legs across my lap, I put my arm around her back, we balance there on the tree branch. She looks at me, her parka framing her face. She is smiling but she is not making light of the moment. There is a steadiness to her presence, her ability to be here with me allows me to be here with her.

I kiss her lips, soft and warm in the freezing cold. She kisses me and we lean into each other, pulling each other close through winter coats. Her mouth on my mouth, the last of the light leaves the sky. The darkness takes us into each other. There is just the feeling of her, pulling in closer, warmth in the cold, communication without words.

Fucking Magic

The black water laps against the shore. I can hear the sound it makes. I am here in this moment, here in my body, here in her arms. She makes me feel safe in my desire. She makes her desire known, unambiguous, clear. She wants to be kissing me and I want to be kissing her. The sound of the water is the sound of this moment, our bodies intertwined on this tree branch, kissing hard and soft, deep and light, as time and cold drift away, leaving only the water and us.

Remember

*I*FORGET I AM the ocean. I forget I am the sky. *You can't own the fucking stars.* I forget that I have died and been reborn, over and over again. I forget who I am, what was forged in the fire, the way my brokenness makes me unbreakable.

It was a hard year. In so many ways it was a bad year, and I didn't want to admit it. As I was out there killing it, living my dreams, touring my book, I was deeply disconnected from my power, from myself.

I don't know how to tell you about the way I forget. *You never know what you'll forget.* I become a child again, not even all of the child I was, but the most repressed part. The part that had to take it all into her, that had to make sense of the unthinkable, the part that has no idea who she is, what she is capable of.

The real child that I was stood out in the snow, in the starlight, and I laughed with my sister. I made up a silly song: *I refuse, I refuse to be a victim, yeah.* And we laughed and we laughed and we delighted in our power, the power that is always protected, hidden deep down and untouched by the awful unspeakable thing.

I often wonder what would happen if I could hold onto my power, if I could stop forgetting. I wonder how many books I need to write about it before it finally sticks. I don't know what I need to do to stay with myself but I need to find a way to stay with myself. I need to stop forgetting who I am, what I'm capable of.

I am the ocean. I am the sky. I am a depth of power down beneath and lightyears away. I am the part that could not shatter, the part that spit blood and laughed, the part that protected the rest, snarling and taking the babies under her wings. I am strong. I am capable. I have lived through the unthinkable. I take all my pain and I turn it into goodness. I take all my pain and I do good with it.

I am tired of forgetting. I am tired of feigning helplessness again and again and again. I am tired of acting like I'm not loveable, like I'm not desirable, when I really fucking am. I am tired of tiptoeing around the truth of myself, never fully taking it up, taking it on. It's like I'm afraid that if I hold my own gaze I will go up in smoke. It's like I'm afraid to know what I could do if I finally stopped losing track of myself.

I'm tired of asking questions I know the answers to. I'm tired of second guessing my worthiness. I'm tired of acting like I am less than I am. I am tired of it. And yet I keep circling around, having to rediscover who I am. I keep throwing away my power, dropping it and turning all my attention to something else.

It's a terrible paradox. I turn away from myself in pursuit of love. I turn away from myself in the hope that I will become desirable, lovable, worthy. In my forgetting I hope to be loved. But when I remember who I am then I am here in my wholeness, already loved. When I remember the love I receive from others is fully felt and welcomed, it is recognized as congruent with the love I feel for myself. But when I forget I am baffled by love, suspicious of it. When I forget I burn everything to the ground again and again because I'm so fucking crazy about it.

Yet I keep turning away from who I am. I keep forgetting.

Tonight I received a birthday card from my grandmother, and I felt crazy with the grief and confusion and terror of reality never being acknowledged, of having to carry the weight of incest all alone, of never having my pain named and never being told *I'm sorry*. I felt the pull and push of all my different selves and I felt the bottom come out from underneath as I lost contact with who I am.

I asked my community to remind me, to help me return. And they did, they told me. They told me about my laughter and my writing and my prayers, about my kindness and my generosity and my tenacity, about my vulnerability and my courage and my strength. Tonight in a circle, surrounded by a community that stretches through space and time I was recognized. And I remember who I am.

The Only Way to Love

A SECRET LOVE, A longstanding love. Remember breath that comes easy and hands falling open. Remember the sky in all its endless shades and the way it's always been there. Remember what it's like to trust, what it's like to let go.

You in all your complexity. Me, in mine. Lying on my bed, my head on your chest, a tangle of limbs. The rise and fall of your chest, the subtle thump of your heart. This life, this love. I am humbled by the simplicity of loving you. I am humbled by the complexity of being in love with you. I am lost in a maze of hours and months, turning now to years. Like the leaves of a tree or the stars in the sky, they proliferate, become more than I can count. All the times I turned to you. All the countless times I kissed you. The times we fought and clawed through the pain of loving. My triggers and yours, your fears and mine. The way it is so easy now to reach for your hand. The way I am learning to really recognize you. You, you, my love, my friend, my partner. You, here in my arms, you somewhere else away from me.

A secret love, a longstanding love. The earth that gives life to everything else. The ground on which I stand. The place I begin and the place I return to. I can love because I know myself. I can love when I return to myself. I can love when I remember the world, when I remember the magic. I can only love well with open hands. I can only love in freedom, in trust. I try to keep a tally. I try to keep track of what is wild. It won't be tracked and it won't be tamed and I am humbled to remember. I am brought face to face with the hunter in me and I lay down my weapon. I return to the earth, to the great wildness of the forest. There is no way to love you without loving myself, there is no way, no way to love you without loving the world, there is no way to love you without letting go.

 When I don't write I don't know myself. I am afraid to write because I am afraid of myself. I am afraid of the depth of who I am. I am afraid of the sky and the way it's always been there. I am afraid of what I'm capable of, the way that I know that I can lose, the way I have already lost. I am afraid of how unafraid I am. I am afraid to meet myself, but here I am and I have always been here. I can only love when I write. I can only love when I remember the sky. I can only love when I know myself. I can only know myself when I remember that I am not afraid to lose. I love you with every cell, in the depths of my bone marrow, in the future and in the past, in the parts of me that are deep and unspeakable. I love you as a lover, as a dear dear friend, as a confidante and comrade and companion, I love you the way I love this bright and shimmering world in all its changing texture and depth. I love you more than I could ever say. And I'm not afraid to lose you. I'm not afraid to let you go.

 Everything in me buckles and collapses, throws a tantrum and resists this declaration of irrevocable freedom, and yet I know that it's true and I know that this is the only way to love you.

The Same Lesson

*I*T'S THE SAME lesson and I don't want to learn it again. But it comes over me like the dawn breaking, the thundercloud finally letting loose its rain. I read my old writing and I think *I'm here again.* I don't want to have to have the same breakthroughs over and over. I want them to stick. But I get so forgetful. I lose my place. I return to habits and ways of thinking that don't serve me. I have to remember that change is a practice. Not a practice that we decide, but a practice we do. It includes receptivity and intuition, willingness to be open and listen, willingness to feel the pulls and shifts, the thumps and pulse of this beautiful, living world.

I break the surface of the water suddenly, sucking air into my lungs. I've been drowning for almost a year. Despite all the growth and all the goodness, despite my absurdly beautiful, unbelievable life, there was something *wrong*, something not quite right. I lost myself again. I lost my relationship to the deep wild part of myself, and my relationship to the deep wild world. Writing is one way in, so I will write it over and over again. I will write my way back, like casting a line into the darkness, trying to find the connection. It's all around me all the time, it is the very make up of my being, and yet I have to remember how to see it, how to be with it.

I come back to remembering but this time it is something deeper, something more profound. I kept doing the same things over and over, expecting different results. I am tired of doing the same things. I am tired of acting helpless. I am tired of eroticizing men's violence toward me. I am tired of putting up with way way less than I deserve. I am tired of forgetting and undermining my power. I am tired of being terrified of

Fucking Magic

love, going crazy because of it. I ease back into this steady power, this wild vast knowing, and I drop deeper to a new level of it. I want to stay here. I want to stay connected to myself and the world. I want to remember who I am. I want to stop forgetting.

Gay Slut Life 2019

I JOKE ABOUT IT. *Gay Slut Life 2019*. But really this is something deep and hard and powerful and beautiful and terrifying. I joke about it but I can't even tell you the depths of trauma that are encasing my desires.

When I say *Gay Slut Life 2019* what I mean is: I have to heal my queerness in order to survive. What I mean is: My queerness is my magic, it is fundamental and essential, and it is injured, deeply injured. There is no way to heal my trauma without healing my desire, and my desire is deeply, viscerally queer.

It's so hard to have so many hang ups about queer sexuality. I often feel deeply broken and feel deeply depressed about this. I have fucked ten million cishet men and I haven't had even a tiny fraction of that amount of sex with queers and women and dykes and nonbinary people. It's not that I've had none of this sex or none of these relationships, I have. But it is harder and scarier and more work. The desire is deeper and it is encased in so much trauma. It is so difficult to relax into it, to let go.

Trauma from men is something I understand and for a long long time it was something I accepted. Now I'm pretty much over it and I don't want to fuck men unless they go above and beyond to ensure that I feel safe and human. I'm really not interested anymore.

With queer dating and queer sex it's another thing entirely. I go on these 'ambiguous lesbian outings', these dates, but is it really a date? Despite flirting and even literally meeting on tinder, there is so much hesitance and uncertainty. I have been in literal months and months long relationships where we have been unable to actually have sex due to a complex web of traumas and fears. And sex isn't everything, but sex is also important to me. Healing my queer sexuality is important to me, and part of that is having queer sex. (Even writing that makes me feel fucked up! It literally still makes me feel like a creep to openly express queer sexual desire.)

Gay Slut Life 2019 means actively naming and expressing my queer desires. It means going on first dates and saying *Do you want to kiss me?* instead of hugging each other goodbye and leaving wondering if that was a date. It means talking about sex and also actually having sex. It means moving through the fear and the trauma and the shame.

It means trusting in the queer desires of others. It means sinking into the reality that I am hot and beautiful and desirable and my desirability is not for cishet men. I am hot for queers. I want to be desired by queers. And *Gay Slut Life 2019* means rejecting internalized homophobia enough to really honour the desire of other queers. There are lots of queers who want to fuck me, and their desire is good and beautiful and sacred and right.

This is not some little or light thing. This is the biggest healing work of my life. I am a queer person. I was a queer child. I grew up queer immersed in homophobia and it traumatized me. I am an incest survivor and a multiple rape survivor and all that shit traumatized me. I am so scared that my desire will be harmful and yet I need to trust myself. I need to trust in my goodness and the fact that I am extremely careful with communication and also paying attention to nonverbal cues.

I need to heal. I need to know, deep in my bones, deep in my cells, in every part of who I am, that being queer is good and beautiful and sacred and right. That my desire for queer sex is good and beautiful and sacred and right. That thinking queers and girls and nonbinary people are hot and wanting to fuck them is normal and healthy and good.

Queer sex is good. And 2019 is the year that I really want to move through my trauma and have a lot of it. 2019 is the year that I want to actively and intentionally and communicatively move through how hard this is, and to claim the truth of my desires and who I really am.

So Fucking Pretty

You look so fucking pretty. Tonight, in your leopard print skirt and your punk tank top, you look so fucking pretty. Tonight you respond to my question *Can I top you some time?* Usually you top me, but tonight you are my sub. You respond to my direction, you surrender yourself to my desire. You let me have you.

You're lying on your stomach, laid out in front of me, I sink into a desire I have never known before. This is the desire of Dominance, of being in charge. This is the desire that comes not from surrender, but from decision, design. I discover pleasure in myself as I let my hands explore your body, watch you writhe with anticipation and pleasure under my touch, watch your body succumb to the movements I impose on you, watch you do what you're told.

Turns out I'm a very nice top. Turns out I get off on telling you how good you are, how pretty, on making you know that I am relishing this access to your body, on watching you give yourself to me. Turns out I like to be in charge, I like to take my time and make you wait, I like to watch you want it. I love the look of the leopard print fabric stretched over your ass, I love the curve of you. You're perfect and right now you are mine.

You are in service to my pleasure. You do what you're told and I like that. I am unafraid of my desire, which is expansive and directive. I am unafraid of your submission, your willingness to make yourself into what I want you to be. You give me exactly what I want, exactly how I want it. I tell you *You're being so good* and you thank me. You are desperate to be good, and I understand that. I know the feeling.

Fucking Magic

When I cum it's of a different kind. This is a pleasure that has thoroughly liberated itself from shame. This is a pleasure that makes no excuses, that does not hide behind the pleasure of another. This pleasure is mine, and you give it to me.

The Fire and the Swan

*I*DREAMT I THREW a book I'd written into a lake. I saw it there, floating on the surface of the water. I jumped in after it, swam through the waves toward it. When I got to it, it had changed into a dead swan. I grabbed the body of wet feathers and began to drag it back to the shore. Then I saw the swan wasn't dead, it was almost dead, on the very edge of life, but it was still alive. I released my grasp and let the desperate creature continue on its way. It was clear to me that she wanted to be in the water.

I awoke thinking of the swan's face. The expression of desperation, the need to escape my grasp and be allowed freedom, even that close to death. She trusted herself, she trusted her struggle, and she was willing to die in the water if she had to die in the water. The water was where she needed to be. I awoke depressed, a lingering nameless sadness. Visiting Toronto for work, sleeping on my friend's couch, the sky thick with snow. I spent the day travelling around the city, stocking the stores with my zines and books. All along I carried with me this sadness.

My skin is on fire. My entire body is covered in psoriasis. Dots of bright red cracked skin which blur and merge into each other creating large patches of psoriasis. It is everywhere. My feet, my legs, knees, thighs, my pussy, my butt, hips, belly, my breasts, back, armpits, my neck, ears, face. It hasn't been bad like this since I was a teenager. I try to understand why. I try to understand the fire that is burning inside me, the desperate urgent message across my skin.

I went to the *Unruly Bodies* event while in Toronto, to read a piece of my writing. It felt so good to be in a chronic illness and disability centred space. It felt so good to be in a space where unruly bodies were recognized as wise and beautiful and powerful, even in their pain and their distress. Liz Leia, one of the writers, talked about those of us with chronic sickness as attuned to and feeling the pain and distress of the world. She talked about inflammation as a sacred fire, a cleansing and purifying fire, a fire that is shining a light and igniting a process. I understood what she was saying. I felt my rapid cells stirring in recognition.

What am I burning, besides myself? What is this muted anger that I feel inside of myself, that is unspeakable and yet speaks through my skin? Who is this dying swan whose very body is a book of my words? There is a juxtaposition of these images, fire and water, the fire that burns and the water that carries away. I feel both energies, the burning consuming fire, the desperate sadness of the swan. I am trying to understand what my body and my dreams are trying to tell me. What part of me is smothered and dying, trying to return to the water, trying to go up in flames?

I spend way too much time on my phone, scrolling, scrolling, refreshing the same two apps. This is a boring problem not worth writing about. We're all addicted to our phones, whatever. But it's not whatever. I feel this strangle, this desperation, this quick and steady, repetitive and compulsive, looking away. Because I don't want to look. I don't want to look at what's right in front of me. My body is crushed under the weight of unprocessed emotions, of things I won't let myself know. So I look at my phone, I look at my phone.

I remember the face of the swan. Her desperation and her resolve. Her breath was barely coming but she was insistent on staying in the water. She was willing to fight for it. I think about Liz's words about the sacred fire, about our receptive sick bodies listening to the world. I try to remember where the water is that my swan is trying to get to. I try to remember what it is that the fire is trying to clear away.

I carry my books and zines in my backpack and trek across the city in the snow. The staff at the queer bookstore who know me well tell me they respect my hustle, as they buy zines and books from me. Other stores aren't so accommodating and make me pitch myself every time. The struggle of trying to make enough money to survive, of declaring myself a writer, of saying *yes this really is my work.* Trying to structure my days in a way that honours my wildness but also keeps me accountable to my practice. Trying to remember, under the crushing weight of capitalism, that I am a witch.

These words are my magic. *The swan is my magic.* And the fire is the repressed rage at every time I have denied my power, swallowed my no, refused to ask for what I want, accepted less than I deserve. The fire is the result of learned helplessness, bargaining and manipulating instead of being strong and direct and clear.

The fire and the swan are redirecting me, returning me. Where do I abandon myself? Where do I speak or act in ways not in alignment with my truest deepest integrity? What in me is dying from lack of access to water? What in me is burning in protest against that which I quietly accept?

I keep coming back to the same questions, the same quiet pains. But I know now that there is an urgency, a need to finally hear what it is that I'm trying to say.

Still Alive

She contacts me to tell me that she dated the person who abused me. She tells me he told her about me, that he said I was a liar and she believed him. I don't blame her for this. I understand. She says that in time he did the same to her. She tells me what he did to her and she asks me to tell her what he did to me. We exchange horror stories. Both of us saying *I'm sorry, I'm sorry, that's so awful.*

I feel sick and slow, the world is round, globular, and it slides away in my peripheral vision. There is thick heavy space all around me and I move through it like water. I feel the impulse in me, the physical feeling of preparing for the attack. I feel the space collapse on impact, my body the animal remembers and responds like it is happening now.

I walk to the café to meet my partner. It's 2019, it's 2019. The snow is bright white, sparkling and brilliant, hard to look at. The people and the cars move like they are under water, a slow chaos, a distant presence. I try to breathe. I try to feel the cold air warmed by my body. I try to breathe it down into my guts where he kicked me. I say to myself *it's 2019, it's 2019.* I count five blue things, five green things, five red things. I know this feeling will pass as it has so many times before.

His last attack on her was two years ago, last contact was one. His last attack on me was nine years ago, last contact was one. This time last year he showed up in my inbox again calling me a lying bitch, threatening to get the transcripts of the rape trial and make them public so that everyone can see what a liar I am. I sat on my partner's bed reading his threats and his rage on my phone screen, feeling the world turn into slow motion again.

Still Alive

Violence is intimate and of the body. My body, this body, all those years ago, on the floor, screaming and crying. And still now, my body has memorized those moments, floating in time like time is a pool not a river, opening like a pupil dilating, I am inside it again. But I am also here, in 2019, alive and escaped, safe. I am here and I got out, and so did she. I tell her *solidarity*, and I feel a deep resonance and connection with her. I tell her *I'm here if you need to talk*. She got out. I got out. And we are here, alive, still alive.

The Forest

WHEN I WAS a kid I dreamed about the forest overtaking the little cottage. Especially my grandfather's bedroom. I imagined the trees growing up through the floorboards, breaking them open and claiming the space. I dreamt of letting the whole place go wild, the little cottages on the edge of the lake, the forest interrupted, now uninterrupted. I dreamt of the strength of the trees, the power of their numbers, their ability to take the land back into themselves. I dreamt of that little cottage overtaken from the inside out. Trees upon trees.

The wild survived in me. Somehow, I managed to keep it like a secret seed. Even as parts of me were thoroughly domesticated. Even as I was trained to abandon myself again and again. Some part of me stayed wild, and this part of me takes me over sometimes, comes up through the floorboards and turns my whole life into a forest. This is when I am most happy, most free, most alive. It doesn't matter what is going on in my life. I feel good because I am connected to who I am and my true wild nature.

But then the trees become like ghosts, invisible to me. I forget about the forest. I think I'm in that cottage again. Helpless and terrified and desperate and trying to be good. I hate this amnesia, this constant forgetting of what I've already learned. I don't know how to stay in the forest, or more accurately, how to remember that the forest always stays in me. It is impossible to kill off the wild in me, that is clear. It has survived despite all the violence, everything that happened. The forest still thrives. It still flourishes. I just forget.

My body is crying out for me to remember, but even with my skin ablaze, I have such a hard time remembering the forest. It is easier to

The Forest

forget. Forgetting happens of its own accord. It feels natural and obvious to be in that cottage, with all the doors and windows closed, no idea that the forest is still here, all around me, inside me. I lose my power. I lose myself. Again and again I wonder what the problem is. I know something is wrong but I don't know what it is. I don't know how to get back to myself. I don't know how to remember what I already know. I don't know how to remember the forest, how to see the trees right in front of me.

The forest is right here. The trees are thick and green. Sunlight filters through the leaves. The sky comes through in snatches. There's a cool respite from the heat. Fallen logs and dead leaves cover the earth. The air is electric with bird sounds and flickers of movement. Mushrooms pass their messages. The deep, deep roots drink up water. It's all here, alive and pulsing with its magic. It's all here despite the orders and commands from the cottage. Here in the forest is the place where I was born, the place I belong, the place where I keep myself, still here, still alive. Here in the forest I am safe and I am powerful. I know who I am.

Femme4Femme D/s

I COME OVER WEARING one hot slutty gay outfit under another. The top layer is black jeans and black t-shirt, because it's winter out there. But underneath this I'm wearing a tiny, too small, black stretchy dress and fishnets. And of course I'm wearing my collar.

You're sitting in your bedroom when I arrive. Red miniskirt, black tights, red knee socks, black tanktop. You look amazing. You ask me to come to you and I do. We kiss and I lie in your lap and you stroke my hair. You are beautiful and I want to be good for you. You are always so good to me.

You tell me to get you a tea and I make sure to make it exactly how you like it. I stand in the kitchen waiting for the kettle to boil. I bring your tea back to you and you are lying on your bed on your stomach reading a comic book. You tell me to strip down to my second slutty gay outfit and I do. I tie my hair up into a ponytail so it won't be in the way. I sit next to you on the bed and you clip the leash to my collar, holding it in your hand as you continue to read.

You pass me a lint roller from your bedside table and tell me your tights have been in the back of a drawer for a long time. They need to be worked over. While you read your comic book, I use the lint roller, carefully and meticulously removing all lint from your tights, savouring your legs and your curves while I do, touching you through the black fabric, feeling lucky and grateful and good.

This is a practice of devotion. Every action is electric with intention, precision, and care. Every action is an act of service. I love to see you lying there, beautiful and perfect. I love to know that it is good and right that you should have exactly what you want, that it is my job to give it to you. This is a game we play, a carefully negotiated scene of submission and service. My pussy aches from the pleasure of being yours, from the pleasure of doing what I'm told.

Later you take me by my leash and position me on a pillow at your feet as you sit on the couch. Your newly cleaned tights are gone and I lie with my face against your skin, savouring the feel of you. You pull me closer to you with the leash, the red fabric of your skirt against my face. I am squirming with eagerness and excitement but I remember to do only what I'm told.

You take out a bottle of black nail polish and start to paint your nails, focused on the task at hand, mostly ignoring me. I can barely contain my excitement and desire but I breathe into it and await my instructions. You tell me I can pull up your skirt and I do, releasing your beautiful cock. You say I can kiss you and I do, feeling grateful and lucky while you look at me only occasionally, pausing to take in my devotion, then returning to what you are doing.

I suck your cock while you paint your nails. This is femme4femme D/s, blazing hot and perfect. I am chained to your couch by my leash, on my knees on a pillow at your feet. I am your slutty gay submissive and you are my gorgeous femme Dom. I suck your cock with complete devotion and care, caught up in the pleasures of both service and desire.

Still Crazy

It's amazing to me what my traumatized mind can do, how I can completely rearrange reality and turn it into something else. It doesn't feel like I have changed, it feels like the world has changed, like what's possible has changed, or that it has always been this way and I was just wrong about it before. This change comes over me. I become negative, suspicious, overwhelmed, hopeless, helpless, like a desperate caged animal, trapped. I look at my beautiful life and I can only see what's wrong with it.

I don't want to keep sliding into this place, but I also don't want to keep pretending that I don't go there. I want to practice integration work again. Integration, wholeness, integrity. I want to bring together all the lost selves and return them to each other. I want to bring together my body and my mind. I want to bring together my past and my future, and this moment right now. I'm scared and I'm exhausted and there are so many beliefs that I'm holding onto that really don't serve me or do me well.

Change is slow and it's a practice. I know this. There is no easy, quick solution to 25 years of trauma. And then some. There is only the work, showing up for it, consistently. I use the insight timer app on my phone to do guided meditations. I google "affordable yoga in Montréal." I admit that I'm triggered. I admit when I'm having a hard time. I start to notice when I'm triggered instead of just feeling it take me over. I start to slow down enough, distance myself enough, to see that the feelings are not all of who I am, that the story I am telling myself does not accurately reflect the world, my life, the people in my life.

Still Crazy

I'm too fucking hard on myself. I don't know what I'm looking for that would finally be enough, when I have this beautiful beautiful life. I just get so sucked down into the feeling of being unloved, into the feeling of being broken. I get so swamped by the terror and the grief and the thwarted rage. I need to remember the process, the magic, the work, and all of the rewards. Those moments when I am laughing, when I am here in my life with the people who love me. Those moments when my breath drops down into my belly, when I can feel my body, when I can see the person I've become.

Something I Can Trust

I'M EXPLAINING TO my roommate about the conversations I've been having with my partner, about the things I'm learning about love and loving and she says to me *You're doing it, you're earning secure attachment.*

Things have been crazy and things have been scary but I feel like I can finally exhale. A combination of hard work in therapy, soul searching, writing, friends, community, deep conversations with my partner, and reaching out to my metamours is creating this massive paradigm shift. It feels expansive and relaxing and deeply good.

I open up the notes in my phone and write *What if I'm safe?* I stare at the words and I feel this openness in my chest, this sensation like melting, like breathing, like letting go.

I am a survivor of a lot of abuse. A lot of really bad and scary and fucked up things happened to me. Trauma is embedded deep within me and it shapes the way I think and feel, the way I perceive things and what I think is possible.

I am just learning about love. I am in a safe, loving, long term, polyamorous partnership. We have been together for almost two years. And being in love like this has been one of the most triggering experiences of my recovery. Feeling safe and happy and loved can be profoundly triggering. Learning how to breathe deep and accept love, deep in my body, in my nervous system, is some of the hardest work I've ever done.

I am grateful. I am grateful to my partner for loving me through this, for learning about c-ptsd and being able to have conversations with me about it, for understanding the context of my life and my trauma, for being generous and patient as I move through massive triggers and fears. I am grateful to them for loving me, and for believing in me, and supporting me. They show me that the hard work of learning to love is worth it, that there is peace and joy and pleasure and safety and freedom to be found through that work.

I am grateful for polyamory and for the vulnerability of reaching out to metamours to talk about my fears and feelings, and to be met in that vulnerability, to be held. I am grateful for community, real community, where I don't have to be alone anymore, where I don't have to be perfect or have everything figured out. Where I can reach out for help and show up as I am.

I am grateful for therapy and meditation and witchcraft and deep breathing. I am grateful for twelve steps and sobriety and patience and practice. I am grateful for chosen family, a home that really feels like home, and a community of survivors, addicts, and queers. We are growing and changing and moving through it and doing the work, and I am not alone in any of it.

I am finally beginning to see. Love isn't something I have to struggle and work for. Love isn't something I have to hypervigilantly monitor. Love is something free and safe, something I can relax into, something I can trust.

Fucking Magic

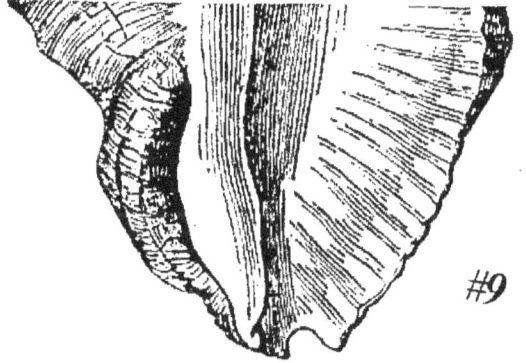

#9

Love in the Apocalypse

THERE'S AN EXPANSIVENESS in my chest, an exhale, the movement of breath. I facilitate workshops on trauma informed polyamory and I ask the participants *What do you desire about polyamory?* I ask myself the same question. Where is my desire in my body? What does it feel like? It feels rooted, it feels expansive, it feels like breath.

A long time ago when I tried to do polyamory I insisted on a complex list of agreements, attempts at control, attempts at feeling safe. I come across this list in my email inbox and I am full of relief that I don't do this anymore. The way I do polyamory today is different. It isn't always easy but it has ease. It is grounded in trust, trust in myself and trust in my partner, trust in the universe, trust in my breath.

I desire freedom. I desire trust. I desire intimacy. I desire community. I desire the particular relationship metamours share. I desire serious commitment to friends and chosen family. I desire the work of love. I desire the work of healing. I desire intentionality. I desire communication. I desire care webs and networks of relationships. I desire anarchy. I desire love freely chosen again and again. I desire love with open hands. I desire the breath that moves through my body, roots in carefully tended soil, safety, and being loved for exactly who I am.

I love this beautiful life I'm building. I love the person I'm becoming. I'm grateful for the freedom and possibility in my life, for the intentionality and care. Love is practice, love is process. Love is laughter, love is conflict. Love is returning, remembering breath. I am grateful for my friends and my home and my dates and my partner. I am grateful for building home and purpose and meaningful work in the apocalypse. I am grateful for us.

I desire the work of polyamory because I desire the work of intentional love, the work of meeting myself. I desire vulnerability, I desire care. I desire freedom and trust.

I don't know what my partner is doing right now. I don't know if they are on a first date, if they are in a café working on the book they're writing, if they are wrapped up in the arms of their other partner who they love and are deeply committed to, if they are having sex with their friend. I know that they love me, that they are committed to me. I know that I'll hear about new dates when we talk about our weeks. I know that I'll see their partner when we go out for coffee and have a work date. I know that their friends and lovers care about me, just as I care about them. I know that I trust my partner. This is love. This is community.

I know my partner will want to hear all about my new crush, and will be deeply excited for me. I know that my date and my partner hanging out is a singular joy. I know that my sexuality is healing and my capacity for love and relationship is healing. I know that I am deeply loved and completely safe.

Trauma magic is the process and the practice: so much of it is the work of love. Polyamory is part of that magic for me. Building family and community and connection and love.

For Mary

I'M LISTENING TO an interview with Mary Oliver on the On Being podcast. I'm crying in the grocery store, looking for a can of maple syrup. I listen again. I listen to the words of this old woman, the interview just a few years before her death, speaking of her life as a poet, her one wild and precious life, her life loving the world, listening to the world. I listen to this woman and mourn the lack of elders in my life, how badly I wish I had elders to learn from, to be in relationships with, and how grateful I am to have access to her words, elder, ancestor, poet. And then, I listen to this woman, whose poems I have loved for years, speak about her childhood, the violence of her father, the pain, the suffering, how she got out, how she survived. I am gutted. Tears are sliding down my face and my body is electric with the shivers of recognition. These aren't tears of pity, they are tears of resonance and recognition and gratitude. Mary Oliver: *one of us*. I listen to her talk about her life, her pain, the process of her healing. I listen to her wonder if she would have been a poet if she wasn't a survivor. I feel the tears sliding down my face.

She understands, she knows, she was surviving and practicing trauma magic before I was even born, creating for us, the world, the massive gift of her poems. I understand that she loved the world the way survivors love the world, in wonder and awe, surprised again and again by the miracle of living, rooted deeply in intimacy with unthinkable pain.

Mary, thank you. Thank you for showing us a way, for reminding us again and again of the world which always turns toward us, offering us love, offering us wonder, offering us belonging, no matter what we have lost, no matter what we have endured. Thank you for reminding us of

Fucking Magic

our wild and precious lives, the lives we defended and kept, the lives we protected. Like you, we know the pain. I want you to know Mary, that we are with you, in gratitude and recognition, we hold the pain with you. And we carry on your legacy of survivor poets practicing trauma magic, deeply in love with the world.

Swamp Milkweed

I WANT TO ASK you about the flowers, the perennials I planted in the backyard. The swamp milkweed that grew strong and tall for the many-coloured bees. I want to ask you if any of them are still growing, since I've been gone. I want to ask you about the mushroom patch. Is it still there? Does it keep coming back? Do the squirrels still chase each other around the trunks of the trees? It's been years since I've stepped into that yard, a place I used to call home, a place that meant so much to me.

Under the anger, there was pain. And now that you have apologized and set things right, now that the anger has started to dissipate, the pain remains. Just a dull throb. Just the remnants of loss. I'm not sure if grief ever goes away, maybe our relationship to it just changes. With the anger there was bitterness, a certainty that you never cared about me, that you just used me and abandoned me, that none of it meant anything to you. I watched you move on with what seemed like ease, leaving me to deal with the wreckage of our relationship alone.

Now I see that you were hurting too, in your own way. Now I see that it did mean something to you. Maybe I'll never know exactly what, maybe you won't either exactly. But I know now that it wasn't nothing to you. It wasn't nothing to me.

Now that the anger and the bitterness are releasing, I can feel the grief that I was never quite able to feel. It doesn't come on like a torrential downpour like it used to. It's more like an ache, a slow sad ache. For what we lost. For what we never were able to give each other. For how we tried. For the ways we were so good together.

I think we were better off as friends and that we should have stayed that way. I miss when I could call you a friend. I miss the way we were collaborators, the way we dreamed things up together and made them real. I miss the way I trusted you, when I trusted you. It hurt me so much that you betrayed that trust, but now I have forgiven you.

I want to ask you about the flowers but I am sure they have died. I want to dig my hands into the earth again, feel the sun on my skin. I know it isn't my home anymore. My home is somewhere else, far away, in a life I've built full of abundant love. A life I created after I escaped the lie of the life we were living. And I am happy here. This is the life and the love I deserve and it is something we were never able to give each other.

But we did try. And we did give each other something. And now that I'm not so angry and hurt, now that I can breathe down into the parts of me that were so hurt, I can finally say that I'm sad for the loss of our friendship. I can finally say that I miss you. I miss the good that we could do together, as friends.

The Beginning of Spring

*I*N YOUR BED I come to the feeling of your tongue against me. I feel the pleasure take root in me and grow heliotropic, turning toward the sun. The stories I tell myself about who I am and what my body is capable of fall away to the feel of you. I am responsive and awake. I am wordless and present. I am with you. Your motions make meaning of my nerve endings, I feel myself glowing from the inside. I don't stop it. I don't rush it. I ride it as it builds. The pleasure extends past the boundary of my body and I stay, I do not turn away.

Later, in the shower, we are laughing in the darkness, the only light a scrap coming in through the window. Steam rises around us and hot water feels good. I stand on my tippytoes, throwing my arms around your neck. You hold me there like that and kiss me, rainbow water splitting the spectrum of the little light there is.

I'm already awake when your alarm goes off in the morning in your windowless room, some hilarious classic rock song which you snooze several times. You roll around mumbling incoherently in French, our naked bodies twisting and turning into the morning. I am awake, the dreams I was dreaming falling away. You smile at me with your sparkling eyes as the world settles in on us.

You make us coffee with soymilk and oatmeal with blueberries and we lounge on your couch each of us wearing only one of your oversized sweatshirts. You kiss me between sips of coffee and spoonfuls of oatmeal. I feel happy and at ease, here in your living room, at the very beginning of spring.

My Beautiful Fucking Life

*I*N THE LIVING room with the big window, books and zines and flyers filling the ledge that circles the room, a bookshelf bursting with the combined collections of the people who live here. The cat, the dog, the little fairy lights. The posters and the art. There are two couches packed full. There are nine of us in total, nine queer and/or trans addicts, anarchists, witches, atheists, survivors, in a network of relationships (sponsors and sponsees, partners, friends, chosen family). There are the four of us who live here. I cast my eyes across the room and see us, the four of us happen to be sitting in a row. I feel this swelling in my heart. These people are my family. My partner on the other couch, and the friends who filled the table with sweets and chocolate and blueberries. All of us drinking chill tea: nettle, lavender, holy basil.

 I am a storm of pain. I am a nervous system hijacked and on fire. I have been spending whole days in bed crying. I have been sabotaging my partnership with the terror of trauma that spills up and over. I have been isolating and feeling unspeakably bad. Flashbacks in my body, writhing in my bed, feeling something wordless (*my twelve year old body on the floor pressed between the bed and the wall*). I have been suffering, and I have been feeling like I will never be happy. I will never feel safe or loved. I will never escape or outrun my mangled nervous system, my structurally dissociated personality, my crushing terror and pain. Then suddenly, slowly, I see where I am. I see the room unfold around me, and here are the people that I love. Suddenly, slowly, it dawns on me. *These people love* me. Every single one of them. They love me and they want me here and they care about how I feel. I am a part of this, an integral part. This is my home, my real home. This is my family, my real family.

Then the anger comes, but it is a different kind of anger. It's not the self-sabotaging suspicious anger that assumes I am being violated again. It is not the anger of shame turned inward on myself in annihilating self-hatred. It is the anger of healthy boundaries, of self-respect, of knowing who the fuck I am. I am angry that my parents are robbing me, right now, of my ability to be here. I am angry that they took from me not only my childhood, not only my safety and autonomy and sexuality, not only my past, but that they are taking from me the present, this beautiful moment right here, right now. It suddenly hits me. My complex ptsd, the profound injury to my nervous system, my personality, my sexuality, my ability to love and form relationships, my body, my mind, the meanings I can imagine, this profound injury which was caused by childhood sexual abuse and neglect and the compounding trauma of being retraumatized, is still stealing from me right fucking now.

The anger feels like power. All the anxious energy of my sympathetic nervous system suddenly shoots into the ground like big fat strong roots gripping the earth. Suddenly I know, I know who I am and where I am and what I deserve. I know what was taken from me and what is still being fucking taken from me. I share these thoughts with my friends. I say *Look at this room, this beautiful room, look at these beautiful people, look at us. This is my life, this is my beautiful fucking life and it is so good and I worked so fucking hard for it. I had to drag myself out of a literal gutter to get here and I did. And still, I can't see it, I can't feel it, I can't know the power and beauty and safety of this life. Because my injured nervous system thinks I'm still in the past. And my parents did this to me and I am fucking mad about it.*

I can feel myself breathing. I can feel the room breathing. We talk about this. We talk about the incredibly hard work of living in reality, of breaking the cycle of intergenerational trauma, of deciding to heal and fighting with everything we fucking have. The walls fall away and

Fucking Magic

I understand that I am not alone. I am not under a blanket on the front lawn pressing my terrified body into the earth, I am not alone in the woods in the night because it's the only place I feel fucking safe. I am here. I am in this beautiful room filled with abundant love, filled with addicts and survivors, people who understand deeply and intimately the pain that I am in. People who are here with their pain, fighting like I am fighting, for a better life, for real love, for the present moment. For this.

This is what I always wanted and I want to know that I am here.

Split Personality

I TELL MY THERAPIST that I periodically decide that I don't have multiple personalities, that it just seems weird and fake and I decide that I don't need to think about it or believe in it. And yet, when I actively acknowledge and work with my structural dissociation, when I acknowledge and name my ANPs and EPs, my recovery deepens and I make so much more progress. I tell my therapist that it's hard, it's hard to have this experience, it's alienating because most people don't know about structural dissociation and don't understand what it is and don't know what to say when I talk about my split personality and my parts. Movies about it create a really sensationalized idea about it. People think it's fake. And people also don't understand that it's on a spectrum, ranging from mild to more severe, and that structural dissociation is actually a pretty common component of complex ptsd.

My EPs are ruining my life. They are dominating my personality and putting me into a constant state of emergency. I am cycling hard between hyper and hypoactivation, I am rapidly switching between parts. I am saying and doing things that I regret and I feel drunk on it, crazy with it, coming out of an EP like I'm waking up with a hangover, with that sick dread regret at the behaviour that so recently seemed to make perfect sense. I am in therapy and I am working hard to try to find a way to get my EPs under control, a necessary harm reduction step on the way toward integration work. Part of the problem with this is that in order to calm my EPs I need to be in my ANP and I don't have one ANP, I have two.

I've done a lot of integration work on my ANPs and they are not as split as they used to be. There is no more animosity. There is relationship.

Fucking Magic

And as a result, there is much more overlap than there used to be. But it is also true that when I switch into Violet (since Indigo has been dominating) people notice. The way I move and talk is different. I am so much more easily able to let go of things. Violet actually doesn't give a fuck. And while both of my ANPs are super necessary for getting out of my EPs and starting the process of integration, Violet in particular has a lot to offer. She isn't anxious. She doesn't care about being 'good'. She is brazen and daring and wild and she can make shit happen. Both my therapist and my partner have suggested that I should put her in charge.

There's some cognitive dissonance to putting her in charge because for so many years I thought of Violet as the fuck up, the drunk, the bad daughter, the run away. She is very good at burning shit to the ground and she has lit my life on fire more than once. But it's true that sometimes things need to burn, and it's also true that Violet has grown up, her wild energy has wizened and matured. Like the rest of me, Violet has been sober for almost seven years.

When I wrote the first issue of *Fucking Magic* I was deep in ANP integration work and Violet was more active than she has been for my entire recovery. People noticed this. They commented on how I had suddenly switched from an anxious introvert to a brazen extrovert, how I moved differently and laughed differently and used my energy differently. You can see it in my writing and it is the wild energy that created *Fucking Magic*, got me out of an unhealthy relationship, allowed me to rediscover my sexuality, and moved me to Montréal. But then I fell in love and falling in love is my greatest trigger and it activates all my EPs like crazy. Then Indigo becomes dominant because Indigo is the anxious one who tries to manage the EPs by strongly identifying with them. So, for the last two years, Violet has slowly begun retreating to the background again.

I come into my therapist's office fully activated in an EP. I can't stop crying. I can't see any options. It all feels terrifying and hopeless. I can't calm down. My therapist walks me through the grounding exercises and I do my best, but I can't relax. As the conversation unfolds, somehow, I bring up Violet. Somehow there is this instinct, this knowing, and I don't

Split Personality

know if it's coming from Indigo or Violet, or both of us, but I know that Violet is needed. I start to talk about Violet, about how Violet saved my life when I left that unhealthy relationship. Deep in integration work, I was able to let her take the reins and she pulled it all together. She found an apartment and got us to therapy and fell back in love with life all while holding Indigo together and holding space for their pain.

Maybe I can let Violet help me like that again. Maybe Violet can help Indigo become less identified with the EPs and more identified with Indigo. And maybe Violet can reignite that wild spark, that *fucking magic* which I love and need so much. Part of this work is letting Violet grow, deepen. Because I have repressed Violet through most of my sobriety I haven't had much time to find out who Violet is and what she likes when she's sober. I haven't given her the opportunity to be fully herself in sobriety, though I did start this process.

Violet loves intensity and pleasure. She loves sex and kink and bdsm. She loves consensual pain and crushes and deep intimacy. She loves music and poetry. Music is one of the fastest ways for me to bring Violet out. She loves to socialize. She loves to go out and be in the world. She loves to laugh and flirt. She loves looking hot and being super femme. She's a writer and she gives no fucks about the haters. She wants to feel, she loves to feel. She goes to the gym to soak in the hot tub and lies sweating in the sauna. She goes to the river and the train tracks (Indigo goes there too). She loves alleyways and abandoned places and she loves wandering the city for hours listening to music on her headphones. She revels in her senses. She loves the night. Her body is awake and alive.

Indigo is more than the EPs, they just over-identify with them. I need to let Indigo mature and deepen too, to find out who Indigo is without that EP dominance. Indigo is ambitious. They are a writer and they love their job. They work hard, meet deadlines, and are deeply motivated about the hustle. Work is the best way for me to bring Indigo up from the EPs. They love to read and to think. They're an academic, a rebel scholar, and they love to think through and talk about ideas carefully and deeply. They love finding the connections between disparate ideas and bringing different types of knowledge into conversation with each other. Their politics are deeply important to them and they care a lot about justice and working hard to help heal the world. They're introverted and relish time alone. They also love the river and the train tracks, for some of the same reasons as Violet and for different reasons too.

All of this is me, and so are the EPs. The EPs aren't bad, they are just frozen in time, caught in the visceral emotions of trauma. They are terrified for our life and trying to protect us. Violet and Indigo are my ANPs, the adults, the ones who got out and survived (although they survived in very different ways). I need to draw upon the strengths of my ANPs, and their relationship with each other, in order to get control of my EPs, and eventually to do the extremely hard work of integration. And in order to do all of this, I need to talk about it. It is so much easier if I am not too afraid to admit that I have a split personality.

Structural dissociation integration work is trauma magic. All the parts of who I am, the different ways I learned to survive, the experiences that were too awful to integrate, all of this has been split off from each other. I am fragmented but it is all still me. Trauma magic is the work of becoming whole again, unafraid of myself, unafraid of my completeness. I can't exhaust myself with the shame of hiding structural dissociation. I am so much more effective in my recovery work when I can talk about these things openly. This is who I am, all of it, and I am becoming myself in fullness. Violet, Indigo, and all the rest.

Love Water Always

I GO TO THE water. Lake Ontario. The Atlantic Ocean. The Saint Lawrence River. All of these are colonial names. I search out the true names. Niigaani-gichigami. Gta'n. Kaniatarowanénhne. I think about the lake from my childhood, the lake in my dreams. I don't know the true name of this lake, the Anishinaabemowin name. But I remember the water, the way it held me and my secrets. I remember cutting my foot on a rock as I swam from the sinking pedal boat. I remember the way the cottagers dumped sand onto the bottom of the lake, trying to crush the ecosystem, the squishy muck, the home of seaweed and fish eggs, to make it more swimmable. I remember the rock bass with their razor fins and bony bodies, an introduced species that pushed out many of the other fish who used to live there. I think about the water I called home, the way the loons and the mist and the muck and the fish were more family to me than my family and I want to call this water by its true name.

I lost touch with that lake once I told the truth of what happened to me there in the cottage on the shore. After the police and children's aid were involved, I didn't go back. And when I think of all the losses I endured, the loss of my safety and bodily autonomy and dignity, the loss of my childhood and my sexuality and first sexual experience, the loss of a family of origin that could have loved me and kept me safe, when I think of all those losses I think of the loss of that lake. Because the lake always loved me, always held me, always listened to my pain. The lake was my true family, my true protector, my true home. I told the truth and I saved myself from further violence, but in the process, I lost the lake. In my dreams I find myself in the water. In my dreams I return to the shore.

Fucking Magic

I'm visiting Halifax and I go down to the water. I don't know the Mi'kmaq name for the Atlantic Ocean. The closest thing I can find is the name for ocean, Gta'n. I see the sign which says the water isn't safe: *Swim at your own risk*. I see all the birds swimming in the water, swimming at their own risk. The seaweed is tangled among the rocks, the seashells are purple and mixed with purple plastic. I feel a numbness in my heart, a subdued panic at the ecological crisis we live in. I feel my unspeakable love for this world and my sense of helplessness in the face of its destruction. I want to show the water my love and it guts me. I want to show this world who has always loved me that the love is returned. I touch the seaweed and the rocks. I put my hands in the cold water and lick the salt off my fingers. I know its poison but it is also my body, my blood, my life, my world.

At home in Montréal/Tiohtià:ke I swim in the river, Kaniatarowanénhne. I'm not the only one who does, but a lot of people tell me it probably isn't safe. I know there is poison in the water, but my need to be enveloped in its wetness is stronger than my fear. I float on the river and my heart is at peace. I am inside the water and I am inside the world. I think about drinking water, water straight from the tap that is safe for me to drink. I think about the basic need for water, the way that water is life. I think about Indigenous communities across Canada without access to safe drinking water. How it would never fly if the city of Montréal lived under a perpetual boil advisory. I think about the Wet'suwet'en land defenders on the West coast, the Mi'kmaq grandmothers being arrested on the East coast. Water protectors trying to protect the water and the earth from the ongoing violence of capitalism and colonialism, pipelines for profit when the world is already dying and we all know.

I don't know what to do with my anger or my grief, my despair which stretches to the horizon as I stare out over this injured ocean. I touch the water and I let the water touch me. I listen to the water and let it into my heart. The water has always held me. That little lake with its invasive rock bass and long long seaweed, that bottomless lake that I swam in and walked on and loved through the changing seasons. I don't know how to save the water the way that the water saved me, but I am trying to be with the water, to be in relationship with the water, to remember that the water and I share the same fate. I am of water, and I am listening to teachers who hold the knowledge of these waters, the names and the relationships which are smothered under the amnesia of capitalism and colonialism. I don't have the answers but I can let the water into my heart. I can let it pour through the numbness and open me back up. I can remember myself, as water, as human, as in relationship. Here. Now. Always.

Incest Survivor Magic

I WANT TO READ books about pleasure by incest survivors. *I never want to think about incest again.*

I don't want to talk about it. I feel my body possessed. I think about the hotel bed but then: think isn't the word for it. I am living *it.*

I don't want or need you to tell me that it isn't true, that my body is jumping to conclusions.

This isn't about my grandfather, it is about my father.

The evidence I've collected might seem small or it might be compelling. I feel the outlines, the edges of the well. I go into the well where there is water.

I want to read books about pleasure by incest survivors. I want to be in a room full of incest survivors. I don't want us to be milling around saying things like *It wasn't that bad, other people had it worse, I'm not even sure if it counts but...*

I want you to scream in my face *I'm alive I'm alive I'm alive.* I want to feel the heat of your aliveness to feel it pulsing in you and to feel it pulsing in me.

It is exhausting, this secret. How do you know? I know in my body. I know because this is the way of my family. Like father like son. The memory skips. His hand on my neck.

I can't breathe but it is safer under water.

I want to read books about pleasure by incest survivors. I want to know how you got your body back. I want to feel the shame obliterated in the shattering of your orgasm. I want us to survive. I want us to live.

Incest Survivor Magic

I want you to look me in the eye. I want to know that you know. I want to feel the power of your resurrected body, the way you remembered your way into yourself, the way you stole it back.

Fingers

WE ARE FUCKING and I am wet, dripping. I am cumming against her and she is cumming against me. I am alive and in touch and then after, I feel her fingers push inside of me and I feel myself freeze. I feel her fingers inside of me and it makes me want to puke. I feel myself pulling backwards into the wordless space of silence, behind my body, somewhere underneath the mattress.

How many times did this happen before I even noticed, before I even named it as a problem? For years I couldn't use a diva cup or tampons. I didn't want my fingers there, inside. The thought of it made me sick, made me feel pried open, brought me to this place I can't speak, a violation. And yet even then, all through the years, I have loved being fucked. I love cocks filling me up, flesh or silicone. It's one of my favourite types of sex.

I didn't understand what was happening and so many times this ruined sex for me. Especially queer sex in which penetration with fingers is a normal, expected act. But nobody asked. And if they had would I have known to say no? Could I have articulated the sickening silence of flesh and bone fingers inside of me?

I finally say it out loud. *I know I've been raped a lot of times and a lot of the times were a lot worse. But, if you count non-consensual penetration with fingers as rape then that's how I was raped the first time I was raped and it was also the first time I had sex.* My partner looks at me. *Yes I count that as rape.*

I was fifteen when it happened. It was sudden, unexpected. An escalation that took on unstoppable force when the eighteen year old who wasn't even my boyfriend, who had never even kissed me, realized that I wasn't stopping anything. I'm an incest survivor. I wasn't stopping anything. And so then his fingers were inside of me, pushing and stretching. Afterwards I danced around his room naked and laughing because I didn't understand what was happening. I didn't understand the electric panic, the wide open violation.

There were other traumas too, finger-specific traumas. Like the time that same guy, now my boyfriend of more than a year, decided to try out fisting on me after I had talked about hearing about it in queer spaces. My mentioning of it was not an invitation for him to try it on me. Again he did not ask. Again it was not wanted or expected. Again I could not stop it. Afterward I went into his little bathroom and sucked on my own fingers. Somehow the warmth of my own mouth, my own fingers going in, prevented me from completely disappearing.

And then there was the first sex I ever had with a woman. She was twenty-one and my cooking class instructor. I was a seventeen year old wearing a *this is what a bisexual looks like* pin on my coat. We started dating. At her place she cooked me a fancy dinner. I got a migraine and I wanted to go home. She offered me a tylenol and I told her I couldn't take it because I had recently tried to kill myself using pills and I didn't want to take them anymore. She offered me another pill, one that dissolved under my tongue. She told me it was all natural and would get rid of my migraine. I now understand that it was something like ativan. I felt calm detachment as she stripped me naked and fucked me with her gloved hands. I didn't understand why I felt nothing, not nervousness, or fear, or excitement. I went home and my friend explained to me that I had been drugged.

These particular traumas are just a few in many years of rape. And I don't understand why I still love to be fucked by cocks even though I have been raped by them so many more times. I don't know why fingers in particular are tied to the experience of violation but they are. This has contributed to my feelings of being a failed queer, of being unable to have what I believed was 'real' queer sex.

It is only recently that I have learned to just say it. *I don't like to get fucked by fingers. I have a thing about it. But I like to be fucked by cocks.* This has gone over well, dildos and harnesses have appeared, or sex has gone forward without penetration. And I have been able to feel safe and in control, avoiding the dissociative disappearing into the mattress.

I was talking to my friend about how I prefer cocks and she talked about loving to feel her lovers' body inside of her. And I felt a pang of regret or grief at my inability to experience that with partners who don't have flesh cocks. I read erotica by Kaleigh Trace that describes a flaming hot sex scene involving finger fucking. The active desire of the penetrated partner called out to me, the way she longed for and pulled in the fingers. It felt like medicine for the rapes, to imagine sex like that, but it also felt like grief.

Now I can put my diva cup inside myself. I can twist it around to make sure it's popped. I can even reach my fingers way up inside and grab it and pull it out. All of this used to be impossible, used to bring up the sick feeling of violation, the desire to puke. Now I can and it makes me feel like I'm healing.

I want to heal. I want to take my body back from the people who enacted violence on me. I want to experience the pleasure of active consent and real desire. Carefully and slowly, when I feel safe and ready, I want to try to feel fingers inside of me in a way that is wanted and good.

Power and Desire

MY HAIR IS greying. I am 32 years old and I feel it. I feel the power I've developed through all my hard work and all the years I've lived. I'm growing into myself. Growing up. I feel my competence, the way I've learned to trust myself. The way I go after what I want, chasing down my dreams, not with desperation but with ease. But in some areas of my life I easily revert to learned helplessness.

I tell my partner I feel insecure about my grey hair and they tell me how hot they think it is. They tell me how hot they think I am, 32 years old, a competent, powerful, ambitious adult. And I think about what it means to be an adult. What it means to be desired in my fullness, my power. I wonder what would happen if I could fully connect my sexuality to my power. What would happen if I finally took my sexuality back, if I completely eroticized my adult, powerful, capable self?

Listening to Black Metal in My Therapist's Office

I'M DOING SENSORIMOTOR psychotherapy with my therapist. I am walking around noticing my spine, noticing the way it curls over, the way I hunch my shoulders and bow my head. I straighten up, I feel my vertebrae align. I raise my chin, look straight ahead. I notice how these changes feel. I am aware of how small I am. I am a small person. 5'1, tiny. I think about my body. I remember my body active, my body trying to fight back. There is both power and terror, the sensation of crumpling. I notice these things. I breathe through them. I return to my spine, to my straight forward gaze.

In my therapist's office we start with the simple question *How connected do you feel to your body?* My body, the animal. My body, the living creature. My body, the place where the bad things happened. My body here, breath. It's hard to answer these questions but we are making room for my structural dissociation. I laugh with my therapist that sensorimotor psychotherapy makes room for the holy trinity: trauma, insecure attachment, and structural dissociation. My splits have different answers to these questions. My EPs are right there on the edge of consciousness. I reach my arm out to hold them back.

It feels like a flood and I don't want the flood. We are trying to stay in the window of tolerance, firmly rooted in my ANPs. How connected do I feel to my body? Well, a little connected, pretty connected, not connected at all. There's a storm coming in through the window, the thunderous

Listening to Black Metal in My Therapist's Office

clap of a thousand hands. There's a fire in my chest, a contracted ball of energy, a black hole.

My therapist asks me if I need to ground. So we try to ground. We count colours in the room. We count the plants, the framed pictures on the wall. She asks me how I'm feeling and I tell her the ball in my chest is contracting further. *My EPs know what I'm doing, they know I'm trying to calm them down, and that doesn't feel safe.* She asks me to invite my ANPs fully into the room. *Use your intuition. Ask Violet, what do you need?*

I listen and suddenly a little smile breaks across my lips. I know what I need. Lately, I have been listening to ambient black metal. This anarchafeminist band called Ragana. And I have been obsessed. I have never listened to black metal before but listening to Regana fills me with this feeling of calm power. I take my phone out of my coat pocket and right there in my therapist's office I put on a black metal song. We listen to the screaming. The guitar. The drums. My shoulders drop. My breath comes back. The contracted ball in my chest eases and opens, expands.

The lyrics: *A voice I couldn't see / A dream I didn't need / We asked you to leave.*

I talk about boundaries, about my active living body, about the pent up need to say no. To scream no. To ask them to leave. I talk about music. Despite my fraught relationship to music it is one of the only things that can consistently bring me back to myself. Listening to black metal in my therapist's office is hilarious and that is not lost on me. Neither is the fact that I am resourceful, brilliant, capable. I know what I need.

I feel the drums in my body. I feel the guitar. I feel the resonance of screaming voices, voices that sound like mine. I feel the power of my breath and my breath moves through my whole body, releasing me. I unclench, I open, I drop, I exhale. And at the same time I am moving, my body is seeking out the rhythm of the music, my body is remembering aliveness, remembering action.

I tell my therapist maybe what I want is to be in a black metal band. Maybe what I need is a space for my voice, for my body, active, emotive, alive. Sensorimotor psychotherapy is opening me, bringing me here to my body, to the repetitive motions and postures that keep me stuck in the past, and orienting me to different motions, movements, that connect me to my power, that empower me.

My intuition knows the secret power that I have been taught all along to disavow.

Straight Girl Trauma

I WAS NEVER A straight girl. I was a queer child traumatized by sexual abuse and pervasive homophobia. My queerness was a little flame, an entire night sky kept secret in my heart. It was painful and hard to be a survivor queer child and I barely made it out alive.

Later in the city, in the alleyways and bars, I became a straight girl. A drunk, fucked up, traumatized, compulsively sexual straight girl. I guess they call it traumatic re-enactment but I needed men's desire. I chased it down and consumed it the same way I did with the booze. I prioritized it over everything, except the booze.

I let men use me and hurt me and fuck me and refuse to kiss me and walk by me on the street pretending not to know me. I got excited about their 5am texts *u up?* believing with all my heart that it was love. It had to be love because I needed love and I had no idea what the fuck love was.

I didn't care if they were married or had girlfriends. I felt no guilt to be the one they were cheating on their partners with. I got a twisted kind of pride from it. Because I knew I was in competition with every other straight girl.

Whether we liked it or not. We could not love each other. We didn't know what the fuck love was. All we knew was how to glare at each other, how to stare each other down for looking at a particular man, how to covet what passed as affection from men who treated us as interchangeable things.

It was hard to be a straight girl. It was hard to need the desire of men so badly. It was hard to fear them and their violence while constantly surrendering myself up to them, taking them home, into my arms, into my bed. It was hard to be driven wild and crazy with the impossibility of wanting anything else as much as I wanted their attention. It was hard to feel shame for this but also to know that it was true. It was hard waking up not knowing where I was, turning over to find some man already touching me.

It was hard to know they didn't love me. It was hard the way they said awful things to me, the way they openly rated my body and compared me to other straight girls. And it was hard to defend them, to know that I had known queerness and turned away from it, to know that I needed this more than I needed anything.

I couldn't explain it. I guess they call it traumatic re-enactment. I guess I was a queer child brought up under explicit patriarchal rule. The rule of the father. And his father. The rule where I had no control over what happened to my body. The rule where there was no easy way to get love.

When I was maybe twelve I wrote in my diary *I hate myself for how much I need attention. I crave it like a drug.* I wrote those words after trying to get my father's attention, after trying to draw him in, after being shut out and rejected again. When I was maybe twelve I slid my body off the side of the bed and slept in the crevice on the floor between the bed and the wall because I was so sickeningly terrified of my father's body sleeping next to me.

I knew what men could do, what they did.

I tried to explain this to my ex-boyfriend. The person who I believed at the time to be the love of my life. Queer love even, because we were both queer, but it turned out that he demanded I be a straight girl. He raged over the fact that I was such a slut. I tried to tell him I never had a choice and so now I chose it. He told me *that's not how it fucking works.* He told me I should have chosen something else.

But little did he know that I was choosing the same thing even then. I was choosing the same thing by choosing him. My willingness to love him more than anything or anyone, my willingness to love him even after he put my whole body through the drywall. I was choosing the same thing.

Straight Girl Trauma

Sometimes I still feel it in my body. The straight girl logic. The entrapment of compulsory heteronormativity. The way we learn to fight each other, compete for scraps. The way we carry these fucked up beliefs with us, as trauma, even after we leave straightness behind. We bring them with us into our queer worlds and our queer relationships.

I want to heal my straight girl trauma. I want to recover from the years and years I spent prioritizing men. I want to be queer, thoroughly queer, down in my bone marrow, deep in my mitochondria. I want all the neuropathways in my brain to sing with deep pure queer love, affection, and desire. I want to know my worth, inherent, unshakeable. I want to dig the binary, hierarchical, competitive thinking the fuck up and out of my body. I want to take myself back from the trauma of the straight world, from the violence of men. I want to love and desire in freedom. As an anarchist. As a queer person. As a survivor. As a femme. As a witch.

I want to love the straight girl in me and all the straight girls in the world. I don't want to turn straight girls into the enemy. I want their freedom, their safety, their pleasure and joy, not matter who they desire and want to fuck. I want that for myself too. I want desire and love to be safe for all of us and I want compulsory heteronormativity and gendered violence to burn to the fucking ground.

I Choose to Live

*I*T'S 6AM AND I'm crying in my bed. I'm so sad. I feel so rejected. Every little thing hurts. Every little thing feels like an attack. My mind keeps circling around. Why do I have such bad luck with dating? Why do people get so excited about me and then totally flake? I'm thinking about all the little heartbreaks of the past year, all the times I've put my heart on the line, only to be hurt again.

The pain comes in waves and it sinks me under water. I don't understand the depths of my grief. I don't understand that I am grieving. I feel this shame which moves through my body. Self-hatred and self-contempt. Why am I so perpetually unable to be loved? This is what I'm asking myself. I hold myself responsible for my loneliness, my inability to develop the kinds of connections that would really nourish me.

A little later I stare at my inbox, the message I've marked as 'unread' even though I've already read it. The message from my aunt which, while claiming to be loving, dismisses and invalidates all my rage and pain, coaxes me to be forgiving, accepting. *Your parents love you so much.* My aunt, my mother's sister, who wasn't there and didn't see the sexual abuse I experienced. She tells me what my experience was. She refers to the sexual assault as the 'incident'. She describes my grandfather as a sick man, says that my father is grieving the loss of the healthy father he once had.

The numbness is more painful than anything else. It writhes inside me like a living thing. I feel the resonance, the layers of meaning. The way I hate myself for being unloved. *The way I hate myself for being unloved.* I hear my own voice in my Trauma Informed Polyamory workshops explaining that *Shame is an attempt at control, an attempt at feeling safe, because if the problem is me then maybe I can fix it, if the problem is that there is something deeply wrong with me then maybe I can become good, maybe I can become safe, maybe I can become loved.*

I open my aunt's email again and stare down her words. I press reply and I tell her *You have incorrect information about my childhood.* My fingers slam against the keyboards as I tell her what it was. I write out the truth. I feel myself cracking open as I break all the rules. I say the things I was never allowed to say. I don't try to protect her or my parents from the reality of what was done to me. I don't hide or diminish the depth of the violation and the reality of whose responsibility it was to protect me. I tell the truth.

The anger comes. The sweet good protective anger. And the numbness releases and the grief is held. I understand. I understand that I've been crying not about all my little heartbreaks. I've been crying about the big heartbreak, the massive one. I've been showering contempt and shame over myself not because I'm having a hard time in my dating life but because I'm a survivor of incest. That's the truth. That's the reality. The loss of love I'm grieving is the loss of my parent's love. And even greater, I am grieving my own self-protection, the way I was domesticated into abandoning myself.

I come back to myself with a vengeance. I feel myself, fierce protector. I feel myself, good healthy rage. I am angry. It is not pathological. It is not unhealthy. It is the right and good response to what has been done to me. And in the light of my healthy anger my shame melts away. In the glowing heat of my anger I understand that I am not and never was unlovable. I understand that other people don't ever and can't ever dictate my worthiness. I understand that people's flakiness or lack of interest is their own thing. And it's fine. It's not about me and it cannot revoke my deep inherent worthiness.

I don't know when I will be able to know and recognize that I'm having an emotional flashback. I don't know when I will be able to come to the child in me with that fierce protective anger, immediately,

Fucking Magic

consistently. But I feel it now. I feel safe with myself. I feel loved. I understand who I am. I understand what happened to me, what was done to me, and what it did to me. And I feel the expanse of my incredible power, the way I survived, got myself out of there alive.

Now I insist on the truth like my life depends on it because it literally does. I tell my aunt the truth. I write the words. I say exactly what happened and why I can't pretend that it didn't. I write the words *I choose to live.*

Nervous System Love

I AM IN THE bath, my body lying against my partner's body. The hot water enveloping us. My partner holds open the science book we are reading together. They read to me about molten magma in the earth's centre. They read to me about the earth's magnetic field. Their voice is familiar and soothing. We are slippery and wet and warm. Our nervous systems are in sync. We are regulated. Our bodies, alive. Hearts beating. Breath moving.

I have spent most of my life in the electric danger of the sympathetic nervous system. I always thought love meant those cataclysmic surges of adrenaline, that racing heart panic. Even now, two years into a safe and secure relationship, I need to practice the work of regulation. I need to remember and remember again how to feel safe.

There is nothing more frightening than finding danger where I expect safety. There is nothing more frightening than misrecognizing my partner, seeing in them not the person that they are but the terror of my past. Every time these misrecognitions happen, every time some miscommunication or conflict activates my sympathetic nervous system, I have to find a way to come back. I have to realign with the present moment, with my body here and now, with my partner's body, with the person my partner is. I have to find the courage to return to safety, to trust the safety that is here.

After a conflict that sent both of us out of our windows of tolerance I lay next to my partner on their bed. I'm not touching them because I know they don't usually like to be touched when they are triggered. I am triggered too and part of me is dissociating and floating away. Another part of me is here. Another part of me understands what has happened, the way I got triggered and started living in the past in my body. There is a part of me who recognizes my partner, who remembers my nervous system, who knows what's going on.

My partner and I talk. We talk about what we are feeling in our triggered bodies. They ask me to come closer, to touch them, and I do. This act of trust de-activates me completely. I understand that my partner feels safe with me, even in this threat to safety, even in this sympathetic nervous system situation, there is a part of them that recognizes me, that asks me to come close. We lie together, touching each other, trusting each other, remembering each other. Each time we are able to do this we move further into the present. The past has less control.

There is such pleasure in love. Real, trust worthy love. Love where I don't have to be perfect. Love where my grey hair and my messy room and anything I'm feeling insecure about is not a threat to my extreme worthiness. Love where I am known, and known, deeper and deeper as time unfolds. And I am still loved. Love where we change, we each become more of ourselves, and we are still loved.

I love feeling safe and loved. Omfg I love it. I can't even explain the pleasure of safety, the way my very bones sing with it. Learning to move through conflict with my partner, learning to move through my nervous system and return to my window of tolerance, finding myself in safety breathing against my partner's breathing body: there is nothing more beautiful than this. Real love. Safe love. Recognition. Remembering who I am, who my partner is, where we are, what year it is.

I don't think there is enough written about the pleasure of learning real deep safe love. Especially for survivors. Especially for queers. Especially for polyamorous people. We know all about excitement. We know all about danger. We know all about fighting for the recognition that the ways we love are legitimate. Queer love, polyamorous love, love between addicts and traumatized people, this is real love. But we don't have a lot of space to talk about the staggering beauty of learning to feel safe. We don't have a lot of possibility models for long term deep safe regulated nervous system love.

    Learning attachment theory and polyvagal theory has helped me so, so much in my journey of learning to love and be loved the way I deserve. I want everyone to have access to that information, which is why I do the teaching that I do. I lie in bed with my partner in the morning after a night of our bodies entangled in the sheets. I tell them I'm teaching another workshop tonight and we talk about that. I make us our morning coffees and we talk about our days.

Fucking Magic

#10

Be Gay Do Crime

A*RE YOU COMFORTABLE facing arrest?* I read the words in the email reply. I reached out to a group doing direct action around the climate emergency we are all facing. They ask me if I'm comfortable facing arrest. The truth is, I'm not comfortable with it. No one is comfortable with it. But there are people who are willing to face it. I feel the fear in me, the razor edge of terror. I want to be unafraid but I'm not. The colossal size of the police, the state, the corporations going on wild killing sprees in the face of all this death. They have a monopoly on violence. I know this. And I know we are living in dystopia when the cry to save our dying planet is met with arrest.

It's a careful balance. Letting the fear and the love drive me but not falling off the cliff edge of despair. I keep reading about the end of the world and it sends me into this animal panic. My nervous system is sending off an alarm and I can't answer. I feel like the dog in the cage that they kept shocking over and over again until the dog just laid down and took it. I try to let my grief and fear and anger act as fuel. I try not to collapse into inaction. I try to remember that the actions we are taking now are important, even in the face of our powerlessness. We have power. And I still don't know what the answer is.

I'm sitting next to her on the little couch by the train tracks. It's the back seat of a van that someone left here for people to sit on. It's spray-painted and covered with sticky seeds. The wind is wild today, whipping my hair up in a frenzy. She is spared because she recently shaved her head. We sit there in the bright light and the wild air and we talk. I have to go soon. I have to meet someone to pick up the keys to the studio

Fucking Magic

I'm renting. I know I'm running late but I just want to sit here on this couch with her, here at the end of the world.

I feel the fear in me, the frozenness. We talk about trauma and queerness and I've been brave several times by being direct about how I feel about her. But in the moment, in real time, I can feel the nothingness inside me that eats up everything. I can feel my inability to speak, to say the simple things, to give voice to my heart, my attraction, my desire. She breaks that thick ferocious ice inside of me by saying she wants to kiss me. We are flustered and laughing but also full of care and wanting. And we switch sides so that my hair won't blow in her face.

We sit on that couch by the train tracks and we kiss. I slow down and bring my traumatized bodymind into the moment. I let myself be here, right now, with her. I listen to the language of her movements, the way she touches me, her lips on mine. I breathe into it and I let myself go. We don't have a lot of time. Not as much as I'd like. And I wish it wasn't so hard for me to arrive at this moment. But the two of us, against all odds, against trauma stacked against trauma, against a queerphobic world that does everything to prevent this, found our way to this moment. Right here. Right now.

As we walk away from the tracks she reaches out and holds my hand. I like that so much that I don't even have words for it. The wind is blowing us around and we are walking together, holding hands.

At the anarchist bookfair I sit at my table selling zines and books. The room is full of queers and anarchists and people trying so hard to dream up and live another world. All around me are signs and patches that read *No Borders, Abolish Prisons, ACAB*. Everyone is talking and full of chaotic anarchist fair energy. And most of the people I talk to feel the impulse toward criticism. I feel it in myself. The impulse to focus on what is wrong here, to qualify our joy and our pleasure by acknowledging that we know it isn't perfect. Acting somehow like we are above this anarchist fair and yet at the same time we are here. We are here and we are full of pleasure and joy and anxiety and fear.

It isn't perfect and I could tell you all sorts of things that are wrong with it. But I feel a shift inside myself, a deep desire to focus on what is good and right and profoundly beautiful about this place. I want to give my energy, myself, to this new world we are building and I want to believe in it with all my heart. *What is this but an act of faith?* And I feel that faith inside me, breaking me open, shattering the numbness that has been protecting me from my despair.

A group of anarchists do a giant grief ritual in the main room where I am tabling. They call up our grief, they name our dead, they ask us to mourn. They pass around bowls of flowers and ask us to pour our grief into them. We pass the bowls from hand to hand. People are crying. People are holding silence. I feel the grief in me like a wall of water rising from an endless well. I feel the grief in me like a violent storm that might tear me apart if I'm not careful. All that comes is the edge of tears and I breathe with what is, and I know that it's here.

Later someone comes to watch my table for me so I can walk around and check out the other building. In the other building I overhear a conversation about a book called *Be Gay, Do Crime*. I go to the table where I hear it is sold and I buy it. I come back to my table and my friend who was watching my table tells me someone came by and left a zine for me. I look at it. *Be Gay, Do Crime*. It's the introduction from the book I just bought in zine form. I feel the resonance, the ripple in the fabric of spacetime as I receive an important message from the universe: be gay, do crime.

I sit down at my table and read. I feel the shiver of recognition, the waking up of my cells, opening onto a power that has always existed. The words on the page ask me to remember the first time I called myself an anarchist, the first time I chose freedom, the first time I found my refusal, that powerful word *No*. I breathe and I read and I remember. No I don't want my grandfather to touch me. No I don't want to cower beneath my father's screams. No I don't want to do what I'm told. No I don't want to follow rules that make no sense. No I don't want my freedom restricted. No I don't want my agency taken from me. *No*.

Fucking Magic

The words on the page paint an anarchist mythology, pull together a history, a legacy of queer refusal, of resistance to the state, the police, the corporations, the domination and violence that we can enact on each other. The words on the page invoke solidarity, the capacity to act collectively, to find pleasure and joy in our refusal. I remember that my pleasure and joy is refusal. I remember the pleasure of resistance, the pleasure of crime. The words on the page pull up from me some deep truth that I've been refusing to remember because it is too powerful and beautiful and breathtaking and true. They aren't afraid to call it magic.

You Are Sucking My Cock and I Can Feel It

*M*Y MIDDLE FINGER is on my clit running slow circles. My thumb is just above the bone of my pussy. You are kissing me on my hips, on my stomach. Your breath is warm, your movements slow. Your mouth finds my thumb and I am surprised by the warmth and wetness as you take me into yourself. I gasp at the sensation. You are sucking my cock. My thumb becomes my cock and the warmth and wetness of your mouth connects with the feeling of my finger on my clit. It all becomes one feeling. *You are sucking my cock and I can feel it.*

We ride the pleasure together. You work on my cock, taking me in, feeling me fill you. My finger on my clit pulls the pleasure of your mouth down my cock and roots it deep within my body. I want this. I have always wanted this and here in this moment there is no question about who I am or what my body is capable of. There is no contradiction. It is good and it is right and you are so fucking sexy working away on my cock, letting me have your mouth.

The numbness and impossibility of my body gives way to pure presence and sensation. My ghost cock becomes a real cock and I don't have to explain it or justify it. I only have to feel it. You give yourself to my cock the way you would give yourself to any cock you love. You are enraptured by my pleasure. Your pleasure extends from my pleasure. It all becomes one feeling.

Fucking Magic

We ride the feeling until the dam breaks and I cum, shuddering, feeling the orgasm deep in my bones and all the way through my cock. You press your mouth down and let my orgasm explode inside of you.

River Slut

WE MATCH ON tinder. You're only in the city for a couple more days. What the hell, I ask you on a date. You're too cute and anarchist and femme not to. The summer is finally heating up and I want to be in the water. We meet in Verdun and grab coffee and head down to the river.

We talk about our lives, our lives which overlap today but probably won't again. We talk about being gay and doing crime, or as you put it, being crime and doing gay. We stretch out in the sun and listen to the river and the birds. We talk about the end of the world.

The water is cold and you don't go all the way in. I tell you I'm a seal and I live for the water. I go out and dive in. I feel the shock that opens me, the cold that completely recalibrates me. I feel my body make the choice between the warmth of the sun and the cold of the water. I choose the cold.

Then I join you on the shore. I throw my dripping body down on the towel and let the sun dry me. I feel the anticipation between us, the femme4femme nervousness. Even though I'm a perpetual bottom, I'm learning to be a top. Even though I'm trained in passivity I am learning about assertiveness.

I breathe the sun and the air into my body. I feel the electric energy of excitement and fear. *What's the worst that could happen?* I ask myself. *What if I just go for it?*

And so in my classic queer way I start to talk around the subject. I say *Thanks for hanging out today.* You say *Yeah I'm so glad we could meet.* I say *How are you feeling?* You say *I'm feeling really good. How about you?*

Fucking Magic

I say *I'm feeling good*. And then I spit the words out of my mouth before they have the chance to retreat into the secret depths of shame inside me. *Can I kiss you?*

You smile. You say *Yes*. You lie beneath me and I kiss you. You pull me close and kiss me hard. You have no hesitation. There are no ambiguous signals. You make your desire clear and I lean into it, feeling you, feeling my body, feeling pleasure which I am learning how to feel without disappearing.

As we make out my body slips toward the water. I feel my toes touch the river. I am tangled between you, the water, and the earth. I feel the rise of pleasure in me and I push my body into the ground to stay with it. I feel your mouth and your movement. I feel the bone of my pussy pressing hard against the ground.

I stop and pull back to look at you. You are beautiful. We kiss some more, long and slow and intense. Then I feel the water call me, the cold that I need to feel safe, to come home to myself. The water which knows me, knows how to make me stay. I look at you lying in the sun and say *I want to jump back in the water*. You say *Okay*. And I do.

Queer Sober Dance Party

MY FRIENDS AND I rush from the 12 step meeting to a fast food place to buy fries and burgers before running to the metro so we can get to the sober queer dance party before it ends. I'm dipping fries in ketchup and shoving them in my mouth as we laugh and rush and hurry. I didn't know if I wanted to go to the dance party. I'm scared of feeling frozen and stuck in my body and then spiralling into shame. But the meeting was good and my friends and I are laughing and having fun and I feel safe and happy and at ease. I don't want to go home alone. I want to join them.

The bus ride is long and hectic and all of us are feeling tired by the time we make it to the party. We get inside to see a lot of people standing around. We run into some friends and they tell us that people haven't really been dancing. Everyone is too shy and it has an awkward high school dance feel. I feel nervous too and the giddy excitement of running and eating fries is falling away. I worry about getting triggered. But I get a grapefruit sparkling water and stand with my friends out front. Socializing, talking, being together.

More friends arrive and we greet them enthusiastically. The energy is starting to build again and I am feeling the glow of love and community. These are my people, my community, my family: queer and trans sober addicts in recovery. We're all here together and we're all happy to see each other. Hugging, laughing, talking, catching up. A few people head inside to start dancing, to break the silence of the dance floor. I hang back because I'm worried. What if I can't move? What if I freeze? What if the shame gets me?

Fucking Magic

After awhile I get up the nerve to go inside and I find my friends dancing together and laughing and joking around. Now a lot of people are dancing and there is ease and joy in the room. I approach the circle of my friends and take my place among them. I begin to move, to feel the music in my body. The laugher of my friends, the way they are being silly and having fun, it makes me feel safe and it helps me relax. I don't freeze. The shame doesn't get me.

Now everyone is dancing. The energy in the room is alive and electric and building. Everyone is doing their own thing, together. Everyone is enjoying the pleasure of music and movement. Everyone is expressing themselves, their genders, their bodies, their movements, in a way that feels good for them. I feel myself start to enjoy the music and the movement. I remember how I used to love dancing when I was drunk. How I was unafraid and just moved. I begin to feel that movement again but this time I am sober. We are sober. The room is sober. And so many of us are traumatized addicts and alcoholics in recovery. So many of us are learning for the first time how to find pleasure and joy in our bodies, the present moment, now.

I feel this freedom and this joy. I feel deeply attached to and in love with the people in my life while also feeling uninhibited and relaxed. That means I feel safe. I feel safe knowing that my friends love me, that they want to see me free and happy and at ease in my body. We sing the choruses of the songs together. We cheer and laugh and build the energy until it breaks us open.

I'm so happy that I'm here. I love being sober. I love being queer.

Do You Want to Kiss Me?

It takes me awhile to have sex these days and that's okay. I went through a slow transition from being a bisexual who hooked up with men on first dates to a trauma gay who takes my time and spends a number of dates kissing, making out, talking about feelings, learning about each other. I was shocked by the transition and a bit dismayed at first. I wanted sex to be easy. But it turns out sex isn't easy. Sex is a process and it's hard and there are a lot of skills involved and a lot of careful risks. Sex seemed easy with men because they initiated it and made it happen. I just had to say yes, and often they didn't even wait for that. Sex with men was often a roll of the dice to see whether I would be traumatized or how traumatized I would be. And there were times when it was hot and nice and other times when it was truly fucked up. But either way, I'm gay now. That happened slowly and on its own accord and I resisted it and tried to continue to want men's desire. But turns out I don't fucking care about it anymore.

But I can't just have sex with women and femmes and queers the way I had sex with men. Especially because I am often dating people with the same fraught history as me, people who are very traumatized and have also been socialized to be receptive to other people's desires rather than to be forthcoming with their own. For a long time I was really stressed about this and I would shame spiral about it. *Why is it so hard to have sex with women? Why do I keep going on all these dates and never having sex? Why is it so scary and hard?* But now I feel differently about it. Now I don't expect sex with women and queers and femmes to be the same as the sex I had with men. Now my trauma is invited into the room, and so is theirs. Now our femmeness and all the baggage that comes with it is welcome. Now we communicate and we take our time. And I'm still a slut. This is what being a slut looks like for me today.

We sit next to each other in the summer sun and talk about art and writing and our lives. We talk about polyamory and dating and queerness. We talk about biphobia and femmephobia and being queers with lots of experience dating men. I say *Yeah and now I'm really intentionally prioritizing queer dating. Dating men was always easier but now I don't want easy. I want to work at my gayness, commit myself to it.* I say *There's this thing that happens where I go on dates with girls and so often I can't read their signals and it ends up feeling like a friend hang out and I want desire to flow between us but I don't know if it's wanted.* And she says *Yeah I know exactly what you mean. I go on dates with girls and nothing happens and then we hug and say Okay bye! And I'm left feeling like I don't know what happened.* I say *Yeah exactly. I've felt this way so many times and I'm realizing like, we have never learned how to be direct about our desire. We are used to men making all the moves.*

We sit in silence for a second watching the wind in the bright green leaves, feeling the sun on our skin. I look at her and I say *Do you want to kiss me?* She laughs, *Yes.* And then she scootches closer to me and we look into each other's eyes and brush each other's long hair out of our faces and then we kiss. We are slow at first, careful. Her kisses are delicate, cautious, exploratory. I respond to her, listen to her body language, feel her lips on mine, play close attention. We stop to look at each other again. Without words we are checking. *Is this okay?* We smile at each other. She looks at my lips and moves in to kiss me again.

Now we are making out and we are both moving into it, sensing each other's desire and feeling safe in it. She moves closer to me, her arms are around me. She is kissing me and I am lost in it. We are claiming this space. We have found a way through the trauma and the socialization to each other. We recognize each other. We name our desire. And now like so many queers before us we have found the pleasure of each other.

Making out is slutty as fuck and queer as fuck. Making out is not less than sex. This make out session is so much more powerful and hot than so many hook ups I've had that followed the predictable script of heterosexual male desire. This is desire without script. This is desire as daring. This is desire as care. We are careful with each other. We take our time. We create the space we need to meet ourselves and each other.

And it's fucking hot.

Violet

THERE'S A SECRET part of me, a part of me that knew the truth but at the same time was untouched by it. There is a part of me that did not consent, that was never broken, domesticated, tamed. There is a part of me that knew the wild world, that felt the poetry in my blood, that knew the shame was theirs not mine. I didn't take it on. There is a part of me who refused.

This part of me was kept separate and safe. She has no shame. She is not desperate and helpless and full of anxiety. She is calm and full of laughter. She is smug and certain and full of herself. Full of myself. In the sense that I know where I end and another person begins. In the sense that I know who I am and I do not betray myself. I have nothing to prove to you.

This part of me comes over me like magic. She comes over me and shows me the world through her eyes. She is powerful and competent and unafraid. She doesn't flinch away from the truth. She holds it steady in her gaze. And I am so grateful that she survived, that I was able to split her off and protect her, keep her alive.

I put on bright red lipstick. I put on the Plasmatics, Hole, Patti Smith. I catch my own eyes in the mirror and I see myself. This is the part of me who made the other choice, the part of me who didn't walk into his arms that day, who looked him dead in the eyes and said *No, get the fuck away from me.* She is wild and free and my parents did everything they could to destroy her.

I am learning how to invoke her, conjure her, bring her to the surface, call her back. I am learning to feel her in the background, watching,

Violet

having her own opinion of the situation. I am learning to let her help, to let her take charge, to let her show me the way back to myself. Because I am her. She is the part of me who always knew it was wrong. She is the part of me who survived in the wilderness. She is the one who chose freedom over love, who chose the wild sacred world, who chose herself.

Punk in My 30s

*I*WANT TO SMILE at the queers I see on the street. I want to say *How are you? Who are you? Can we be friends?* I want to feel that solidarity. Sometimes I do. I don't want to be shy. I don't want to feel suspicion. I want to be in this together. Because we are in this together.

I'm becoming a punk in my 30s. I'm growing into the punk I always was. I tell people I wasn't a punk in my 20s and people disagree. I tell my date I've been making zines since I was twelve and they say *That's punk.* I guess it's true. I'm a literary punk. DIY magic. Never waiting for someone to say my writing was good enough. Never waiting for approval or permission. Writing because I needed to write. Publishing with what I had. I still make zines with scissors and glue, just like I always did.

Now I go to the studio twice a week. An hour and a half all on my own. I plug in the mic and the amp and tune up my guitar. I drink my coffee. I take it easy. I let my body feel the music. I let myself enjoy myself. I feel the calluses on my fingers thickening again. I feel the deep love I was always afraid of, always running away from. I remember who I am and I'm a fucking punk.

I forget who said it but I read somewhere that punk is the creative possibilities that open up in the context of limitations, whether that be financial limitations, or limitations in training or skill. Punk is making with what we have, doing what we can, and it's the beauty and power that comes from that. Punk means I don't have to wait until I'm good enough, until I prove myself.

I was always so afraid to claim my place in punk. Getting beat up at that hardcore show when I was nineteen fucked me up real bad. Being an anti-social alcoholic for so many years fucked me up real bad. And now I'm 32 and I'm supposed to be growing up and aligning my life with capitalism and heteronormative bullshit. But I don't want to and I can't. As I age I am becoming more and more radicalized and the simple pleasure and joy of punk rock is something that means so much to me.

I want to play music with people I trust. I want to sing and press my fingers into strings. It doesn't have to be good and I don't have to be good. I want to show you what's beautiful inside of me. I want to show you what survived. I want to show you my refusal, my pleasure, my desire. I want to take the words that have always poured from my fingers and I want to let them out of my mouth. I want to make noise and I want to move and I want to take my body back.

I want to lie on my back in the dirt. I want to feel close to my friends. I want to feel safe in my body. I want to feel safe expressing myself. If it's the only thing I ever accomplish in this life I want to be free.

Feel It All

SLUTTY OUTFITS. PSORIASIS on my arms and legs. Grey in my hair. My body, alive. My body come back. I lose the connection. I find the connection. I come back to myself.

In my dreams I remember the repressed rage. It's right there at the surface. It's waiting to explode. Violation, humiliation, helplessness. *I'll fucking kill you I'll fucking kill you I'll fucking kill you.* It's right there. *When I was a kid I used to think about killing him. I used to think about soaking his dentures in poison. I wondered if that would kill him.*

I can't feel this so I can't feel anything. If I feel this I will feel everything. I am so sick of being so mentally ill. For the first time I want integration. I want to be one person. I want to feel all of it. I want to feel it all and I don't want to die from it. I don't want to do anything fucked up.

My fingers are magic. They are fast and they are sure. I put your hand on my clit. I am full of rage and helplessness. I want to smash something. I try to breathe. I try to relax. I try to show you the movement, the way to unlock the pleasure in my body. The numbness brings on the shame, brings on the rage. I want you to stay with me and move with me through numbness to sensation. I want to feel.

I want to get off on my own pleasure not just on yours. I don't want to feel shame and rage and disgust at my body for how hard it can be for me to have sex. I want to feel the pleasure and I want it to be easy. But it isn't easy at all.

I will feel it all. I will feel those feelings and I will be gutted by them.

Feel It All

I am crying in the rain and I know the church is closed but I go anyway. I sit outside the locked doors in the pouring rain. I am trying to be close to my mother (the queen of heaven). I am trying to find a secure base. I need to feel safe. I don't feel safe. I read in attachment theory articles that I need to imagine someone from my childhood who made me feel safe and loved and I just cry and cry and cry. There is no one.

If I unlock the doors to my heart will I survive it? If I trust you will you betray me and violate me like everyone else I trusted did? If I don't try so hard will I still be loved? If I don't struggle will I still be safe?

I wake up to a thunderstorm. I feel it in my body. The rain and bright green leaves. The thunder and the lightning cracking the sky. I come back to myself like the lightning. If I feel this then I have to feel everything. If I feel everything then I can feel this.

Waking from a Dream

IT HAPPENS AT the same time. I start masturbating again. I go months without touching myself. I don't notice. I have no desire. Then one day, I do. I reach for my vibrator and I let myself imagine the thing that turns me on the most and I revel in my fantasy and I cum. Then later, I decide to ride my bike. I went months without riding, a year. Now I pump my tires and I ride. I ride all the way out to Nun's Island, a place I've never been. I find a secret spot in the trees by the shore of the river. I swim. I stand in the water. I pray, not so much with words, but with my body. I come out of the water and lie on my towel among the trees. No one is around. I slip my hand inside my bikini bottoms, feel my pussy pressing against my fingers, let my finger find that rhythm that I like so much. And there, under the bright sun, the green leaves, with the water close by, I cum.

It's like a dam broke. It's like I didn't know I was dissociating. It's like I just passed through a barrier I didn't know was there. I see my tarot cards on the shelf. I haven't read in so long. I take them down. I sit by my altar. I notice that my room is clean. How long was it a mess for? And then I just put on music and I cleaned it. I organized my zines and the top shelf in my closet. Now I'm sitting at my altar pulling cards. The cards start coming. So much Major Arcana. *Strength. The Fool. The High Priestess.* Again and again. The magic comes back. I can feel it. The universe is speaking to me again and it's because I am listening.

Before I know it I am finishing the poetry chapbook that I have been writing for years. I'm going on dates and expressing my attraction. I'm finding words which have been so choked up with silence. I go on a date and I bring my vibrator. I take it out and I show my partner. I tell them how I like to be touched. I feel that old familiar shame rising to the surface and each time it does I crush it with all the strength I possess. I stay with my pleasure, my body, my neon pink vibrator, my partner's intent attention. My voice, like the river, flowing, unstuck, unfrozen. I feel this pleasure and satisfaction at being able to speak. *Here, right here, like this. A little softer. A little softer. Here.*

It happens suddenly and it happens gradually. I notice that I have expressed a desire. I notice that I have expressed attraction and have experienced rejection and unbelievably I am not filled with shame. I brace myself for the impact but it doesn't come. I hear the words *I guess I just feel platonically toward you* after I have braved the conversation of queer attraction, and instead of feeling disgusting I feel fine.

The shame isn't mine. I say these words to my therapist. But then I notice myself living them. I begin to feel the power of myself as an adult, as a worthy, equal person. The repulsion and terror that I secretly feel toward my own sexuality suddenly disappears. It isn't here.

I say these things to myself. *I am beautiful. I am fucking gay. I love myself so much.* I am 32 years old. I am a homosexual. I am alive.

What happened to me doesn't define me. I mean it. What happened to me doesn't define me anymore.

Cutting Fences

THE BOLT CUTTERS close down on the chainlink fence. I feel the pressure and then the easy release as the chain breaks away from itself. Snip, snip, snip. Just like that the fence comes away and in its place is an open hole, a passageway. This fence was easy. But there's another one that's harder. Thicker chainlink and a whole other reinforcement second fence, but we cut through that too. Taking turns in the tall grass under the cover of darkness, one of us cuts and the other keeps watch. We restore the freedom of movement which was just recently taken away. We open up the fence, make it passable.

This is work and it is good work. It is meaningful and challenging. There is problem solving as we figure out the best way to cut the second fence. There is strategy in our choice of location for the hole. There is collaboration as we take turns cutting and keeping watch. There is laughter and pleasure and joy as we take back this space so frequently used by our friends and strangers and community members. It's community service. It's refusal. It's affirmation of the world we want to live in. A world of freedom, not fences. A world where we can move.

I make the final cut. *There it is, that's the one.* I take the final big section of fence and throw it away. *That's what I think of your fence* I say laughing. The hole stands before us where there used to be a barrier. Possibility has opened where there used to be a closure. It's a beautiful hole. Nice and big and well placed. So many people will make use of it. And for that we are glad.

You are standing next to me, beaming with success and pride. I lean into you and kiss you. Standing there before our newly made hole, bolt cutters still in my hand, we make out. Our bodies affirming the pleasure of our refusal, the intimacy of our criminality.

It's a small thing but it is everything.

Grief

I T'S UNDER THE surface and it wants to come out. It rushes over me. My mind can get caught in these spirals, repeating beliefs that hurt me. But I want to grieve. That's what my body is trying to tell me. There has never been any ritual, any witnessing, any memorial or ceremony to honour my grief.

I type the words *I am just so sad and full of grief at everything that was taken from me.*

It isn't just the original losses: the loss of love, the loss of safety, the loss of my first sexual experience as something that should have been good and mine not horrifying and forced, or even the subsequent losses: the many years in which I gave myself away to more trauma over and over again because it was all I knew how to do.

In some ways it is the ongoing losses that hurt the most. The way that intimacy and sexuality are still so fucking hard for me after seven years of recovery. The way I have to work so hard at something I want so much, the way it's one step forward and two steps back, the shame that keeps coming out of nowhere and crushing me, the way I see other people access these things with ease.

And so I grieve. Maybe for the first time, I say it without trying to fix it. You listen without offering advice. There in that container of witnessing the tears come hot and full, they release from where they have been waiting for so long.

It isn't right. It isn't okay. It fucking sucks and it's awful. I am sad and I am angry and I am heartbroken. And all this hard work, I shouldn't

Grief

have had to do any of it. And all the things that were stolen from me should have been mine.

It's that simple. So I let myself cry. I let myself grieve.

La fin de leur monde

*I*CARE ABOUT THE train tracks because they are a common. I care about the train tracks because they are a place where things still grow wild. I care about the train tracks because people use them, cut across them, walk along them, write messages, hang out, fuck. They are not a public space. They are a common. And now there's train track cops coming up and down the tracks giving people tickets. They're repairing the holes in the fences and keeping people out. It's a small thing but it is everything. This awareness of the way that our movement is restricted, the way we aren't even allowed a small space to do what we want without the presence of cops.

It took me awhile to realize that I'm an anarchist, to realize that anarchism is the blood in my veins, the heart of my politics and my spirituality. I was raised to believe in reform, to have some kind of hope that the system could be changed. I was brainwashed into being unable to imagine a world without borders, without cops, without a government telling us what to do. But even as a child I hated the imposed authority of my school teachers who controlled me and never had to offer any explanation for why they made the rules they did. Even as a child I rebelled deeply against the abuse in my family. I saw the way that power worked, the way that I was denied autonomy on a bodily level, and I fucking hated it.

I became a vegetarian at the age of six, and even then I was able to articulate that I didn't think killing for food was wrong. What was wrong was the caging, what was wrong was the way the animals' freedom was taken from them. They never had a chance to be free. And I empathized

La fin de leur monde

with those captured animals because I knew that I was captured. I was a child and I had no power. I was made to submit to the rules and desires and whims of the adults in my life no matter how fucked up it was. That refusal deep in my bones was a tiny anarchist seed, the anarchism of a child.

Unfortunately it took me a really long time to connect to a politics that articulated this love and longing for freedom. I had to move through years in activist scenes where most of the people I knew also could not imagine a world without cops, borders, governments. We relied on state intervention and even worked to increase it. Carceral feminism that encourages survivors to go to the police. Trying to get the government to domesticate queer love through gay marriage. Hate crime laws that bolster the prison industrial complex as some kind of symbolic justice that actually does nothing to make us safer. Nonprofits relying on government funding and accepting government rules eating up all the radical grassroots initiatives.

Even as we decried the violence all around us we were like children dependent on our captors. We thought we needed them.

I look at the world burning around me, the governments committing atrocities left, right, and centre, sometimes with a smile on their face. I listen to Justin Trudeau say yes to a pipeline days after the declaration of climate emergency, days after being forced to face the reality of ongoing genocide of Indigenous people (which he still denies, calling it 'cultural genocide'). He says that the money made from this pipeline can be used to invest in environmental solutions. This is the bullshit that a man who liberals and even leftists put their hopes in is saying as we literally face the end of the world. The governments don't work for us and they never have. Those who have lived with the most atrocious violences of governments have always known this.

I feel the extreme sense of powerlessness in facing down the massive power of the state with its cops and military force. I feel the extreme overwhelm of the clock running out as another pipeline gets built. But all my hope and all my power comes from anarchism, from the thorough internal refusal of their authority, and the decision to turn to each other and to figure this out together. We need to learn how to imagine another world. We need to stop hoping that the governments will get us out of this situation which they created.

They won't save us. They never have.

I Still Think of You

*I*N MY MIND I see you standing on the metro platform. I remember my back against the wall, your hands in my hair, your smile cracking the world open. I remember you kissing me. In my mind I see you standing by the river, November grey all around, burst open by your exuberance and laughter, your blue hair. I remember sitting on the ground, talking to each other. Then laughing and kissing, and the pleasure of being in your arms. I remember the man who passed us on the path saying *Make it sexy girls*, and the way we recoiled.

I remember cooking dinner together in my kitchen. Buying groceries at the store and stopping to kiss each other in the aisles. I remember the way you looked at me, the way I loved the way you looked at me. It felt so good to be with you and I was always a little afraid to believe in it but eventually I did. I remember accidentally stumbling on a Free Palestine demonstration together and joining it. I remember lying in your arms in the bath. I remember walking by the canal in the snow and hoping we still had a future even after you left the city.

I remember being in your apartment in Montréal, just before you were set to move back to Toronto. The way you said to me casually that your boyfriend was thinking of going monogamous. You said *I asked myself, would I go monogamous for him? And I think that I would.* I remember feeling like you said that to me as if I were your friend, as if I wasn't your date, someone you'd been dating for more than a year, someone who would be impacted by this decision. I remember your face when you saw the sadness in my eyes and started to backtrack, telling me things wouldn't change. But I knew that they would.

Fucking Magic

I told my therapist about this, this strange dissonance. The way that I felt like your friend not your girlfriend or your date or your lover or your partner. The way I judged myself for feeling upset by that. I mean, of course I was your friend, of course I wanted to hear what was going on with your boyfriend. But the casual way you told me made me feel unimportant. It made all that old internalized homophobia in my body ache. I don't know what it would have taken to make it real, to show you that you meant to me what you meant to me. I don't know if it was ever real for you, the way that it was real for me.

I haven't let myself grieve the loss of our relationship. I tell myself it was my fault for getting too attached, that I should have known it was nothing serious. I felt the danger of wanting, the danger of letting my heart open, and I wanted, I opened to you. I felt the danger of believing, and somehow that danger is heightened when it's queer love.

I was going to tell you I loved you the next time I was back in your city but by that time it was over, you were with him.

You didn't even break up with me officially. You just let me know after awhile that you and him had become monogamous after all. And I told all my friends that it sucked and that I was sad about it. But I don't tell them that every time I get off the metro at that stop, I still think of you.

Naked

WE STRIP OFF our clothes at the edge of the field. We can see from horizon to horizon, just farmer's fields, occasional trees. There is no one around. Under the bright July sun we are completely alone. We climb down the steep drop to water and step on the stones, hurting our feet. We wade out into the moving water and learn that the river is shallow. So we sit down in it. We lie on the rocks and I float on the surface. Sometimes we let the current take us away.

You are sitting in the middle of the river, naked and happy and familiar and covered in sun. I wade over to you and sit on top of you and kiss you, holding you in my arms, feeling the rush of cool water and the warmth of bright sun. Feeling your arms around me and your mouth on mine. We kiss deep and full, our bodies pressing together, cool and warm and safe and full of pleasure. Love is so disarming, so terrifying, it makes me crazier than anything else. And yet here we are, naked in the river, in love with each other, happy and safe.

I feel the pleasure in my body, the secret electric language, deep like the water in a well. I feel it surging through me and I kiss you and press myself into you, more, more. I feel the pleasure in your body, the rush between us. The pleasure is rooted deep inside us, in our living animal bodies. The pleasure is rooted in the water, in the big open expanse of sky. The pleasure is rooted in the courage of longterm love, of growing and changing and being crazy and imperfect and scared and learning how to love through it all. The pleasure is a prayer, a rebellion, a refusal, a criminal act. The pleasure is magic and we believe in it.

Fucking Magic

    I love you so fucking much and love is different than I ever thought. I fumble in love with all the terror and confusion of trauma. I get so wound up. But then I breathe and I relax and I see you. My partner, my lover, my friend. This person I love deep in my bones, familiar and warm. I love you for being exactly who you are. You love me for being exactly who I am.

    After awhile we lead each other from the water, stepping on stones, hurting our feet. We clamber naked back to the shore, laughing at our nakedness, laughing with our joy. And right there in the sun, in an open field under wide skies, we make love.

Hitchhiking

I GO HITCHHIKING FOR the first time at 32 years old. Everyone's surprised that I seem to be taking up all the things that they are letting go of as they age. I try to explain how my teenage years and my twenties were subsumed in a thick swamp of trauma, how I didn't do much but cry and drink and fuck strange men who treated me like shit. I was too fucked up to even be a punk. I was terrified of everyone, alienated from everything.

My partner and I fly a sign on the side of the highway. The July sun beams down on us, hits the pavement making rainbows. The wildflowers explode in colour behind us. I eat an orange. It's sticky sweet in my hands and in my mouth. We wait for a ride. I feel safe because my partner is with me. I feel happy to be doing this thing I've never done. I love being out here, tired from carrying my bag, fed on apples and peanut butter sandwiches. My hair full of saltwater and sweat.

It isn't long before a car stops and we pile into the car with our giant backpacks. We go a ways and are let out again. One car after another. My partner conversing with the drivers in French while I sit in my Anglophone silence in the back, watching the world rolling by and trying to catch snatches of the conversation. A driver asks me in French if I understand anything they're saying. I shrug, *Un peu.*

I'm amazed at the kindness of these strangers. The way they open their cars to us, the way they move things over and make space for our stuff. As an extremely traumatized person who has learned to expect the worst from people it is amazing to be shown such kindness and generosity from strangers. It is amazing to experience the mutual trust, the way the interaction is an assumption on our part and the drivers' parts that people are basically good, mostly trust worthy. Two drivers have their kids in the car with them and pile us in among them. One driver takes the wheel off his bike so he can put the seat back up and fit us in.

Sometimes there are long hot stretches walking in the sun, with no luck at all. But mostly we are surprised by how fast people pull over. Once we barely have time to put our bags down before another car rolls up. My partner tells me that a lot of the drivers share stories of their own days hitchhiking. They know what it's like being on the other side of the dynamic which contributes to their generosity and their willingness to trust us.

My partner and I sleep in a tent at the edge of the fleuve after being dropped off right at the beach. We watch the wild tide go way in and way out. A place in the water that is up to my knees a couple hours later is over my head. We make a fire and we swim and we make out and we sleep. The sky is lavender and violet and the grass is glowing green. The water is deep and wild and holds me when I lay my body on top of it.

I lie in the sand. I read my book. I breathe. I say a prayer of thanks for all the strangers who brought us here, for every little bit of goodness I've been shown.

If I'm Going to Be a Musician I Need to Practice Freedom

I'M ANXIOUS WHEN I arrive at the studio. There is this energy I feel when I don't want to face myself. I am terrified of being present, of being here. I am terrified of being in my life, picking up the guitar, feeling the storm of emotions that I'm always trying to suppress. Fear, shame, regret. Always mourning the life I didn't have, the things I wanted but couldn't have. Being drunk in an alleyway, being unable to believe in anything.

But I'm here now. I'm 32, I live in Montréal, I've been sober for more than seven years. This is the studio I'm renting to work on my music. This is my guitar that my ex-partner smashed when I was 23, breaking the internal wires, which I recently had repaired and now it plays perfectly. But there is a feeling of fear just being here, a feeling that it is too late, that I will never arrive in the life I long for, the life I've worked so hard to build. The fear edges onto the shame and that's when I pick up my phone to scroll and dissociate and move away from this pain that I don't even have words for.

Instead I lie on the floor. There's a big carpet in the centre of the studio and I lie on it. The lights are still off. I haven't set up the amp or the PA or the mic yet. My guitar is still in the bag, leaning against the wall. I only have so much time here and there's pressure that I put on myself to use the time wisely, to break through all my fear and shame and learn how to make music. But I lie on the floor instead.

Here on the floor I feel the solid weight of my body, pressing down with the power of gravity. I see the room, darkened and familiar now, the ceiling, the mic stands. I feel my breath moving through me and my breath is a passageway into and through the thing I am so afraid of. So I breathe. I breathe and I let the feelings move through me. I breathe deep into my body and I let myself relax. I tell myself *This is your time, and there is no rush. Just be here.*

Of its own accord my breath turns into sound like something moving and living inside of me. Formless strange deep and wild, sound moves through my body. And I am alone here so I let it happen. I don't worry about what anyone would think. I vibrate with the sound, my voice which is always so trapped, is rising like a creature from the water. It is strange and un/familiar. And suddenly I feel this power. This great expansive power. I remember my power. I remember who I am.

This will take practice. It will take returning over and over to my body and my voice. Learning to become uninhibited and free when my body was trained through violence and domesticated into hypervigilant silence over years and years will take time. But if I listen to my body the answers are there. My body is a wise animal and my voice is a passageway between my body and this world. My voice as sound, not just as words and verbalized thoughts, but as embodied sound.

Words are not the only way important meaning is conveyed. There is a whole language of body and voice. And it is this language, of gesture, of cry, of expression, spontaneous and genuine, that was punished, domesticated, silenced. So, I need to return to it. I need to lie on the floor and let the sound pour out of me. No one told me to do this, but my body knew. My body knows.

If I'm going to be a musician, I need to practice freedom. If I'm going to have the life I want I need to listen to my body. I need to be here, exactly where I am.

Family

I'VE STOPPED SAYING 'chosen family.' Now I just say 'family' to describe the people who are more family than my family of origin ever was. I'm liberating the word 'family' from its associations with trauma. I don't need to reply to questions about my family by triggering myself and explaining that I'm estranged. I can just answer the question in reference to my real, actual family, the queer and trans sober addicts I surround myself with. The people I live with and share my life with. The people who know me.

I am starting to relax my hypervigilance. I am starting to see who I am in the eyes of the people who love me. I'm having long moments of letting my guard down, not watching my every move, feeling uninhibited, unencumbered and free.

We have radsob meetings in our beautiful living room, walls and surfaces filled with books and zines and pamphlets. We sit in a circle and take turns talking about our lives, our feelings, how we are coping, what we are struggling with. We really listen to each other and hold space for each other and show each other that we are loved. We have a place where we belong. And I am learning that I can be all of who I am here. Crazy and anti-social and depressed. Exuberant and loud and playful. I get to be Clementine and I am loved for being Clementine.

The other day I was crying and my partner was holding me. And usually I feel so much shame when I am sad, but I listened to them when they told me *Clementine I love you, you are perfect exactly as you are.*

I listen to my roommates and my friends when they tell me they want to know me, when they welcome me back over and over again.

Fucking Magic

    I think about how sad I was as a little kid, about how no one noticed or took care of me when I was sad. Either that or I was yelled at. My life isn't like that anymore. Today I am loved, I am loved, I am loved, just as I am, for all of who I am.

    These people are my family. They are the ones who deserve the name.

Fucking Magic

#11

Lipstick

YOU COME OVER in a purple velvet dress and fishnets. You texted me earlier saying you were rushed leaving the house and didn't feel put together, but you look amazing. You texted me asking if I have any nail polish because you didn't have a chance to paint your nails. I don't but I borrowed some from my roommate.

We go to my room and sit on my bed and you tell me about your day as you paint your nails. I eat vegan chocolate and share it with you while we wait for your nails to dry. We're about to head out to the amateur trans strip night happening close to my place. I'm wearing a slutty black dress and bright red lipstick. Your lipstick is dark purple to match your dress.

We talk about mercury retrograde and how everything seemed to go wrong for you today. You tell me you feel like your lipstick makes you unkissable and we both laugh at this. You're looking into my eyes and I'm looking into your eyes and we should really leave because the event has already started and it's true, we are both wearing bold lipstick.

But I'm gay and I don't fucking care. So we lean into each other, let our lips brush against each other a little bit. The energy is electric and it pulls us closer together but we pull back to survey each other's lipstick. It's still okay. So we kiss some more, gently, carefully. But the energy between us keeps heightening and before we know it we are kissing each other hard and long.

We're making out, our bodies are pressed together, our lipsticks are smearing all over our faces but we don't care. All we feel is the pleasure of each other's lips, the pleasure of the energy moving between us. It feels

Fucking Magic

good. It's so nice to make out with you. And honestly, it's an honour to have your lipstick all over my face.

But then we think about the time and how we do really want to go to the amateur trans strip night. So we pull back from each other and survey the mess we've made. It's hilarious. Dark purple and bright red, speared and smudged all around our mouths.

Laughing, we go to the bathroom. I bring a salve and grab some toilet paper for each of us. Next to each other we go to work on ourselves in front of the bathroom mirror, cleaning up the smudged lipstick and reapplying it so it's perfect.

Fucking by the Train Tracks

YOU TEXT ME and tell me to meet you by the train tracks, at our spot. I go and I get there before you. I sit on a rock and watch you walking from the distance in your leather jacket. You look so punk rock and I'm so excited to slide my hands under your jacket, around your waist.

The trees have changed their colour, they are red and orange and quickly losing their leaves. After you've crossed the distance between us and I've wrapped my arms around your waist, after you've held my face in your hands and looked into my eyes and kissed me, you comment on the fallen leaves. *Our spot isn't as discrete as it used to be.* You're right, I noticed it too. In the summer we had the secrecy of the lush green leaves. But we're brave and we're scandalous and we're sluts and we're here, so.

We walk among the trees stepping over piles of garbage and find a spot that is mostly sheltered by the trees. You look around, we can't see anyone. It's quiet on the tracks. This is the spot. I'm already dropping to my knees, greedy, smiling, my hands on your belt. Your attention splits between looking around and looking at me. You're giving me that look, and I'm drinking it up.

On my knees, on the ground, amid the fallen leaves and trash, I suck your cock. Taking part in the proud gay tradition of public sex, I earn the dirt on my knees with my passion and my desire. I take my time and savour the experience, trusting you to keep an eye on our surroundings. I feel safe and I feel loved and I feel fucking good.

I watch your face as pleasure moves across it. The air smells like autumn and fallen leaves and dirt. Your hands are in my hair. I take you in. Tears run

Fucking Magic

from my eyes and drool pours from my mouth and I know I'm a messy slut and I love it. I love you. And I love that you let me have you here, like this.

I Need to Write

I HAVEN'T WRITTEN IN months.
    I am walking home from the Blessed Hysteric show, something has split open inside of me again. I can feel it moving through me like electric shocks, or more like an animal thrashing, trying to tell me the story that can't be told.

At the show I saw a performance of femininity and trauma and madness. I saw the embodied pain of being disposable, of being feminine and crazy in the same body, of being unstable and out of control. And I feel it in me. The parts of me I've moved on from, the parts of me I've disavowed. The crazy drunk girl screaming, cutting herself, destroying everything. But that was a long time ago, that was a long time ago.

I have been thinking about drinking and cutting and suicide. Bright torrents of impossible escape. I've been holding up the glittering possibility of past oblivion even as I know I can't. These aren't options for me anymore, these aren't real possibilities. But in the muted numbness of my impossible pain they shine like the bright light of a train coming. They offer me escape.

I am staggering through the city. I can't breathe properly. I am muttering to myself and crying. Words and images escape my lips and mix with the night and the falling snow. I feel visibly crazy and exposed, like I used to feel all the time. It feels dangerous. Everyone can see me and I am so afraid of getting locked up.

I duck into a dark alleyway, hide myself in the shadows. The movement is still split through me, the embodied memory of terror. *I want to be safe. I want to be safe. I want to be safe.* I listen to this body of

Fucking Magic

mine because right now it will not be silenced, right now it rises with nervous system energy that I can't repress or deny. I am sick with it. I am terrified.

I think about cutting, about drinking, about the things I used to do to answer the call of this body, to engage with it, to lean into the pain so hard that I broke through it to the other side, to oblivion. But the pain only magnified, becoming more and more of itself. The pain took on new depths and proportions, became a monstrous spell of a pain unspoken, acted out.

I think about writing, about the impossibility of writing. I can't believe I'm a writer, that is an impossible thing. I am so fucked up scared to write, but I feel it moving through me. The writing does the same thing for me that the cutting and the drinking did, but without the shame filled hangover or regret. The writing opens me to my body and lets my body speak. It pushes me through the pain and turns it into something else. Spoken rather than acted out. Processed rather than pantomimed.

What if I try to write and nothing comes? What if I'm left alone with these unbearable feelings? What if the thing I need doesn't work this time? What if I can't face what I write? What if I am destroyed by the writing? What if it doesn't work? What if it doesn't work? What if there is no power, no magic, no transformation? What if it doesn't work?

I shudder and squirm and make incoherent noises as another wave hits me and then another. I am huddled in an alleyway riding out this storm. I am 32 years old. I am seven and a half years sober. I've been in therapy for eight years. And sometimes I'm still this fucking crazy. I don't know why because it isn't something that can be answered. It isn't something that can be said with words.

But that's not what writing does and I know that. Writing is not the answer to the question. Writing is not the explanation, the pinning down, the proving of the point. Writing is something else, something wild, something of my body. Writing is not the disconnection, the dissociation, it is the opposite. Writing is the bridge, writing is the river, writing is the opening, bringing the unspeakable sensations up and up

I Need to Write

and out. It comes through me like electric shocks, like the wild thrashing body of the animal I am.

And I want to run. I want to hide. I want to fight. I need to write.

Turn Back Into Stars

I DON'T WANT TO let it go. I don't want to surrender. I'm terrified. I want you to understand: I need this. I think about the ability to sever attachment, the ability to turn the familiar, the beloved, into the enemy. *I feel nothing.* You hear it in my voice, you see the change in my face. And it scares you. You say *When you're like that, I don't recognize you, when you're like that I feel so alone.*

I remember smashing glass bottles against concrete. I remember destroying everything. I remember the years and years I survived without love. The way I hardened myself to it. The way I found an abject power in denying my need. *I don't fucking need you.* And when I'm scared, when I'm terrified, when I feel cornered and trapped, that part of me can come back.

I can turn love into contempt, I know how because I know how to do it to myself. I know how to sever all connection, to let my eyes harden, to become untouchable. And all these years I've kept this part inside me. I've hidden this part of me, I've pretended it isn't here anymore. But it is. And sometimes when I'm scared you can see the change in me. Hard as ice. I can turn anyone into an enemy.

I walk alone at night, the winter is arriving all around me. The air is cold and I'm ashamed. I know that I did it again. I turned everyone into enemies. I cut off love because I don't trust it. I became angry and accusatory and I dissolved all memory of connection, affection, trust, feeling safe. You said to me *I don't like it when you talk to me like that.* And when I come back to myself, when the hard ice begins to melt again, I'm left with the feeling I used to get when I woke up with a hangover. Shame, regret, remembering. I did it again. Why, why did I do it again?

I am full of regret because I do need love. Because I do know that I am loved. Because I am safe now, I know that I am safe now. Because this fight response has nothing to do with my life today and everything to do with the abject terror of being a helpless unloved child. I react with the same defensive terror I felt then. Some switch gets hit and I feel like I am in profound danger. I react as if it were true. *I don't need you. I don't feel anything.* But I need you, and I feel everything.

How do I find this part of me that lives like a ghost in my neural pathways, in my nervous system? How do I chase down the traces of this part of me that hides out in the alleyways of my heart, waiting? How do I find this part of me, and face her? How do I tell her, we don't need you anymore? How do I look her in the eye and say *I know you are trying to keep me safe but you are hurting me, you are hurting the people that I love*? How do I disarm her? How do I take her apart, bit by bit, steal back the energy she has stolen from me and give her power back to the rest of me, turning her back into stars?

There are two timelines happening simultaneously. I am the happiest and healthiest I've ever been. I am wiser and braver and more adult than I ever have been. I am loved. I have my home. I have my work. I have secure relationships. I am having crazy breakthroughs, reaching levels of healing that I didn't believe possible. I'm dating. I'm having sex. I have a partner who I love, who loves me. I'm asking for what I want. I'm transforming my shame. It's incredible.

And then it comes over me again: I want to destroy. I want to destroy everything. Myself. My life. All my relationships. I want to show everyone: I don't need you, I don't trust you, you don't know me. I don't feel safe and I don't know how to be safe and so I'm going to attack and I'm going to destroy. I hate the weakness of need, I hate the vulnerability of love. I feel like a dog, belly up, and now I'm snarling. Because I don't know what you're going to do.

I don't know how to arrive in the present and stay here. I don't know how to find this part of myself and release her, undo her, transform her. I don't know how to stop this cycle from repeating itself, how to let the lessons

Fucking Magic

I'm learning sink down into the deepest parts of myself. But I have to. I have to find a way. Against all odds. Against everything I believe to be possible. I have to change. I have to release her. I have to turn her back into stars.

This is the Change

THE CHANGE IS slow and it is a practice. The change is nervous system education and attachment work. The change is recognizing that I am triggered. Developing nervous system literacy, reading the sensations in my body, the quality of my thoughts. Understanding that I am time traveling. Noticing that this is what's happening.

I am triggered. This feeling in my body, this sense of urgency, this anger, this panic, this terror, this is me being triggered. This is me having an emotional flashback. The stories I am creating out of this place are not indicative of what is really going on. These stories are a response to my nervous system state. These stories and these sensations don't have to drive my actions. I can make a different choice.

I keep trying to notice when I am triggered and make a different choice. Take the opposite action. Break the pattern. Sometimes I don't know what the opposite action is. Sometimes I don't know how to break the pattern. Sometimes resisting the story that my trigger is creating is like trying not to be swept away by the force of a breaking dam. But I am practicing. Over and over again. I am paying attention, I am noticing.

I am triggered. This feeling in my body means that I am triggered.

I am trying different things. I am finding the language to talk about it. I am bringing the language of polyvagal theory and attachment into my relationships. Instead of repressing my feelings or hurling accusations I am saying: *I'm feeling triggered. Can I check in with you about how I'm feeling?* I'm saying: *This is the story my trigger is telling me, and I know it's not true, but it is still really scary.*

Fucking Magic

When I approach the experience of being triggered like this, with recognition and honesty, I am more able to get the help and support I need. I am more likely to be reassured, to co-regulate, to come up the polyvagal ladder, to return to the present, to return to feeling safe. This is the change and this is the magic. It isn't sudden and spectacular. It is slow and it is hard and it is a practice.

I ask for what I need, using the language of the nervous system, using the language of attachment. I let the people in my life be collaborators in my recovery. I stop turning them into the enemy. I risk showing them what is happening with my nervous system. I build the trust, bit by bit, to move through the process with them. Little by little, I learn how to let them help.

Each small success is a huge victory. Each time I make a different choice, break the pattern, experience different results, I try to savour it. I try to let it sink in. This is the work and I am doing it. This is the change and it is happening. Again and again. Again and again. Again and again. Repetition. Practice. Putting in the effort even when it is really really hard.

And here I am. I find myself in the present. I feel the rush and panic of my nervous system. I notice it and I name it. I do my best to ground and regulate. I communicate from a place of honesty rather than accusation. We co-regulate. I climb the polyvagal ladder. I feel safe. I feel safe. *I feel safe.*

Cancel Me

I KEEP TRYING TO apologize for the girl I was, for the harm she caused, the things she did and said. It comes back again and again, the fear based thinking, the shame. But then I remember: I don't believe in repentance, I don't believe in confession, I don't believe in performative guilt. I accept myself and love myself unconditionally. I believe in integrity, transformation, compassion, change. And I have changed. I am finding myself again, and not as a disavowal of everything I was. This self is the outgrowth of that one. The person I am today could only have come through that transmutation.

There is no purity. There is no original sin. There is no secret terrible thing inside of me that makes me bad or unlovable. There is nothing to repent. There is nothing to confess. There is the work and process of change. There is the complexity of being a human being. There is the tangle of intergenerational and collective trauma. There is the decision to heal.

I'm tired of internet call outs posing as justice. I'm exhausted by the frantic attacks and the numeration of our pain. Trauma response after trauma response, nervous systems in distress. Each of us trying to be good, trying to exile the bad in ourselves, the bad in each other. Pointing fingers and casting blame. Turning conflict into abuse, blocking resolution by overstating harm, believing we will only have our boundaries respected and our pain validated if the other person is punished, marked as the bad guy. I'm tired of living in fear. I'm tired of being told that this culture of disposability is the only thing protecting survivors. It isn't protecting us. It isn't promoting transformation. It isn't teaching us how to keep each other safe. It isn't teaching us how to intervene in harm or how to resolve conflict. It's just making us live in fear and shame.

    I've done these things. I've participated in these call outs. I've refused to be friends with people who have been nothing but kind to me based on rumours and the fear of social consequences. I have refused to take part in the hard work of conflict resolution. I have overstated harm. I have pointed the finger hoping the finger wouldn't be pointed at me. I have lived in fear of my fucked up past coming out and destroying everything I've built since getting sober. I have tried so hard to be good. To exile the bad from inside myself. But being good will never solve the problem because the problem is not that I am bad. And casting people out of my community, participating in campaigns of harassment, will not solve the problem either. Because the problem, also, is not that these people are bad.

    If you wouldn't be friends with someone who's been abusive then I guess you aren't my friend. If you need me to list out every harm I've caused in order to decide if I am worthy of forgiveness you will be disappointed because I will not be performing any confession. If you want to know if I am a trustworthy person you can assess that based on my actions, the way I treat you and the other people in my life. If you want to know if I've 'been accountable' I can tell you that I've repaired the harm I've caused to the best of my ability, grounded in my integrity and dignity, out of respect for myself and for my fellow human beings. Beyond that, it's between me and those I have made amends to, it is between me and the living universe.

    I can't live in integrity and honesty if I live in perpetual fear of being honest. I can't practice honest self-reflection and responsibility if I am motivated by shame. When I am grounded in my inherent worth, my integrity, my ethics, my principles, my spirituality, when I am connected to my community who love me and also lovingly challenge me when needed, then I am free to speak my truth, and it doesn't matter if I am liked or not. Because my intention is not to be good, my intention is to live in reality and to act with integrity. I am not here to earn something that is already mine. I am here to effect as much positive change in the world as I can, to do my work, to love and be loved, to heal and transform, to grow, to help build the world we are trying to build.

I have been subjected to campaigns of harassment framing themselves as righteous calls for justice. I have been lied about and sent aggressive messages from strangers who have no interest in what really happened. I have watched friends and loved ones being harassed and exiled for disagreements and conflicts. I have watched the exile and harassment spread to those who publicly take a stand and defend those being targeted. I have been asked again and again *What about serial abusers? What about serial rapists?* whenever I have dared to challenge the way we handle conflict and harm in our communities, as if you could really think for a second that I am suggesting we shouldn't intervene in abuse and rape.

I have put my body between men twice my size and the partners they are trying to assault. I have had my clothes covered in a stranger's blood as I dialed her mom on her bloody phone and asked her to meet her daughter at the hospital. I've got onto the ambulance and talked down the cop. I have gone along to the hospital. I have helped plan safety strategies. I have been the safety call. I have knocked on the door when I heard screaming. I have answered phone calls about how to support a friend in an abusive relationship. I have communicated boundaries between people who aren't speaking. I have been a safety buddy. I have brainstormed on alternatives to calling the cops. I've warned community about people who are actively causing harm, and I've sought support for people who are actively causing harm. I've had the hard conversation of *I know you are friends with my abuser and I need you to never pass on any information about me for my own safety, but I hope you stay his friend and I hope you help him change.* I've worked closely with people who've caused harm, and with survivors of harm, and with people who are both of these things, holding their experiences with compassion and helping them towards the life of integrity that they want to live.

Fucking Magic

I intervene on violence whenever I see it. I help with the communication and implementation of boundaries whenever I'm needed. I do the hard work of transformation in my own life and help with the hard work of transformation in other people's lives. This messy, complicated, hard work is the work of justice, it's the work I believe in, because I am deeply committed to supporting survivors and ending interpersonal violence. This hard work isn't simple, it isn't based in binaries of good and bad, and it is far more effective in both stopping and transforming harm than any internet call out I've ever seen or taken part in.

I don't believe that the culture of fear, shame, harassment, punishment, and exile that we currently use to address everything from disagreement and conflict to severe abuse is effective in intervention or transformation of harm, or in the resolution of conflict. I believe we can build the communities that we deserve, where we are supported in being responsible and compassionate, where we heal the massive collective trauma we are grappling with, where we resolve conflict and truly transform harm. And in order to do my part in moving toward these communities I so long for, I have to live in my integrity, I have to tell the truth of what I feel and believe, and I have to risk the harassment that is often directed at people who say these things. I can do that with love and compassion for myself, and for the people who disagree with me or feel triggered by what I'm saying. I can live in my integrity, even though it is scary, because I am brave, and because my desire for the world I want us to build is stronger than my fear.

The Fucking Pleasure of Being an Adult

Who am I without the shame? (I remember my search for love, my hungry eyes, the way I sought it out and was refused. I remember the terror that drove my body to panic and then to deathlike stillness. I remember the shame that grew inside me like a fungus underground, passing electric messages, but the message was always the same. *It's me. It's me. It's my fault.* My body collapses and the shockwaves move through me. I am writhing like an animal. These were the motions that my body couldn't make. I was too small, too collapsed in on myself, too unable to express the desperate panic, the need for protection, the need for love. The terror went underground. It had nowhere else to go. I remember what made the shame inside of me. My father's cruelty. The humiliation of desperation. The humiliation of trying to be loved, trying to be safe. I remember, but I don't identify with it anymore.)

Because I am someone else. I look around and I see suddenly that I have become someone else. It took years and years to get here. Twelve step meetings in church basements. Therapist after therapist, so many of them not very good at their jobs. Shame upon shame. Seeking absolution in social justice spaces, seeking absolution in love. Coming closer and closer to the truth, the truth I know deep down now. The shame isn't mine. It's the passed-on shame of my parents, and it wasn't theirs either. The shame just keeps getting passed along, desperate unloved child to desperate unloved child. Until one day someone wakes up, someone does the work and puts it down, passes another message through the electric currents.

Fucking Magic

Oh god there is such fucking pleasure in being an adult. There is such fucking pleasure in being almost eight years sober, thoroughly therapied, deep in nervous system and attachment work, responsible, competent, healing. There is such fucking pleasure in loving myself, trusting myself, being good to myself, cleaning my fucking room. But not from a place of shame. Not from a place of trying to be good. I'm already fucking good. I'm already worthy worthy worthy. I am already deliciously irrevocably deserving. And I know that now. Being good to myself not in a desperate attempt to be good, a masochistic flipping of the healing script, but being good to myself because it feels fucking good. Being motivated by pleasure and desire rather than shame. I have no fucking time for shame anymore. It still comes up, the familiar story, but my god it is so much easier to put down than it used to be.

I'm not out here like a kicked dog, tail between my legs, sad eyes, love me, love me, love me. I need love like every living creature does but I don't mistake abuse for love anymore and I don't settle for less than I deserve. I know how to rise in love, how to meet the challenge of love: grow, grow, deep and high, roots in the earth, branches in the sky. I know how to love as an equal, as an adult, worthy worthy worthy. I know how to bring my child self with me, my rattled nervous system, I know how to take the hand of that terrified part of me and show her love. My own love and the love of those I love and trust, those who love and trust me. But more and more I am able to prevent this terrified child from driving my actions. More and more I can lovingly take control back, I can be the adult she needs. I can say, *shh baby shh, you're safe*. Something no one ever said to me when I was a child.

The breath moves through me and more and more I accept my power with grace. More and more the shame falls away. I don't have time anymore for the crazy games I used to play, all the tricks and traps and attempts to be loved. My date says to me I have grown dyke energy and it's hot. My partner says to me I'm integrated as fuck, embodying my adult self, and it's hot. They reflect back to me what they see. All the hard work of recovery is paying off. I'm not a desperate mess trying to earn it anymore because it's already mine. Worthy, worthy, worthy. Loved, loved, loved.

It isn't always forward progress. Sometimes I get sucked into the panic of my past with unbelievable force. But I am getting so much better at coming back to the present, at returning to my adult self. It is starting to feel comfortable and familiar to be an adult. I am starting to trust it. It's becoming my default, and the triggered panic is the aberration. I am learning to recognize my agency, my power, my capacity, my choice. And in this state of adulthood I can welcome and recognize the nourishing love of trustworthy people. The love I have always so desired.

Shame is a trap. Shame is a lie. And I love this lesson maybe more than I've loved any other. I am finally beginning to see what it means to be free.

Yours

YOUR LONG HAIR *falls over your shoulders, your lipstick is everywhere, our breathing has taken on an urgency. We don't speak beyond the quick check in:* Is there anything I should know? Is there any way you don't like being touched? *Otherwise the conversation is happening between our bodies, our breath, the sounds we are making.*

I love your desire and I'm dizzy with it. I'm chasing it down, I'm collapsing into it. I love the way you push your body against mine, grinding, trying to get the exact angle, trying to find the right rhythm. I'm on my back, hips angled for you, giving you my pussy so you can use it to make yourself feel good. You are on top of me, slamming your pussy into mine, taking what you need from me. I know I'm going to be bruised in the morning and I know I'm going to savour it.

Later you're on your back and I'm fucking you with my hand, noticing what you like, what makes you want more. I'm listening with my whole body, watching every movement, every shift in your expression. You are fucked up beautiful in your pleasure and I just want to give you what you want.

Do you want me to fuck you with my cock? *I ask and you eagerly nod your head yes.* Do you want me to use my hand or do you want me to strap it on? *You look up at me and say* Strap it on.

I get my harness from the drawer next to my bed, take my reluctant eyes off of you just long enough to get the straps adjusted and my cock in place. Then I'm back before you, watching your anticipation. I ask you Do you want to suck my cock? *And you get between my legs and do. You take me into your mouth, rhythmic and deep, beautiful. Then I grab a condom and slide it onto my cock and you lay back.*

Yours

 I slap my cock against your pussy, enjoying your anticipation as much as my own. I bring your hand and place it on your clit, get you to rub it for me while I slide into you. I listen to your breath and watch your face as you take me into you. I kiss your beautiful mouth while I fuck you.
 That energy takes you over again, and you rise up and meet me, my cock still inside you. I lean back and give my cock to you the same way I offered up my pussy. I watch you fuck me, hard and deep and exactly the pace you want. I watch you driving my cock into you, taking exactly what you want, driven by your desire. And it's yours.

We Went to the Ocean

I'M AN ADDICT that means I know how not to feel this. *I'm an addict that means I can numb out, chase oblivion, find the thing that will take me out of myself.* I scroll my feeds endlessly, feel the little hits of dopamine. I feel the ache in my heart and the panic of my sympathetic nervous system. I work till midnight stapling zines, then I go home and collapse into bed. I haven't cooked myself a meal in weeks. I'm not looking you in the eye. I go days without showering. I forget I love the water. I forget a lot of things. All I know is I don't want to feel this.

I don't want to feel a lot of things. I could collapse and fall apart under the grief and panic of climate chaos, all the new phrases we have to try to communicate the urgency and numbness of watching species going extinct, people dying, places changing beyond repair, tipping point after tipping point as the billionaires go on business as usual and the governments protect them with their guns. What can my body do with the feeling of the end of the world? My body doesn't know. And I'm an addict so I know how not to feel this. I know how not to write, how not to sink into my body, how to stay in low grade panic and despair, just bearable.

And if my heart is broken then so what? It's not like my heart hasn't been broken before. It's not like I let myself love you. Not completely, not ever, no. I'm an addict so I know how not to feel this. Loving my friends was always too dangerous. I never understood love without sex. I never understood how to keep a person close if they weren't fucking me. And so I awkwardly ask *Are you trying to hug me?* And so we sit in the kitchen

We Went to the Ocean

at 2am talking about our lives. You say *I love you* so easily to everyone but those words are a blade to me, slippery and sharp.

We went to the ocean and we stood under the moon and you drove the rental car for way too long and we slept on an air mattress as the air slowly escaped it. And you stood on a ladder to hang the sheet for your art project and I worried about your safety. We went to the ocean and we went into the freezing water and we got sand in our clothes and in our hair. We laughed like children. We slept in a tent. We ate salad with our bare hands because we forgot utensils. And I'm an addict so I know how not to feel any of it. I know how not to let it get into my heart.

Of course I'm being dramatic. Of course I'm being avoidant as fuck. Of course the feelings I never feel, the feelings I repress and disavow are a panic beneath my skin. Of course I'm not really losing you. Things are just changing, as things do. But things change too fast for someone as slow as me. Things change so fast that I never really had time to find a way to say I love you.

You'll move down the street and I'll panic and move somewhere else too. I'll avoid the places I know that you'll be and then eventually I won't and we'll act normal and everything will be fine. We'll still see each other sometimes. But we won't sit in the kitchen at 2am. We won't have the endless, normal, mundane time that roommates have. We won't expect each other and take each other for granted. And maybe that's the problem. Maybe I should never have taken you for granted. Maybe I should have been brave in my love. Maybe I should have told you.

Coming Back to My Body

I GO TO THE gym for the first time in months. Suddenly I just know that it's time. I go and I tie up my hair and I put on my floral leggings and I work out on the machines for 20 minutes. I feel my body moving, my heart pumping blood. I feel myself sweating. I'm listening to King Princess on my headphones and I am *moving*.

I forgot what it's like to have a body again. It happens over and over again, for months or years at a time. I move around in a dissociative haze, scrolling on my phone, shoulders hunched and bunched, I don't feel anything. I have no awareness of what I'm feeling. There are a million stories and a million chaotic sensations that I make meaning of or push down into numbness, but I don't show up to my body. I don't listen to the living animal that I am.

But here I am, moving. And in this movement I feel this return to myself, this sinking into my skin, this breath. I feel relief. I feel power. I feel pleasure. I feel my capacity and my agency and my beautiful wild self.

I get off the machines and stretch. Oh yes, it has been so long since I've done such a simple thing. I feel the stretch and breathe into it. I feel my body elated with the attention, with the presence, like a child yelling *Look at me, watch this, did you see?* I am seeing, I am present, and I am here with my body. *I am so sorry I've been ignoring you. I'm so sorry I've been so focused on other things.* But here I am again, returning. Here I am.

I go downstairs to the change room and take off my clothes. I get into the shower and feel the water on my skin, hot, cold. I get into the hot tub, sink my body down into the wetness and the heat, feel myself enveloped. Yes. I always try to find a gym with a hot tub. The hot tub is better than the workout. The hot tub is everything to me.

I sit in the water. No cellphone. No distractions. No conversations. Just the heat. Just the relief. Just me, here, in my body, by myself, present. Doing this for myself. This sacred ritual that I have neglected for far too long. But I'm here now, I'm here. And I can feel the relief of it, the pleasure and joy and security of returning to myself.

Trauma took me out of myself. Again and again I learned to disappear, and now I do it automatically. I have learned to be everywhere but my body. I have learned that it is safer to be anywhere but my body. I am thoughts and disconnected words and the blur of disembodied hours never touching down into my skin. It becomes normal and I forget the way back in. I forget how much I miss my breath, the sensations, the aliveness. I forget how to be present, how to be here, and then I remember, and then I come back.

I know that it all comes back to this. I know that all my magic and all my power is rooted in my body. I know that my ability to resist the call of dissociation, to find a way to return to my wild living body, over and over again, that's the answer, that's the key, that's the magic I've been looking for my whole life. I know how scary it can be, how impossible it can feel. I know how easy it can be to just forget about it, to just drift away, to be gone.

But I come back to my body. I come back to myself. I feel the pleasure and the power and the capacity that I have locked away and become terrified of. I welcome it back. I return to myself. I let out a long breath. I am here. Here I am.

My Wild Precious Life

When I was fifteen I was crazy and brave and I wanted to die. I wanted to live. But the impossibility of living weighed on me. I knew that something was wrong. I didn't know what was wrong. I had no words for all the ways I was trapped. So I stared at traffic. I cut my arms. I took too many pills. I lit things on fire. I ran down the street at full speed without any shoes on. I tried to feel nothing. I tried to feel anything. I fell in love with random boys and then panicked when they liked me back. There was a chaos inside of me that I couldn't speak. I was fifteen and I wanted to die.

But I wanted to live and the drive for life was wild and impossible. I kept skipping class. I kept sitting on the bathroom floor making myself bleed. I kept 'getting into trouble', being a 'bad kid'. Everyone acted like something was wrong with me, like I was doing something wrong. I would sit down on the floor in the middle of the hall in my high school, rocking back and forth and pulling at my hair. I was desperately trying to show everyone that something was very, very wrong. If you asked me what was wrong, I wouldn't have been able to tell you the truth. I kept seeking something impossible, trying to split reality open, trying to get the truth out of it.

I dropped out of school. I moved to the city. I look back at all those years. The way that crazy girl grew up and became even crazier. The way I didn't have one single responsible adult to help me. The way the pain ate at me from the inside and I would do anything, anything, anything it told me to do. And I did. Over and over again until I was so far gone. Until I lost touch with everything except this drive for death that was also somehow a drive for life. Until I was under piss soaked cardboard shivering and shaking and hiding from something that I still couldn't name.

It took me so long to get the help I needed. I had to wait until it got so bad that my fear of being locked up again didn't deter me from going to the centre for abused women and telling them what was happening. My life was that same old story: incest, child abuse, self injury, suicide attempts, psych wards, dropping out of high school, running away, becoming an alcoholic, intimate partner violence, being abused over and over, chaos, panic, unbearable pain. But then one day through a mix of desperation and luck, I called the rape crisis line and screamed at them that I needed more help than they could offer and they sent me to a service that offered non-psychiatric therapy and I finally started to get help.

Six months later I went to a 12 step meeting and I got onto the path of being sober. Recovery has been a long, long journey. Many years and many many layers. Complex ptsd, structural dissociation, attachment trauma, alcoholism/addiction. I put in so much work. I took that crazy wild impossible drive inside of me, the thing that drove me to survive the pain, that drove me to razor blades and bottles and suicide, I took that very thing and I put it in service of my precious, beautiful life. I fought for myself with everything I had in me. I went to the meetings. I did the work. I went to therapy. I did the work. I didn't know if it would really help, I didn't know if it was really possible to change, I didn't know if my life could be different. But I fought for it with everything I had.

I went outside at night and prayed to the moon. I went to meetings and drank watery coffee. I walked around the city for hours in the pouring rain. I laid on the floor and sobbed gut wrenching sobs, the same floor where he kicked me in the stomach and I curled up in a ball. I found my way back to writing and I wrote, and I wrote, and I wrote. I sought the divine, the goddess, the living universe pulsing in my veins. I remembered the magic inside me, the very thing that made me crazy was the very thing that would make me live. I remembered the magic of foxes and raccoons

Fucking Magic

and trees. I put out my hands and I reached toward the world. I took my crazy brave punk rock wild anarchist heart, my love for poetry and music and the unspeakable beauty of the world, I took my tenacity and my stubbornness and my brazen unshakable faith, and I put it all in service of my life. My precious, wild, irreplaceable life.

Sometimes I forget where I come from. Sometimes I forget the fucking magic of my miracle life. Sometimes I take it all for granted, I get bored, I get complacent, I forget how fucking hard I worked for all of this. I forget how easily it could have not happened, how easily I could still be drunk in an alleyway, locked up in a psych ward, or not here at all. I forget the moon, the way it shone with rainbow light, the way I loved the moon with all my heart because it was what I had to love. Sometimes I forget the magic, the power and the push of my writer spirit, the way I make meaning out of the things that happened to me, the way I transmute the pain into power and possibility and leave a trail of light so that others can find their way. I forget that it's my fucking calling, it's my fucking job.

And things can be hard, things can feel stuck. I can go in circles, learning the same lesson and forgetting it. I can be frustrated with what I want that I haven't achieved yet. I can wish I was more healed than I am or that certain things were easier. I can feel the pain and jealousy when I compare myself to people who didn't have those years, when I compare myself to people who have always been well loved. I can lose the magic, the miracle, the insistence. I can lose the power, the wildness, the connection to the divine.

But then I remember. I cut a hole in the fence and I walk along the tracks and I read about anarchism and I lie in my love's arms. I make myself cum, I fuck other queers, I ask for what I want, I say no to what I don't. I pull the Empress from my deck, I pray, I sit down at my computer and I write. I talk to my friends, I smile at a stranger, I give money when people ask me to. I tell the story of my life and what happened to me and the way I survived. But more than that. I look out my window and I see a bird and I feel a wave of sadness and desire, I feel the crazy wild power of my fifteen year old self.

My Wild Precious Life

I didn't die. I didn't fucking die. I'm here, I'm still here. I'm still alive.

We Don't Crawl Before Anyone

I'M TIRED OF the same old story. I'm tired of being identified with helplessness and passivity. I am tired of conflict avoidance and people pleasing. I am tired of believing that telling the truth is not a real option. I'm exhausted by the ways the same patterns play out over and over and I'm beginning to wake up to what those patterns are.

As queer people we build chosen family. As estranged people we build chosen family. As traumatized people we build chosen family. We work so hard to create the family and love that we need. And yet, so often, over and over again, we reproduce patterns of dysfunction, we watch our relationships crumble under sudden unmanageable conflicts. Things blow up. And we're left wondering why.

It's so crazy to me how deep conflict avoidance goes, how unsafe it can still feel to simply be honest about how I feel and what I believe. I learned young that my best bet was to hide my true feelings and try to get my needs met in other ways. This is a deeply dysfunctional behaviour but it served me well as a child in an abusive home. The trouble is, now, that I want to be able to act like an adult rather than a scared abused child. I want to feel competent and capable and I want to be honest. Yet I'm still so scared. And more than that, I often don't even recognize what I'm doing, I bury my feelings, I don't even see having the hard honest conversation as a real possibility.

I'm going through it again. Interpersonal relationship chaos that I didn't see coming at all. Yet I should have seen it. There were months and months of the build up of resentments, months and months of feeling uncomfortable and not saying anything. My partner would tell me I needed to be honest about what I was feeling and I told them I couldn't, I don't want to lose the relationship. But the result of conflict avoidance is that I lose the relationship anyway. When I'm honest I at least create the opportunity to work through conflict, to see if there is a way to come back to closeness.

I want to show up to my relationships as an adult. *As free people we stand on our feet, we don't crawl before anyone.* I want to live in my integrity. I want to make choices grounded in my ventral vagal nerve. I want to act from the deep trust that I've developed with myself. And I want to trust that I can move through whatever results from the practice of being honest. I want to be done with learned helplessness for good. My trauma will always be a part of me. I will always be someone who had those experiences. But I don't want it to define me anymore. I don't want it to shape my actions. I want to be able to have new experiences.

It's scary to let this learned helplessness and conflict avoidance go. It's scary to think about the consequences of being honest, about how it might mean not being liked, how it might even mean being harassed or attacked. It's scary to think about the relationships I could lose. It's scary to take full responsibility for myself, to step into my worth, my power, my sense of reality, to stop pretending like my worth, my power, or my sense of reality are things anyone could take from me. It's scary to really own that I'm an adult now, to recognize that this life I've built is mine, and the choices I make today are mine. And it's scary to admit that I am powerless over other people: over their nervous system responses, their behaviour, their choices, their beliefs, the way they respond to my honesty. I can't control them. I can only make choices for myself.

Even though all of this is scary, I see that I am at a turning point. I see that I have reached a place in my recovery where I am completely exhausted and done with these behaviours and patterns. I've reached a place where the pain of staying the same is outweighing my fear of change. And so, it's the beginning again. This is recovery. One more lesson. Another major change. I have been working on this lesson for years. Little by little I have grown closer to becoming the adult that I want to be. And I'm here now. I'm ready to take the leap, to own my power, to change.

It is only through this work that I will build the chosen family my heart so desires. I can only let people love me if they know me. I can only build closeness and intimacy on the truth. And, we can only build the world we are trying to build by developing and nurturing real relationships and community. Conflict avoidance doesn't get the goods.

Fucking Magic

#12

Transformation Again

I'M EXHAUSTED FROM moving. I spent the day with my friends, my date, my partner, and my metamour, lugging boxes of furniture down the stairs, up the stairs, out of my old place and into my new one. My new place is a five minute walk from my old one, and it's a music venue/ collective Montréal punk house and I'm so excited to be living here. My third home in Montréal. After shoving all my stuff into my windowless room and saying goodbye to my loved ones and thanking them, I spent a few minutes talking with my new roommates then headed out to the erotic arts market I'm tabling, just a couple doors down from my new place, past my studio.

Sitting at my table at the erotic arts market, third year in a row I've tabled it, exhausted from moving, all my zines and books spread out before me, I take in my surroundings. A dog and a puppy are running around the loft, chasing each other and playing. Artists are setting up their wares: sexy handmade underwear, drawing of people sucking cock and femme4femme bondage, jewelry, books, nipple tassels. The place is already filled with people, punks and hippies, queers and sex workers, straight couples, a whole range of Montréal subcultures and aesthetics fill the busy room. And suddenly I'm seeing this place, and how fucking Montréal it is, with new eyes. And I am grateful, so grateful for this city.

I have lived here for two and a half years. Living here has changed me. I can take it for granted now and forget the particular magic of this city. But the truth is, I love it so much. I love it so much and my heart breaks for the push of gentrification, steadily raising the rent and increasing the cost of living, which will fundamentally impact the cultures here and what makes this city so fucking special. I know we have to fight that push, with everything we have. And I am still so grateful for what is still here, and the fact that I get to be a part of it.

Transformation and change. It happened again. I built a beautiful life and a beautiful home, with chosen family, and I put down my roots and I resisted looking at any indication that anything was wrong, any indication that it wouldn't last. I needed it to last because I invested so much in it, and because I am so tired of all the change. I want something to last. And so when I get something my heart feels safe with, I tend to hold on for dear life, ignoring any signs that it isn't working or isn't serving me anymore. And then it all comes crashing down under the weight of its own internal pressure. The pressure of conflict avoidance and denial. And I'm forced to transform again.

My beautiful sober collective house disbanded in the midst of interpersonal conflicts. And while I was able to save most of the relationships involved, I lost a lot and my heart broke open and I grieved. And it was more than just the pain of this loss. It was also the pain of being a runaway, an estranged traumatized queer, a person who has no safe family of origin, a person with nowhere to call home. And so of course I spiraled out, of course the pain of loss brought up all the shame of being an abused child: *Why can't I be loved? Why can't I have a home?*

Even though I resist it so hard the transformation is amazing and life giving and always preferable to the denial and desperate holding on. The transformation has come over me time and time again and I have resisted it and rebelled against it but ultimately when I surrender to it I find it gives me what I need. Moving into my new place, opening a new chapter in my life, extending my story into new territory that I didn't expect, it is a sigh of relief, it is invigorating. I can feel myself opening to possibility again, instead of being closed off in fear.

I do have a home. I have homes. Montréal is my home. My partner is my home. My body is my home. My community is my home. My writing is my home. The river is my home. The train tracks are my home. The magic is my home. Being alive is my home. I am my home. Now, this

Transformation Again

new place is my home too, this place where people come and go and play music and make culture and hold shows and events and where life unfolds in all its beautiful busy chaos. And so the transformation comes, wild like a storm, tearing me from what I cling to, and reminding me of who I am.

I breathe. I breathe into the incredible magic of this city and the incredible magic of my life. I am 33 years old. I'm an adult punk. I'm an anarchist. I live in a collective punk house and venue in Montréal. I am a writer, it is my job and my calling and how I pay my bills. I am extremely therapied, almost eight years sober, and experiencing so much healing and growth in my trauma recovery. I am growing up and this is what my beautiful adult life looks like. I love to read. I love my bolt cutters. I love to swim in the river. I'm polyamorous. I'm queer. I'm not going to outgrow these beautiful things, I am growing into them.

It might not be the life for everyone. It might not be what someone else wants. But it is my beautiful fucking life, hard earned and built through desire. Pulled from the nothingness by the power of my will to live, by the power of the living universe, always transforming me, always giving me new ways to grow. This is my home. Here with the puppy and the dog chasing each other around my feet, the joint passed my way that I turn down, the cute queer flirting with me across the table, all my work laid out before me. My life. My beautiful fucking life. Mine.

Wild Living Mourning

*I*T STARTS WITH grief. It starts with what never was. It starts with the years that disappeared in a blur of nothing, not nothing but: plain-clothed cops in my bedroom while I'm naked in my bed and the hole in the drywall where my body went through and park benches I passed out on and the smell of stale piss and beer bottles and repetition and guys whose names I don't remember and the power of imagination to turn this nothing into something, to turn it into everything.

Every time I hear some beautiful story of adventure, of lives fully lived, of times that were maybe a bit fucked up but still powerful and present and alive, I am gutted. I am gutted, because I'm 33 and I spent the first half of my twenties in the nothingness of trauma upon trauma and the second half in the misguided struggle for redemption, giving up my life force in the quest to be good. I was 30 before I arrived at myself, sober and finally ready to put down the shame. And even now, it continues to be work, cyclical and continuous.

So, it starts with the grief. I can't romanticize my past. I can't make it beautiful. I can find myself in it and I can refuse to abandon that girl that I was, I can refuse to shame her or offer her up as a sacrifice in the search for redemption. But I can't pretend it was cool and fun, I can't pretend it was less painful than it was. And so I need a story that starts with the grief, I need a story that has enough space in it for that level of loss.

I need a story of right now, a story where the present moment opens up in its vastness, and is big enough to hold all my power and all my desire. I can't spend my life lamenting the past or trying to pretend it was something different. I can't shrug it off and act like the wild beauty of my life comes naturally. The reality is that getting free is hard fucking work. I can and I must remember the practice of getting free, and do it over and over again. I can't let the grief keep me stuck, I can't let it harden into shame, I must move through it and let it move through me, dynamic and alive.

I don't know why I'm a writer but I am. I don't know why it's my job to reach down into my body, into my pain and my joy, my pleasure and my desire, my numbness and my loss, and to make something out of it with my words. But it is my job, it is my work, it is my calling. So many times I have wished to be someone else, someone on the receiving end of this message instead of the writer creating it. And I hold the writers who speak to my heart as sacred and precious, because I need to receive. So often, I am here writing what I needed to hear, writing the words that I needed when I was lost in the nothing for so many years.

We can start now, in this precious living moment. We can start right here where we are. We can start with our bodies. I drop my shoulders, shift my posture. I am trying to learn what my body feels like when I feel safe and powerful. We can use the numbness as a guide back to sensation. We can find our pleasure and our desire, in the present moment. We don't need to change the past. We don't need to regret it. But we must mourn what was lost: mourning as a dynamic, living act, in the present. Right fucking now.

I won't surrender my life to endless scrolling on instagram. I won't avoid this pain and numbness even though I want to with all my heart. I won't shut down when I feel the grief, I will move toward it. I am the girl who survived all of that, and I didn't survive all of that to give up my power now, to be confused about who and what I am. I will move through it. I will feel it. I will write it. I will let the longing and the desire swell up in me and I will combine that power with the power of my mourning.

This is a dynamic living process. This is my body, here and now. This is a prayer, visceral and of the flesh. This is the motion that went uncompleted, now completed. This is my heart and my animal body. This is my power. I won't deny it anymore. I won't turn away from my pain. I won't turn away from my numbness. I won't use the little hits of dopamine the way I used to use the booze.

I will return to my life. Here and now.

We can return to our lives. Here and now.

The grief is not a wall, it is the surface of a lake. The grief is not static, it is always moving and very much alive. The grief is not what we lost, it is the wild living mourning, it is the aliveness of what is here right now.

Safe Enough to be Curious

THE GOAL IS just to feel safe enough to be curious. It isn't easy to feel that safe. There is a powerful chaos inside of me whose sole purpose is to keep me distracted, to keep me from looking straight into the face of my pain. There have been many times when I have arrived at a place of feeling safe enough to look, there were even times when I could go down there, down into the deep endless well, and it was okay. I could handle it.

But things have been hard. It isn't just my own trauma, it's the world all around me. It's capitalism and how inescapable capitalism feels. It's Canada going in with guns to force a pipeline on Wet'suwet'en land. It's the global pandemic. It's the forest fires in the Amazon, in Australia. It's climate apocalypse. It's the newsfeeds bursting with both urgency and alienation. It's the panic that becomes numbing. And yes, it's always been bad. There's always been extreme violence and exploitation and unthinkable harm for as long as I've been alive. It's just that lately, especially with environmental collapse on a global scale, it feels especially urgent and especially impossible.

And so my standard c-ptsd level of not feeling safe is amped up to a higher level and I shut down and I dissociate and I scroll my phone and I distract myself. I try to take a pause but the chaos inside of me says *You dare not look at your pain*. It feels dangerous. It feels impossible. It feels bigger than I have the capacity to address. I don't feel safe enough to be present to my life. I don't feel safe enough to be curious. I don't feel safe enough to begin to ask the questions.

But it's coming back to me. Little by little. I have these moments of connection, sudden and unbidden, and I cry. Tears flood my eyes. Because

Fucking Magic

I remember, I remember the feeling that I've been avoiding: the feeling of being alive. It happens when I listen to my friend Tara McGowan-Ross read her poetry at an event. It happens when I'm listening to a local band, the Pudding Chomeur, playing country music at a show at my house. It happens when I'm reading *How to Do Nothing* by Jenny Odell. And it happens big time when I start to read *Upstream* by Mary Oliver. With that last one I start to sob. I feel what I've been pushing down begin to rise up within me.

Today it feels like spring. Everyone is doing social distancing because of the pandemic. I'm walking in the sunshine. I look down and see green leaves on the ground amid the dirty snow and garbage. I stop and I stare at those leaves. I feel my very soul respond to them. I feel the human animal that I am shouting shouting *I am alive, remember! I am alive!*

And so difficult things happen, things are confusing and hard, there aren't always easy answers. I try my best but it is so easy for me to collapse into shame or spiral into panic. It is so easy for me to be so hard on myself. But more and more, here and there, I am beginning to remember what it feels like to approach myself with curiosity and kindness. I am beginning to remember what it feels like to live without condemnation or avoidance, to simply show up to what's here with curiosity and kindness.

Are my actions in line with my integrity? Not all the time, not in every way. Capitalism makes that extremely hard. But instead of spiraling into shame I approach with compassion. I look at the context, the larger systems and I try to approach with the same compassion I would show anyone who is sick, unwell, living out the realities of mass imbalance, which we all are. I try to get curious about what might bring more integrity, not just for me personally but for all of us. And I ask these questions not as a desperate panic about redemption and being 'good', but as a human animal feeling of *aliveness*. How do I honour the aliveness? More and more each day.

Trauma can make things extremely scary and hard. And the world being what it is, it's already extremely scary and hard. But there is a part of me who is ancient and wise and connected to a lineage of ancestors, of blood, of community, human and nonhuman, and this part of me anchors and roots and says: What if we were curious? What if I felt safe enough to ask the questions?

And in asking the question I begin.

Ferris Wheel

We sat on the ferris wheel, side by side, watching the world move in its circular movement around us. We were kids, sisters at the summer fair.

There were things we talked about, and things we didn't. There were things we could say and things we only communicated in knowing glances because we did not have the words.

We sat there, in the August heat, at the end of another endless summer, and we said to each other

Imagine we get off this ferris wheel and we go back to the cottage and the rest of our day happens and then we close our eyes and open them and we are back on this ferris wheel and all of that was a dream.

We laugh at this, we consider it. We let the story unfold further.

Imagine we get off this ferris wheel and we go about our days and summer ends and we go back to school and then we close our eyes and open them and we are back on this ferris wheel.

Imagine years and years pass, imagine we grow up, imagine we have whole grown up lives and then we close our eyes and open them and we are back on this ferris wheel.

Imagine we open our eyes and we are back on this ferris wheel.

There are some responsibilities that we shouldn't carry, and we carry them anyway because no one else will. There are some regrets I can't speak or name even though anyone would say I did the best I could.

I did the best I could with what I had and that wasn't much. I was only a child and so were you and we did the best we could. And yet, I wish

Ferris Wheel

I could close my eyes and open them and be back on that ferris wheel, I wish I had the chance to do it all again.

I would take you by the hand and look you in the eye and I would hatch a plan to get us out of there.

We would escape, we would run through the forest, until we found a safe place to land.

We wouldn't grow up to be drunks, teenagers without parents drinking in alleyways, getting into fistfights. We wouldn't compound the trauma over and over again because we found a way to escape.

We opened our eyes on that ferris wheel and we knew what to do.

We Did What We Were Capable Of

*I*THINK ABOUT YOU in my arms. I think about you on top of me, straddling me, pressing your body into mine. I think about my hands on you, our hands on each other. *We did what we could, we did what we were capable of.*

I think about walking across the city, talking about trauma and the group sex we were each having with our own partners and dates. Talking about how hard it is to watch pleasure be easy for someone else, how hard it is to not have the secret key for unlocking our bodies. I think about how I wanted to reach for your hand, reach out and kiss you, but I didn't. Despite everything I still waited for you to make the first move.

I think about sitting in the hot tub, you sitting on the edge with your feet in the water, me listening to you talk about your other dates, your other crushes. I almost canceled that date. I was so angry for some reason I couldn't understand, but at the last minute I threw my bathing suit in the bag and went and met you. I sat there in silence listening to you talk to me like I was your friend, not your girlfriend or your partner or your lover. I felt the ache in my heart and I knew.

I think about kissing you outside the metro, feeling your body pull close to mine. The way all the confusion melted away in the simplicity of our embrace, in the purity of my desire, in my patient devotion to a seed I hoped would grow. I think about the electricity of our hands touching in the café, back at the beginning, the way holding hands was an act of sabotage against a world which had worked hard to slaughter our sexualities at the roots. I think about how we tried.

We Did What We Were Capable Of

I broke up with you sitting on a ledge on a day that was almost too cold to be outside. I didn't want to do it in the café, in front of everyone, so I asked you to sit with me in the cold, holding our hot drinks in our hands. I said my piece with as much kindness as I could, carefully and deliberately. I wanted to be careful with your heart. I wanted to be responsible and mature and do the right thing. I wanted to end it in a way that acknowledged there was something to end.

I also wanted to thrash against the limits of our capacity, to become a storm powerful enough to shake us from our ambivalence. I wanted to love you without it hurting so much. I didn't want to disavow the pain, ignore it, pretend to be okay with our inability to really meet each other. But I didn't want to end it either.

I wanted a way to open to each other, to move past the wall of disorganized attachment that made us both incapable of really being together. No matter how hard we tried.

We did what we could, we did what we were capable of.

But I wonder if there was another way. I wonder if I didn't try so hard to be good, to be safe, to protect us both from the avalanche of my heart. I wonder if I was braver, more reckless, less concerned with what was right.

I wonder if I could have shown you. I wonder if I could have seen what you were showing me.

It Starts with the Water

*I*T STARTS WITH the water: this particular lake, which opens and closes with a stream, as I suppose all lakes do. This lake with its muck and its long ropes of seaweed and the shafts of light in the darkness of the deep water.

It starts with the bulrushes at the edges where it gets shallow and marshy. And the frogs, oh my god the frogs. Their slick slimy green-yellow bodies bright with brown spots. Their legs which propel them through the air and their big watchful eyes. Holding the frogs in my hands, letting them slip their way to freedom, throw themselves from my hands and back into the water.

The little bugs that ride across the surface of the water like it's the ground, never going down inside, always staying on top of it, a flat surface, a whole world.

And the horses. Yes, horses. Wild horses galloping down into the water and playing in it like dogs.

Here, this place, is where it starts. My first love, my first home, the water. My body, the water. My words, the water. And here, in this first place, is also where the bad things happen, where the splitting happens, where the dissociation happens that severs me from myself.

I can know and not know, act and not act.

We catch frogs in buckets and my dad takes them and puts their beautiful bodies on hooks. Hooked. I watch them wriggling, trying to get free. I watch them struggle with all their power, desperate to get back to the water. I'm still trying to get free from that hook.

The magic and the violence can be in the same place, and I'll tell you a secret, they probably are. Because the magic grows up like a forest all around the violence, it opens the world and says here, here, right here come inside. The magic is like the lake with its surface and its depths, always offering itself up, always giving a place to go under.

When we were children we couldn't get away but we could be with the world. We could be with the water. We could be with the forest and the night. We could run our hands across the bodies of the horses. We could lie in the fields and eat raspberries from the bush.

The magic is the pulse of the living universe. It is the presence I know is there with me but I always forget and disavow and deny. It is the magic that sparkles and pulses and throbs, this aching openness that meets my gaze, that looks back. This aliveness which doesn't speak in any human language but has its own voice, a voice that I've listened to my whole life, even though sometimes I deny it.

The magic is what saved me, and the magic is here with me now, even though I can't go to the lake anymore.

I remember the frogs and the horses and the loons breaking the surface of the lake, the way they are as comfortable under water as in the air, and I try to remember what they taught me about freedom, about the necessity of impossible freedom, about keeping my connection to the living world alive.

Even as I was trapped in circumstances of violence and danger, a part of me could not be captured. A part of me remained free.

Now as an adult, far away from the lake, I go to the river. The river with the phragmites, unnaturally tall and abundant, an invasive species. The river with the red winged black birds aggressively guarding their nests. And the ducks on the water and the cormorants.

The willow reaches out across the water and I hang onto the branches with my arms while the powerful current tries to take my body away. I lie on the surface of the water and I could let my body float all the way downtown. I don't sink. I don't struggle. I lie on it like the waterbugs. It is a flexible surface that holds me, that cradles me at the edge of the depths.

Fucking Magic

It starts with the water the way it starts with my body the way I turn to the moment and open it. The way the magic is still here, alive and expansive and vibrant, showing me a way to hold onto my power and my freedom, even here and even now. It may feel impossible. I might feel like a frog on a hook, wriggling for my freedom. I might not be able to escape the violences, but I am never without the magic of the water. It is with me always, like it always was.

I remember the depths and the cold and the sunlight splayed in glittering fragments against the moving body of the living lake. I hold that power within me, all the time, even now, even as we live through impossible things.

The magic and the violence can be in the same place, and I'll tell you a secret, they probably are.

Animal

OKAY SO THERE is a wild animal inside of me. She is crawling on the ground. She splits spirit from body, she spits blood with that hungry eyed look like: *I don't fucking care if I die in this fight.*

She is under the blanket on the front lawn. That's where I left her. She is in the crack between the wall and the bed in a motel room and I dare not look into her wild eyes.

She is running through the forest and the night. The moon is the only one who knows her, the only one who refuses to forget her, the only one who returns to her again and again.

She is chasing me through the forest and I know it is impossible to outrun her but I can't let her get me. She'll kill me. She'll split me from my body and turn me into a ghost. She will leave me on the train tracks waiting for a train.

I can't write poetry. I can't look her in the eye. I have to be careful about the pill bottles in case she suddenly swallows every pill inside. She is wildly suicidal: violent. She is prepared to kill and prepared to die. She has a body, it is an animal body, all motions and limbs, all wriggle and shake. She is both hunter and prey. She is both hunter and prey.

I don't know what to tell you. There are earwigs in the crotch of my swimsuit, wriggling wriggling and I throw the fabric to the ground. There's a cup with water and dentures in it and in the dentures: meat. *Meat.* I've always been a vegetarian. Slick with the killing, with the taste of death, his breath and the impossibility of motion and yet:

It gives her a sense of control. It gives her a sense of power. To hold the blade in her hand, to watch it come down again and again repeatedly.

Fucking Magic

This is my body she says in the frenzy of a prayer. *This is still my fucking body and you can't take that from me.* Oh, but I have. I have taken away her access and I don't intend to return it to her, unless she gets me in the woods.

The thing is she is just so much trouble, she is so much danger. I am afraid she will kill me and she might. I am afraid she will start fires that I am unable to put out, that she will create damage I am unable to reverse.

So I keep her. Her wild motion, her body contorted, the way she crawls and runs and hunts. I keep her caged, in the basement, out of sight. But she still runs wild through the night.

This Love

WHEN I TOUCH you it feels fucking sacred. When I run my fingers across your skin. When you aren't here and I pick up your jacket and hang it on the hook I run my fingers over the fabric, I press my face into it and smell you. Oh my god, I love you. I love you in ways and at depths I didn't know possible. In fact loving you has completely transformed my understanding of what love is.

We walk through the alleyways of this city, for hours and hours. I can complain to you uninhibited. You have my back fiercely and unequivocally and I have yours. If they come for you baby, they come for me. We talk about evolutionary biology, we talk about history, we talk about anarchism and communism, we talk about everything we want for this beautiful fucked up world. We talk about what hurts, we talk about our childhoods, we laugh and laugh and laugh.

In my bed I curl my body toward you. I say I love you. You say you love me. I lie with my head on your chest, listening to your heart beat, the rise and fall of your chest. You are my home. You are my friend. You are my lover. You are my partner. You are my co-conspirator. You are my equal. We fuck and the desire moving between us is alive with the depths of our intimacy.

I still cry sometimes, because it still surprises me. But more and more I breathe into the trust of this love.

There were months and months when we fought. Months and months I thrashed against this love in a desperate panic because I was so scared. I loved you and that scared me so much. I had no model to show me what safe love could be, no anchor in my past to show me that it is safe to trust and grow in love. I felt like a failure for fighting with you, for bringing all that stress and drama into this life changing love. But I learned that this was a part of our intimacy too, it was a way to move past the surface and crack open the depths of our attachment injuries.

We were caught in the anxious/avoidant cycle, both of us trying our best to breathe into the love we were building, both of us scared. Both of us reacting to lessons we learned in our past about the inability of other people to really be there, to really know us, to really meet our needs.

We worked hard through those months, through those fights, activating each other's fight, flight and freeze responses, learning how to talk about it, how to hear each other, how to ask for what we needed, coming back and trying again.

Our love deepened through all that work. We grew past the rush and sparkle of new love through the hard work of learning how to really love each other, deeply and in the ways we needed to be loved. And then, we found the shared language, we trusted the work we were doing, we found the rhythm of communication, and then the trust filled itself out, in all its glorious texture and its staggering depth.

I let out a breath and I turn to you. My love, right here and now. In the present, together. I reach for your hand. I know that when I need you, you will be there for me. I know that I can trust you to reach for me when you need me too.

On our three year anniversary we go to the river and stare at the water and lie on the ground and touch the moss and touch each other. We sit on the ground in a parking lot and eat take out falafel in the sun.

We go back to my place on the metro. My bathtub doesn't have a faucet but we fill it with buckets of hot water from the sink. It's the sketchiest bath set up in this very old and questionable punk house, and you climb in and I do too. In the hard earned heat we lie against each other and breathe.

You show yourself to me. You show me the important scenes, the places that you loved and lost. I show myself to you. I feel my heart open in a kind of love that is not scared or desperate or seeking or pushing

This Love

away. I feel this love that is rooted in trust, that is held in the complex intimacy of knowing each other in so many ways.

And my love, I am so grateful for our unfolding story, and everything we will live through side by side. I am so grateful to know you and be known by you, to feel our love dynamic and alive.

Tell Me About Your First Time

*I*WAS SEVENTEEN AND I said I had a headache. Classic escape. Recent suicide attempt and really, I was just overwhelmed. She cooked me a fancy meal. She had latex gloves ready. And I wasn't sure. She gave me a benzo, "for my headache", I let it dissolve under my tongue. She fucked me in her bed and I felt nothing.

Tell me about your first time.

I was nineteen and I brought a magnum of red wine to her apartment. She had shown up at the sex store where I worked wearing nothing under her long jacket. She flashed me there in the store. She came close and said I could touch her. Her gross boyfriend was there, but I did, I came close and I touched her. She gave me her number and I went over to her place with a dildo in my bag and a magnum of red wine. Her boyfriend made one last attempt at a threesome before leaving us alone. I wondered the whole time if we were being filmed.

Tell me about your first time.

Drunk in a park. Drunk in a field. Numbness. I feel nothing. *The reason you need to touch your clit to cum is because you're always fucking dudes. You need to be fucked by a real lesbian.* My body is broken into pieces again. My survivor body, queer in all the wrong ways, already invaded, already numb.

Tell me about your first time.

I was ten and enduring an embarrassing video made in the 1980s, in my sex ed class. All the kids snickering and silently trying to hear something important. Then the relevant words filled my ears: *You might start to notice that you think about someone all the time, you might get butterflies in your stomach, this is called a crush, and it's a perfectly normal feeling to have about someone of the opposite sex.*

Tell me about your first time.

Maybe it hasn't happened yet. Maybe every time is another first. Maybe I am filled with a bottomless yearning that has no name. Maybe I'm tired of the arguments about who is really queer and who is really a lesbian and who gets to call themselves a dyke. Maybe I want to feel your desire, unencumbered by your shame. Maybe I want to feel my desire, unencumbered by my shame.

Maybe for the first time in my life I know what I want, I know who I am. I know what I want. I know who I am.

Tell me about your...

In your bed, your fingers in my mouth. In your bed your hands on my skin, breathless and urgent and hesitant and seeking. There aren't any words or there are only words and no answers. Processing, processing, is that all lesbians do is process? Or is this my own special brand of traumatized gay shit?

The look in your eyes when you flip me over. The look in your eyes as you grind your pussy into me. The urgency and the convoluted desire. The pauses. The conversation. The laughter. Riding across the city on my bike at 2am without lights because I was too afraid to ask you why you didn't ask me to sleep over.

I want to be crushed by your desire. I want to crush you with my own. I don't want a fucking benzo under my tongue or a magnum of red wine or some biphobic bullshit shaming my desire before it has even begun. I want the space and the time to feel the build of desire. I want the safety to reach through the avalanche of shame that has dammed my desire. I want to release it, unleash it, and I want to be here with you.

I want it to be okay to bring our trauma, mine and yours. But I want to bring more than our trauma, I want to be more than our trauma. I want to trust our commitment to desire, our willingness to do the work

Fucking Magic

when it isn't easy, our willingness to show up even when it's hard. I want to know that it's worth it for you, traumatized for traumatized, bisexual for bisexual, we are not less than, our desire is no less important and no less real.

I'm tired of feeling used and not feeling seen. I'm tired of being treated like a therapist or a bestie when I'm actually in a romantic relationship or on a date. I'm tired of queer desire, queer love, not being honoured, not being important, not being treated as real.

I don't want to be the one you come to, to process all the issues in your relationship with your boyfriend. I don't want to nod politely, say the validating thing you need to hear, all the while trying to make sense of the reality that this is supposed to be a date.

I want you to be unafraid of your desire and I want to be unafraid of mine. I want you to be willing to look at me with those eyes. I want you to be brave enough to meet me in the ambivalence of complex trauma. I want us to find what we are seeking. I want to be brave enough not to turn away.

The Abandoned One

THE TWO OF us and the wolf are looking for the abandoned one. The wolf: always at my throat, always trying to tear my throat out. But I looked the wolf in the eye and I understood that her death grip is protective. She's prepared to take us to death, she's ready to destroy it all including ourselves, to avoid the unbearable pain of the abandoned one.

I can't find the abandoned one. I feel her in the morning. I wake up in a state of subtle terror. I don't know why. Images of peanut butter toast. Images of small plastic neon eagles that balance on their beaks. Waves upon waves of pain, deep and fast, edged with fear, sharp and electric. I'm looking for the abandoned one.

She's the one who is defined by her need. She's the one who has not forgotten it, disavowed it, turned it into a million other things. For her it is still simple pure devastating need. It is the voice unanswered, the hand unheld, the news of death left hanging in the air. It is the unspeakable impossible thing that is happening. For her it is still happening, and no one is coming, no one will save her from the thing that doesn't have a name.

She is the child walking there across the wide canyon, unsupervised, head down, carrying a book in her hand.

She is the child who writes in her diary *I crave attention like a drug*. She is the feeling that preceded that writing, the unspoken unmet constant throbbing need. The shame rushes in with its million violences, the wolf does what the wolf does and destroys. But underneath that violence, underneath the destruction and the shame, quiet as the breath that won't come, is the abandoned one and her endless unmet need.

Fucking Magic

I try to let it in: not then, but now. I try to time travel, bring her to surface, and share the love in my life with her now. I try to imagine me, as my adult self, and the person I trust most in the world, breaking into that cottage and taking her hand. *Come with us. We are getting you out of here.*

I don't have a lot of forgiveness for what was done. All the power and transformation I have worked to free my parents from the weight of their failure. But still, even with everything I've given them, they leave the abandoned one alone. They don't answer her, listen to her, have any capacity at all to acknowledge her. And so it is up to me.

The two of us and the wolf, hand in hand with the person we trust most, connected in our blood to the water and the trees, we find the abandoned one where she is hiding, curled up in a tiny ball. We open the door to the cupboard, we meet her gaze, all of us together, and we tell her: *You are safe now. We are here to protect you. We are taking you away from here and we will never let anyone hurt you again.* All of us together we form a circle around her, basically a bunch of adult punks, trustworthy and so different from the adults she knows, plus the wolf circling around her feet, licking at her hands. We say: *Abandoned one isn't your name anymore, we've come to give you a new name, we've come to give you so much love, you are our child, our beautiful perfect child, and we love you more than words can say and we will show you every day and we will protect you and keep you safe, welcome home. Welcome home.*

The Tracks

THE GROUNDHOG RUNS quick and fast past us, toward a network of underground tunnels. Cautious and brave, with sparkling eyes. The groundhog sits by the entrance of the tunnel, thinking about what to do next, aware of our presence but unafraid due to the welcoming depths of the earth, right there, if they need to run.

The squirrels are collecting sticks and leaves, creating nests right in the caged-in part outside our windows. The cat, George, watches from the other side of the glass with murderous intent but the squirrels trust the glass and think the location is safe and convenient, a perfect place for a nest despite George's hungry eyes.

I normally only see the rabbits in the evening, running or frozen in a tableau, camouflaging and waiting for me to pass them unnoticed, but they are out here, they are living their precious lives, in this makeshift ecosystem surviving in the corridor carved out by the train tracks.

My love and I are picking up garbage, filling bag upon bag with plastic and cigarette butts and beer bottles and all sorts of random trash. We are emptying old abandoned flower pots full of earth into the spaces between discarded rails to create makeshift gardens, spaces for weeds and wildflowers to catch root and grow.

We are planting clover on the patches of ground left bare from human treading, scattering seeds with the hope of providing blossoms for the bees. We are leaving seedbombs full of native wildflowers, casting over them our sincerest hopes for their abundant growth.

Fucking Magic

After the rain we crouch close to the earth, see the tiniest new clovers pushing through. We are ecstatic, celebratory, proud of the tiny clovers, abundant in our joy.

We love the tracks. We use boltcutters to make passageways onto the tracks. We crush coins on the rails, creating medallions to celebrate milestones in sobriety. We notice the birds, the brown ones, flecked, and with a particularly pointy beak. We wonder at their names. We walk along the tracks and we fuck along the tracks and we sit out in the sun reading and we take care of the earth.

There are rail cops to look out for and once we had to run from them. There is the city and the self-appointed cops that fill the holes cut into the fences by us and others, like gang d'la track who make signs about their practice of liberating the train tracks. We shout with joy when we see the signs. Gang d'la track!

We see people out there. Taking a short cut or just going for a walk. Graffiti artists throwing up tags under the cover of darkness or brazenly in broad daylight.

We have so many long conversations, walking through this corridor. We spend hours picking up cigarette butts and planting seeds. We feel the spring beginning to explode all around us. We wait for rain and it comes and it soaks the earth.

It's been a hard year. And this is a joy that carries me through. This is a love for the wild world itself, springing forth abundant and criminal, cut right through the city.

Desire is Holy

It can be scary to want, to feel the full power of desire. It can make me feel like I'm not enough or that there is something wrong with me because I am not able to achieve what I so desire. It makes me feel like a failure, that after so many years of therapy, after so much hard work, there is still so much out of reach.

Desire can bring up intense feelings of shame and humiliation, can make me time travel to a time when I was an unloved child so full of desperate desire for love and safety. And so unable to get those things.

But I am trying to change my relationship to desire. I am trying to feel desire as a force of power in my life, as a process that is good and sacred in its own right. The desire itself is the point. Not the fulfilment of it. The desire itself is holy.

The desire takes me places, moves me, and where I end up might not be exactly what I wanted, what I expected, what I planned, but it is something alive and dynamic, something unfolding. I try to trust this unfolding, to stay with it, to feel the momentum of desire. I resist the crushing shame that tries to take me. I move toward desire, again and again.

I'm thinking about the person I'm becoming, the person I am moving toward. The potential in the seed. I am thinking about my desires, what I *want* and how that might shape my actions, make my actions full with intention, vibrant like a prayer.

I can see the outlines of some future self, the hard work paid off, the confidence, the integration, the holiness of moving toward desire. A practice. A process. An intention made manifest.

Fucking Magic

I wrote a list. A secret list of seven, no, eight desires. These desires feel big and powerful and potent. They feel like the dreams I dared not dream, the hopes that felt too dangerous to really want. But here they are. Real and spoken.

I wrote them down, conjured them simply and concretely, in words, in front of me. I took a moment to really read them, to let the want sink in. I shared them with one trusted person. I imagined my life with them fulfilled.

But most importantly, I turned toward the desire itself, expansive and abundant, charged electric and full of power.

It is not shameful to want. It is not humiliating to yearn for that which is not yet manifest. It is not shameful to desire.

I turn toward desire now, unafraid of its potential and its power.

Pandemic

DURING THE PANDEMIC my roommates, my partner, and I read books and work on projects and cook food. It is quiet at our place.

My partner goes to work during the day. They are a frontline worker supporting homeless people, and their work is as important now as ever.

During the day I write and I read and I work on projects that have been gathering dust for a long time. I get some things done that I've been meaning to get done. I submit my manuscript to a press. I create my online workshop.

The cat chases a toy mouse and his little feet make a storm of noise through the main space.

When it gets warmer it is a blessing. The feeling of being trapped lessens when we are able to move out into the world. The train tracks, the earth, the groundhogs are a blessing.

The graffiti that is piling up now that it isn't being regularly washed off, a blessing. The big dog barking in someone's yard, a blessing.

Days are slow. Days blur together. Days are a rollercoaster of mental health experiences, one to another.

Therapy is on zoom. Me in my bed animated and hoping my roommates can't hear the play by play of my complex ptsd. My therapist a little image on a screen.

I miss my friends. I miss the cafes. I miss shows in my living room. I miss crowds. I miss strangers. I miss the busy fullness of life.

And I know how blessed I am. My partner, here with me. This beautiful place I call home. My work which I love, the sun setting now outside my window.

Fucking Magic

None of this is what we expected. And this is my life, as real and full of wonder as it always is.

I can feel joy even now.

Careful and Unafraid

*I*T WON'T BE easy to let go of the old stories. It won't be easy because they saved your life.

The panic, the surveillance, the control, the chaos, the numbing, the void. It won't be easy to let all that go.

But remember: you did all of that not only to live but to keep a secret part of you alive.

You sacrificed so much not only to live but to keep a secret part of you alive.

You feel it at sunset, as the stars begin to pulse into existence. You feel it in the rush of the breeze in your hair as you walk home on the overpass. You feel it in the water, that living creature that pulls you under.

You know all the ways that you survived, and it is a brilliant magic and it is life taking and exhausting. You don't want to survive anymore, you want to live.

It's a cliché but – you don't want to survive anymore you want to live.

And the secret is: you already know how.

You go outside and get on your knees in the dirt or on the concrete. You don't care if anyone is around or if there are people staring. You put your forehead to the ground in a holy embrace.

You remember the way the snow glittered hot bright white. The way it gave way to the sigh of mud. Which opened to the chaos of bloom and bug song. Finally easing into the harvest of decay.

You remember the way you snuck yourself away, kept yourself underwater and in the call of birds and in the secret shivers and in the rush and pulse of living.

Fucking Magic

You know that underneath all that terror you remained: careful and unafraid.

It won't be easy to let go of the old stories, to drop them in the river and let them be carried off, to drop your shoulders, feel that breath you were waiting for.

It won't be easy to stop fighting for your life and start living. But I'm telling you, it's time to stop fighting for your life and start living.

It may feel monumental and uneventful. It may feel impossible and like it's happening right now.

It may feel strange the way you've changed, the way you don't need the old stories anymore.

But you don't.

Acknowledgments

THANK YOU TO Jay, my lover and partner and comrade and friend. Thank you for trusting me to write the story of our love and for encouraging my writing and for loving me like you do.

Thank you to Wallea Eaglehawk and *Revolutionaries* for backing and believing in outsider writing.

Thank you to my readers for being with me through all of this.

Thank you to the river, the lake, the ocean, and to Clover, my dog.

About the Writer

CLEMENTINE MORRIGAN IS an underground writer who has been making zines since the year 2000. She writes literary nonfiction, essays, and philosophy and the majority of her writing is independent. She staples thousands and thousands of zines. She has written a few other books over the years: *Rupture*, *The Size of a Bird*, *You Can't Own the Fucking Stars*, *Trauma Magic*, and *Sexting*. It would be difficult to list all the zines she's published. She has a leftist podcast with her partner and political collaborator Jay Lesoleil called *Fucking Cancelled*. Her life work is in service of survivors, crazy people, the exiled, the scapegoats, and the undefended. She is a socialist and a political vegan. Find more of her writing at clementinemorrigan.com.

www.ingramcontent.com/pod-product-compliance
Lightning Source LLC
Chambersburg PA
CBHW020512080526
44583CB00013B/572